Bill Stewart

Packaging design

Laurence King Publishing

I

In the beginning and looking forward

Packaging in the post-modern era 11
Social and economic changes 12
Technological advances 23
Retailing 27
Changes in design practice 34

II

Understanding the target audience

Defining market sectors 39
Identifying aspirations 48
Techniques for researching target
    audiences 51
Preparing mood boards that work 55

III

The packaging designer's toolbox

Materials 62
Surface decoration 74
Colour 79
Typography 85
Photography and illustration 88

IV

Creating design concepts

Understanding the brief 95
Making research relevant 97
Sources of inspiration 104
Ways of working—concept
    generation 110
Presenting concepts 117

V

Design development

Selecting and discarding design
    candidates 121
Developing concepts 123
Mock-ups and models 128
Presenting recommended designs 135

VI

Working with brands

What is a brand? 143
Brand types and brand values 152
Branding through shape and sound 154
Working with logos 156
Creating brands, sub-brands and brand
    extensions 161

VII

Packaging obligations and responsibilities

Environmental impact—fact and fiction
    169
Issues of age, gender, sexuality and
    ethnicity 181
Corporate responsibility 187

VIII

Finding your role

The future of packaging design 197
Design consultancies 202
Packaging manufacturing 207
Brand owners 209
Down the line... 212

Glossary 216
Bibliography 218
Sources of inspiration 220
Index 221
Picture credits and acknowledgements
    224

LAURENCE KING

Published in 2007 by
Laurence King Publishing Ltd
361–373 City Road, London EC1V 1LR
T +44 20 7841 6900
F +44 20 7841 6910
E enquiries@laurenceking.co.uk
www.laurenceking.co.uk

A catalogue record for this book is
available from the British Library

ISBN–13: 978-1-85669-525-1
ISBN–10: 1-85669-525-5

Design by Catherine Dixon
Diagrams by David Preston
Picture research by Peter Kent

Frontispiece: Courtesy Caffarel, Italy
Cover: Tŷ Nant PET bottle. Photograph by
Tim Marshall

Printed in China

Introduction

Packaging, at its most fundamental level, contains, protects and promotes products. Within this simple definition lie multiple challenges for packaging designers. Packaging is a commercial activity that demands designers have a business sense, as each of the fundamental functions of packaging inevitably has financial implications attached. This applies throughout the packaging lifecycle, from production, distribution and retailing, through to disposal. Designers, therefore, need to be commercially aware at every stage of design to reach the right level of compromise between financial, functional and marketing performance.

Chapter Three reinforces this view, providing practical information on the critical issue of choosing packaging materials, deciding on what graphic techniques to employ and comparing the merits of photography and illustration. Making these decisions always has a financial implication on the overall packaging cost and the subject arises again in Chapter Seven, where environmental decisions also have to be considered. These also carry cost implications, often making it necessary to have a trade-off between environmental benefits and costs.

Equally, packaging is also a technical activity, requiring technical understanding of materials and processes. That, in itself, encompasses a constantly changing and complex series of issues. Making frequently difficult decisions on technical criteria is part of the packaging designer's role. Help is at hand, however, in Chapter Five, where ways of selecting and discarding design candidates are explained, helping to highlight and resolve these important and often conflicting issues.

As if that was not enough, in today's intensely competitive commercial world, arguably the most important demand that designers must address is an understanding of society and the needs, wants and desires of the people within it. Without this, design will have no focus, no matter how technically brilliant or financially sound it may be, and therefore it will have little impact. The importance of this is reflected in Chapter Two, which shows how to identify target audiences and communicate your understanding of them to others. It is a subject that returns throughout this book, emphasizing the need for designers to be socially aware. Chapter Seven expands the theme by reference to some of the obligations and responsibilities designers must bring to any packaging study, including responsibilities for the environmental performance of packaging.

So, in addition to being commercially alert, technologically updated and socially aware, packaging designers are also expected to be creative thinkers and expert communicators. A key area here is branding. Brands have become much more than a graphic device to indicate their heritage or quality. They are often fundamental to corporate strategies, requiring creative yet sensitive design skills in translating brand values onto the consumer interface represented by packaging. The importance of branding is recognized throughout the book but particularly in Chapter Six, which considers branding in depth and, in practical terms, how designers work with brands.

Being able to communicate design thinking effectively is a key packaging design skill, whether the communication is to oneself, as a critical self-assessment, or to colleagues, clients or examiners. Ultimately, however, packaging is designed to communicate visually with consumers and, therefore, designers are encouraged to work in visual media from the outset of a design study. In Chapter Five, for example, information is given on developing mock-ups that allow design thinking to be assessed quickly before creating more sophisticated models and visuals used to present final design recommendations.

In reviewing packaging design, the first question that comes to mind, "How did we get to this point?" is addressed in Chapter One, where the contemporary history of packaging is considered in parallel with social, economic and technological changes. Other important questions such as "What do we do now?" and "How do we do it?" are also discussed throughout this book. Finally, for young designers embarking on a new career and asking "Where do I go—now that I am a packaging designer?", in Chapter Eight the options in this fascinating and rewarding business of packaging design are considered.

In the beginning and looking forward

Packaging in context

It is doubtful whether, in ancient civilizations, those responsible for producing glass in Egypt, paper in China or making containers from woven grasses in other parts of the world, ever considered themselves to be packaging suppliers. Yet every society in history developed containers, which we now would describe as packaging, to meet the needs of its people. Water, honey, seeds, salt, medicines and all the other necessities of life had to be protected as they were transported and stored. As populations began to form into villages and towns, the need increased for packaging to contain and transport these valuable commodities further from their sources, and in smaller quantities, establishing an early parallel between packaging technology and cultural development that still persists today. At its most fundamental level, the requirements of packaging have not changed. It must still contain, protect and preserve products while informing those who use them. Containment and protection are always essential and, for many categories of packed products, for example, surgical dressings, clarity of instruction is a critical function. In consumer markets, however, we may extend this information function also to perform a marketing role, selling the product and representing the brand.

This chapter expands this theme, considering packaging in its contemporary context and looking at technological developments alongside some of the key cultural changes in society. We begin in 1945, at the end of the Second World War, and the beginning of the nuclear age, at a time when technology had developed rapidly, fuelled by wartime needs. It was also a critical time for social and economic development, when, at last, peace could nurture unprecedented social changes and re-establish commerce and business. The theme continues through present times and includes a glimpse into the future with a sneak preview of 2015, just to alert ourselves to likely changes ahead.

The three most significant strands influencing packaging design, both historically and currently, are socio-economic changes, technological advances and retail practice. In this chapter all have been teased out from their interwoven travel through time for separate examination, with a fourth strand considering how packaging design itself became established as a specialist design function.

Opposite The demise of sugar rationing in 1950s Europe allowed companies to introduce new product lines to meet increasing public demand. Competition intensified during the 1960s with the arrival of commercial TV and self-service shopping.

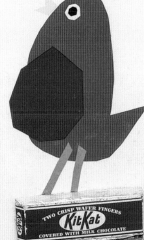

Have a
break...
have a
Kit Kat

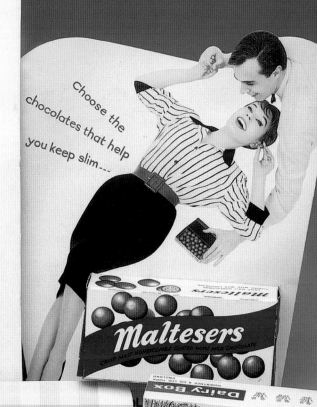

Choose the
chocolates that help
you keep slim...

Cadbury's
ROSES
CHOCOLATES

TWO CRISP WAFER FINGERS
KitKat
COVERED WITH MILK CHOCOLATE

FOUR CRISP WAFER FINGERS
KitKat
COVERED WITH MILK CHOCOLATE

maltesers
CRISP MALT HONEYCOMB COATED WITH MILK CHOCOLATE

Mackintosh's
Good
News

Iced Caramels

CLARNICO   HALF POUND NET

Iced Caramels

CLARNICO

FRY'S
TURKISH
DELIGHT

Paynes 6d
toff-etts
coated in rich milk chocolate

Mackintosh's
WEEK-END
chocolates & candies

Mackintosh's
WEEK-END

Dairy Box

Dairy Box
HALF POUND NET

Soft toffee · milk chocolate cups
Mackintosh's
Rolo 6d
Mackintosh's
Rolo 6d

TOBLERONE
with ALM

Cadbury's
Skippy

1D
OFF
AZTEC

Cadbury's
ROASTED ALMOND
6d

Cadbury's
TURKISH DELIGHT

Cadbury's
DAIRY MILK
CHOCOLATE
CADBURY'S MILK

Cadbury's
Dairy milk chocolate
Buttons
6d
MADE BY CADBURY'S IN THE REPUBLIC OF IRELAND

Cadbury's
Whole
Nut
½ lb
MILK CHOCO

Cadbury's
Fruit &
Nut
½ lb
MILK CHOCOLATE

	Socio-economic changes	Technological changes	Retailing changes	Packaging design changes
1945	• Second World War ends • Post-war austerity in Europe • Manufacturing expansion in USA	• IBM introduce computer system based on punched cards • UNIVAC 1 becomes the first commercial computer. Powered by 5000 vacuum valves, it is the size of the average bedroom • First transistor made in 1947	• Introduction of self-service shopping outside USA	• Packaging recognized as a specialist subject outside the USA
1955	• US popular culture exports rock 'n' roll, jeans and teenage style • Rationing ends in UK • McDonald's founded in USA • 1961: manned space flights; on April 12, Yuri Gagarin; on May 1st, Alan Shepherd	• Ownership of freezers expands outside USA • Sony make the first pocket transistor radio in 1955	• Increase in self-service shopping across Europe • 1963: first hypermarket established by Carrefour in France, sized 2600 square metres	• Became known as packaging engineering—usually by US companies expanding into Europe and Japan • Tetrapak milk carton introduced
1965	• Contraceptive pill available to women • Swinging Sixties morality • 1969: Buzz Aldrin and Neil Armstrong become first men on the moon • 1973: Bertolucci's *Last Tango in Paris* banned in several countries	• ARPANET—precursor of the internet—being developed by MIT, UCLA and Stamford universities in USA	• Louis Delhaize begins first Cora supermarket in Belgium	• 1967: first ring pull introduced • 1974: SiebertHead established in London as first specialist packaging company outside USA
1975	• Punk culture begins • 1978: Sony introduce the Walkman • 1981: AIDS first identified 1984: TGV high speed train leaves Lyons, France for its first journey	• 1977: Creation of bar codes by IBM in USA • 1984: Apple launches its first personal computer	• Beginning of scanning at checkouts	• 1979: First PET bottles produced for carbonated drinks
1985	• Hole in the ozone layer detected over Antarctica • 1986: Chernobyl in Soviet Union sees nuclear accident • Nov 1989: Berlin Wall removed • 1991: Soviet Union collapses	• 1982: Sony launch audio CD with first pre-recorded music reaching the market in 1983 • 1989: CDs outsell vinyl records	• 1989: Carrefour open the first hypermarket in Asia in Taiwan • Consolidation of retail market by major grocery companies with decline in specialist local stores	• Design studios are retained by major brands while retailers begin to develop own-label products in-house, often closely following branded product design directions
1995	• Increase in single-parent households • Global warming attributed to human activity. Despite Kyoto agreement, emissions of greenhouse gases still rise • Natural disasters: tsunami in Asia and flooding in USA sharpen environmental debate	• 1995: Microsoft launch Internet Explorer • 1996: First cloned animal is a sheep called Dolly • Rapid increase in Internet usage. By 1999 there are 150 million users, 50% of whom live in USA	• Rapid growth of non-food products in supermarkets • Walmart, the world's largest retailer, buys ASDA in the UK • Home shopping begins • 2004: Carrefour now have 216 hypermarkets in France and 56 stores in China	• Retailers employ design studios to introduce corporate design strategy for budget, standard and premium products
2005	• Environmental legislation increases • Manufacturing boom in China peaks by 2015 but begins in Africa	• Cost of RFID tags falls to level where widespread adoption is possible • Nanotechnology introduces new ranges of materials	• Supermarkets diversify into finance, banking, legal services, communications, fuel, funerals • Non-food profits outstrip food for the first time	• Environmental packaging design specialists established • Design software simplified enabling easier access to design tasks

Packaging in the post-modern era

Our timeline chart begins in 1945, although packed products predate that by some considerable margin. The end of the Second World War saw a period of austerity across many countries, particularly in Europe and Asia, where economies struggled to rebuild their infrastructures and rationing was still imposed. Packaged products were difficult to obtain and remained largely functional in style, following their pre-war pattern.

It was not until the late 1950s and the introduction of commercial television, together with the increase in self-service shopping, that a new platform for product and packaging development was established. It was, however, the creation of marketing as a new commercial activity that provided the catalyst to allow packaging to become the principle driver in achieving product sales. Key to this would be the brand. Up until the 1960s, brands were largely considered to be the product manufacturer's name. This provided reassurance for buyers that they were getting the original product that would be consistent in quality. Now, it was recognized that brands could do much more.

By the 1990s and on into the twenty-first century, the role of the brand had increased in importance to the point where the product became the vehicle for carrying the brand. Products were now being developed as a way of extending the brand. For example, Richard Branson is the likeable, straight-talking face of the Virgin brand and has created a diverse range of products and services to carry it. Brands are now being forced to reconsider what their core values are and how they can be extended into other areas. British Gas now offers electricity, telephone services and broadband, while the local supermarket offers funeral services and wedding ceremonies along with banking and car insurance. Packaging still has its functional role to play, but the emphasis for the future will not be merely carrying the brand, but also extending and enhancing the brand experience.

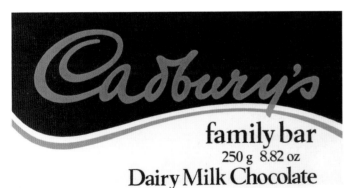

Left The brand is clearly Cadbury's on this 1977 chocolate bar. Later, Dairy Milk would become the brand and Cadbury's used as an umbrella brand.

Above As with the earlier Cadbury's bar, this Nestlé chocolate bar from 1983 uses Nestlé as the principal brand.

Social and economic changes

Designing packaging is concerned with designing for people and, unless we know about the social and economic circumstances of those we are designing for, designs may not find resonance with them. Social changes proceed at a different pace within different cultures and countries, each having their own pivotal moments and consequential new directions. It would require at least one whole book to analyse social and economic changes and chart the consequences for design. Here, we can only highlight some of the more important and contemporary social issues to demonstrate how they interact with packaging design.

Social frameworks

John Grant, in his book *The New Marketing Manifesto*, suggests that the rigid framework of structured societies has largely been replaced by a far more fluid model, where individuals have more control over their own destinies. As the formal framework of state, commercial and institutional control diminishes, we gain new freedoms but at the price of losing safety and accepting risk. In many countries, such as the UK, France and Japan, this change has taken place over a period of time. In Germany, however, the removal of the Berlin Wall in 1989 changed the rigid society of East Germany into the fluid society of West Germany at a stroke. For many, especially those who longed for the freedoms of the West, it turned out not to be the comfortable experience anticipated. The state structure of the East may have been stifling but it did provide support in employment, education and child-care. Some former East Germans found great difficulty in coping without such state support in this sudden change from a rigid to flexible society. This demonstrates that there is a social price to pay for flexibility and, as we shall see, this will be reflected in the audience we are designing for, who, like the East Germans finding new freedoms, have found new doubts.

The chart opposite suggests how some of the most important aspects of our lives have changed. Clearly, the new society appears to be a much riskier place but also one where there are more possibilities.

Right Increased freedom of choice is accompanied by increased decision making, bringing its own pressures to bear.

The changing values of contemporary society

Structured society

Objective

Formal

Ordered

Rigid

Impersonal

Safe

Fluid society

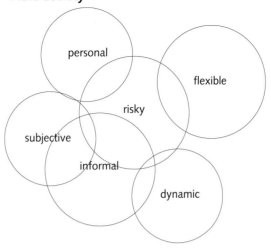

personal

flexible

risky

subjective

informal

dynamic

Changing society

	then	now	responses
Careers (doctors, teachers etc)	job for life vocation	contracts job	uncertainty less involvement
Relationships	marriage for life	partnerships/singles	doubts
Trust in authority (police, politicians, finance)	respect	mistrust/cynicism	anxiety
Life stages (adolescence to retirement)	set pattern	play at all ages	doubts
Pensions	guaranteed	shares/none	fear
Social structure	class system conformity	rich or poor individuality	vulnerability
Gender roles	fixed	flexible	uncertainty
Family	nuclear	dispersed	isolation

As a result:

Plurality	no right way to live and think
Freedom	more choices to make
Informality	less need to be serious or respectful
Tolerance	open to new ideas
Anxiety	stress from loss of certainty

Age, gender, class, background, religion, ethnicity are less important

People are more alike in their lifestyles—a mass middle class

Individual differences are accepted as the norm

We compensate for loss of structure by forming new communities and tribes—health clubs, style followers, team supporters, environmental campaigners, etc

One of the results of these changes is freedom of choice, something we should celebrate, but which brings with it the need to constantly exercise that choice. Packaged goods illustrate the point where, in some market sectors, cereals, for example, the combination of brands, products and varieties extends into the hundreds, providing choice but, at the same time, making it more difficult and more individual.

Social trends

This freedom of choice coincides with the decline of the traditional family unit across North America and Europe. Euromonitor's Global Market Information Database provides demographic and lifestyle information on individual countries around the world and, as might be expected, there are differences between countries at different stages in their cultural and social development. We see, for example, Eastern European countries previously incorporated within the Soviet Bloc are at a different stage in their consumer evolution to the more mature economies within Europe where consumer culture has already been established. Similarly, countries as diverse as Mexico and China are developing their consumer-based lifestyles in a shorter timeframe compared to their European counterparts, as these economies also gather momentum.

As the Euromonitor reports reveal, however, although the timing may differ, many of the trends are broadly similar to those experienced in countries where freedom of choice and consumer power have become established as social norms. Mexico, for example, with a very different cultural heritage to Northern European countries, is seeing more women incorporated into the workforce. This has resulted in the number of men making everyday household purchasing decisions rising from 18% in 1998 to 43% in 2003 (Euromonitor, "Retailing in Mexico", 2004), echoing patterns already established in Europe.

In parallel with this trend, and across Europe as a whole, increasing numbers of people are experiencing more than one relationship, cohabiting or choosing to lead a single life. There is also a significant rise in single-parent families and in the number of women who balance a career with looking after a family. Many young adults opt to remain single in favour of cultivating jobs and careers. Rather than establishing families early in a relationship, it is being left until a considerable degree of financial stability has been obtained. With more singles leading a hectic working life, time is frequently at a premium.

There appears to be further convergence of social behaviour taking place on a global scale that transcends national and cultural differences among the younger generation. The world's teenagers have embraced the same new technologies and fashions, spread globally through the Internet and other media, sidelining many older cultural values and behavioural patterns. In that respect, teenagers in New York and Beijing probably have more in common with each other than they have with their own parents. Lindstrom and Seybold, in their book *Brand Child*, consider "Tween" behaviour across some 14 countries, confirming more similarities than differences in young people's perception of branding. This is an indicator of the global power of brands in cementing social behaviour across cultures.

These are examples of factors that are having a marked effect on the structure of many societies around the world and are fundamental elements in the creation of new markets. This type of information has a message for us all, but particularly for the design community. It offers the starting points from which designers can operate and create designs that are relevant to the segments of society being addressed. It is critical that designers understand and engage with changes taking place in society. You can't design without knowing who you are designing for.

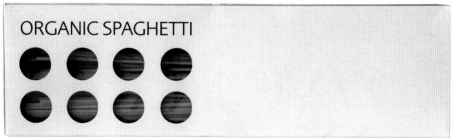

Left Although both products contain spaghetti made in Italy, they are targeted at very different audiences and sold at very different price points. The use of a carton immediately differentiates the expensive product from the day-to-day product. It is important for designers to understand these differences in consumer profile and motivation, even when the same product category is involved.

Eating habits

Looking at the eating habits within specific populations provides a key indicator of lifestyle change. It is the most basic of human needs and one that has also been imbued with social values and codes. The way that food is bought and consumed clearly indicates how the influences of traditional cultural values are, largely, diminishing. It is the influences of changing work patterns, economic conditions, health concerns, imported values and the global penetration of brands that have now become the dominant forces in shaping lifestyles. In most instances, the changes that have taken place in these areas have far outstripped the influence of governments, both in terms of far-reaching effect and speed of change. It is also striking to discover how different countries, despite having very different ranges of traditional and cultural values, are now exhibiting a common pattern of lifestyle change, with only minor deviations attributable to domestic conditions. While this is of major sociological interest, it is also highly significant in design terms, as the consumption of packaged food is rising in most parts of the world. The need for packaging design is, therefore, extending across product categories, countries and continents. This becomes particularly evident when the growth in packaged convenience food is considered.

Consumption of packaged and processed food—grams per capita

Canned meat and meat products	1998	2003	%change
Spain	512.1	587.1	14.65
Mexico	23.5	27.4	16.55
Germany	1,825.6	1,140.6	-37.52
Japan	128.0	127.6	-2.20
UK	1,644.8	1,583.4	-3.73
S Korea	229.0	497.1	17.31
Denmark	453.3	421.10	-7.11

Breakfast cereals	1998	2003	%change
Spain	845.4	1,108.7	31.14
Mexico	1,467.4	1,962.3	33.73
Germany	2,265.4	2,530.2	11.69
Japan	204.5	205.3	0.40
UK	7,046.5	6,819.6	-3.22
S Korea	358.0	503.1	40.52
Denmark	3,171.9	3,513.1	10.75

Chilled food	1998	2003	%change
Spain	5,348.8	9,049.7	69.19
Mexico	1,127.2	1,474.1	33.73
Germany	2,948.2	3,228.0	9.49
Japan	32,733.6	32,845.6	0.30
UK	16,423.2	20,295.7	23.58
S Korea	3,241.3	4,665.5	43.94
Denmark	21,797.8	22,506.0	3.25

Dried food	1998	2003	%change
Spain	9,260.2	9,733.7	5.11
Mexico	10,252.8	12,492.6	21.85
Germany	6,766.8	7,627.4	12.72
Japan	40,301.6	37,889.9	-6.00
UK	4,433.7	4,784.4	7.91
S Korea	39,254.3	46,629.6	18.79
Denmark	9,972.9	10,716.1	7.45

Frozen food	1998	2003	%change
Spain	3,766.4	5,189.9	37.80
Mexico	378.0	481.9	27.47
Germany	10,032.4	12,638.5	25.98
Japan	3,492.1	3,937.7	12.80
UK	23,103.3	24,918.3	7.86
S Korea	1,476.1	2,089.3	41.54
Denmark	34,564.4	37,291.4	7.89

Ready meals	1998	2003	%change
Spain	2,046.3	3,222.5	57.48
Mexico	43.9	58.1	32.59
Germany	3,449.9	3,553.2	2.99
Japan	8,390.3	9,996.8	19.10
UK	12,060.5	14,239.2	18.07
S Korea	29.4	54.5	85.36
Denmark	7,569.8	8,207.4	8.42

Source: Euromonitor (2003)

Convenience cooking

In this chart, selected categories of pre-packed foods are compared across seven countries showing, overall, a trend towards convenience cooking. Taking the consumption of ready meals as the most extreme example of these lifestyle indicators, the chart indicates growth, albeit at different rates, in all seven countries.

As the chart shows, the highest growth in packed and processed convenience food in the countries listed is occurring in Mexico, South Korea and Spain, while the highest consumption of convenience food tends to be in the more mature consumer-based economies of Northern Europe and Japan. Such consumer societies are characterized by some or all of the following factors:

—significant numbers of women in work
—high ownership of microwave ovens
—lack of time due to the demands of work
—less emphasis on cultural and traditional eating patterns
—decline in culinary skills
—increase in eating out
—internationalization of eating habits
—increase in snacking

According to a Euromonitor survey ("Consumer Lifestyles in Germany", October 2004), four out of ten women in Germany stated that they are "not in the mood for cooking" during the week. In consumer-based economies, cooking at weekends has become a hobby where a more elaborate meal can be prepared for family or friends, whereas simple meals or convenience foods suit the time-poor households on week days.

Below The range of ready meals is rapidly expanding to include ethnic foods, healthy options and vegetarian meals. All offer the convenience of minimum preparation and cooking, allowing family members to eat according to their individual schedules, thus replacing the more traditional family meal.

% BMI overweight adults

	%
Saudi Arabia	72·50
UK	66·90
Germany	66·50
USA	66·30
Kuwait	64·16
Israel	62·20
Croatia	61·40
Chile	59·70
New Zealand	57·00
Australia	53·50
Czech Republic	51·73
Canada	49·10
Spain	49·00
Finland	45·00
Belgium	44·10
Sweden	43·90
Iran	42·80
Italy	42·60
Netherlands	41·80
Denmark	41·70
France	41·60
Brazil	40·60
Switzerland	36·61
Cuba	36·42
Ireland	34·00
Norway	33·40
Japan	23·40
China	18·90

Source: World Health Organization (2007)

Note: The national BMI data shown apply internationally recommended BMI cut-off points but data is not directly comparable due to variation in sampling procedures, age ranges and years of data collection.

The chart reveals some interesting information regarding overweight adults, indicating that the lack of dietary control and/ or physical exercise crosses national and cultural boundries and is a complex issue not always directly linked to national economic performance. Packaging will be increasingly used to highlight the fat (and salt) content of packaged food, particularly for snack foods consumed by children.

Health issues

The health record of nations, and sectors of society within them, provides another useful social indicator for designers. National health statistics frequently show trends that are a reflection of social or cultural behaviour. For example, obesity is a health issue in many societies, much of it associated with poor diets, snacking and lack of exercise, particularly among low-income families. Pre-packed foods have been criticized for being a contributory factor, given that they often contain high levels of salt, fats, preservatives and artificial colourings. In addition, packaging has provided convenience, allowing consumption at all times of day with minimum effort, making snacks, in particular, easy to access. In a strange juxtaposition of traditional values, it is now the rich who are thin while the poor get fat. This is not simply a financial issue but one that is often compounded by location, where the recreational facilities are inadequate, education is sub-standard, local shopping is poorly supported and the social environment depressing. It is hardly surprising, in these circumstances, that diets include fatty comfort foods and sugary drinks.

Obesity in childhood is recognized as a precursor to heart and diabetic problems in later life. The advertising and packaging, primarily of snack foods, aimed directly at children has been criticized as fuelling this trend. As packaging designers, we are in the front line of this argument because it is claimed that the design of packs for these unhealthy products attracts children's attention. While one of the prime objectives of packaging is to increase product sales, it is also a little unfair to blame packaging designers who, after all, are not responsible for the product formulations. It is probably less likely that designers will take an ethical stance over a bag of crisps, as some have done, for example, with cigarettes. Nor is such action likely to be necessary as pressure for change has come through governmental action and media pressure, with schools and parents beginning to take action to ensure a healthier diet coupled with more exercise. This has led to a massive increase in demand for low-fat, low-salt and low-sugar products and for healthier organic options. Product manufacturers and the multiple retailers have quickly responded by modifying recipes to reduce or eliminate ingredients considered to contribute to unhealthy eating. Packaging designers are to ensure that the sales appeal of these new product varieties on the shelves will be sufficient to overcome any potential loss of taste appeal experienced by children.

Organics—a broadening market

Manufacturers and retailers now believe that organic food has joined the mainstream. The scale of this in the UK is revealed by a 94% increase in spending on organic products between 2000 and 2005, according to Mintel ("Organics—UK", November 2005). As might be expected by their higher prices, the key group purchasing organic products are professional, well educated and middle class. In addition to an older 35–64 group committed to an organic lifestyle, households with children are also opting for organic products, particularly fruit drinks within the packaged products sector. Increased demand, however, is expected to drive down prices, making organics affordable to a wider market.

While there is general encouragement from governments and the media to move towards healthier eating, time constraints and lack of culinary skills have created a market for healthy pre-packaged organic ready meals. There is, also, a new hybrid generation of ready prepared gourmet meal kits. At the most expensive level, these provide sauces, pre-prepared "fresh" vegetables and accompaniments together with meat or fish, wine, dessert, fresh cream, chocolates etc., with a guaranteed maximum preparation time for conventional cooking (around 15 minutes). There is a packaging opportunity here as many of these gourmet meal kits have an almost industrial catering appearance. Currently, the market seems to be dividing into two sectors with pre-prepared, healthy, so-called "gourmet" meals targeting a busy professional market while simpler organic replacements for family favourites target working mothers. Both markets will be of interest to packaging designers but the healthy "gourmet" meal concept is particularly challenging as it takes pre-packaged food in a new direction. Here the packaging design will have to demonstrate convenience while also conveying the food interest, natural organic content and health benefits—a complex message for packaging to communicate.

Although ethical and food safety issues will also remain important to organic food purchasers, the connection between healthy eating and organic food will become significant in all market sectors. There is, however, a polarization within society where low-income families, on the one hand, cannot afford the healthier organic options, while, on the other, high earners become health obsessed. The lifestyle of the latter includes a healthy dietary regime but also embraces exercise, through membership of health clubs and participation in sports, all maintained by their higher incomes and denied to those with no disposable income. This has inevitably resulted in a health products boom, notably in energy drinks and cereal bars, clearly targeted at "fitness fans" requiring an energy boost "on the go". In general, these new products have quickly become assimilated into the mainstream, broadening their appeal to a much wider target market who also want an energy boost from time to time for other, non-sporting reasons. The energy product market, therefore, now extends to include long-distance drivers and clubbers.

A further specialist market is also developing for "functional food", sometimes also called "neutriceuticals". Functional food products claim to be proactive in promoting health, typically containing bacteria, enzymes, minerals, vitamins or other active ingredients to provide specific health benefits in addition to nutritional value. The challenge for packaging designers will be to move these products away from specialized health supplement sectors and into mainstream market sectors while, at the same time, communicating their complex health/nutritional messages.

Above Designed by Philippe Starck, this instant organic meal just requires the addition of boiling water. Here the combination of exclusive designer brand and instant meal is a difficult proposition for consumers to understand through the packaging alone.

Below One of the first brands on the market, Red Bull has now been joined by a host of competitors. This is Sprite 3G from Coca-Cola, containing glucose, caffeine and guarana. The appeal extends beyond sports and into the mainstream arena for those who need an energy boost.

Alcohol

"Binge" drinking, heavy sessional drinking to get drunk, has received much media attention for both its resultant anti-social behaviour and health concerns. As the Institute for Alcohol Studies points out in its fact sheet (2005), it has, however, been an integral part of Northern European culture for generations, extending at least as far back as the Vikings. Of the 20 or so countries covered in the report, it becomes clear that regular daily drinking is most common in Southern Europe where it is part of the ritual of family eating. There is, however, a growing culture of intoxication, particularly in Northern Europe, where young people have adopted a hedonistic approach to drink and drugs. They actively seek drunkenness for fun, excitement and to fit in with their peer group. There are territorial differences between cultures with regard to alcohol preferences, with regular consumption of wine, often accompanying food, in Southern Europe, whereas in Northern Europe the emphasis has been on beer and spirits within a pub environment. The dark and cold winters in the North also play a part, encouraging the consumption of warming spirits. The volume of traditional alcoholic drinks consumed, such as brandy and whisky, has been in decline for many years, presenting a challenge to manufacturers to develop new products that will attract a younger audience into the drinks market. There are now many pre-mixed alcoholic products on the market, often based on vodka to provide an innocuous taste but considerable "bite". Packaging designers are constantly responding to the alcoholic drinks trade to create packs for new drinks specifically targeted at separate male and female segments within the 18–24 -year-old market. It is difficult to change deeply ingrained patterns of social behaviour through design alone, but a challenge for the future may be to find ways of encouraging a more responsible attitude to the consumption of alcohol. Printing responsible drinking messages on bottle labels is probably not enough and we may have to turn to new technology to find the answers. Could, for example, a neck insert in a bottle provide a read-out of alcoholic units consumed, or could low-alcohol or non-alcoholic drinks be made "cool" and appealing to the target audience?

The cult of celebrity and new tribes

From early times, there have always been celebrities, role models and tribes. The difference today is in the active branding and marketing activities that promote them, using all the tools of the mass communication media, including packaging. Sections of society have become obsessed with the status of celebrity, perceiving it to be a personal goal. Magazines such as *OK!* and *Hello!* specialize in photographing celebrities, often revealing the brands that they buy and creating a brand culture amongst readers. The glamorous celebrity lifestyle as portrayed in the press is often very different from that of the reader and, for many, buying into the brand represents an achievable escape from the confines of a society where other opportunities for personal growth might be limited. It can, however, prove useful on some projects for designers to identify a role model or celebrity that typifies the target market, as expanded in Chapter Three.

JUST DO IT.

Left Nike was among the first companies to recognize that it was offering a lifestyle choice rather than just another pair of trainers. Buying into the Nike brand becomes a statement for personal development and the potential to escape the confines of society.

Our new society with its lack of formal structure is highly tolerant of individual differences, offering us anonymity when, sometimes, we wish others to recognize our differences. True individuality would, however, be a solitary experience and as social beings we are more at ease when we share our individuality with like-minded people. We form tribes. Characteristically, we may choose to dress in a particular way, perhaps as "Goths", bikers or cowboys, for example, to express our personal tribal loyalties. We may choose a more subtle route through brand choice and display our loyalty by the distinctive white wires of the iPod. The iPod tribe is apparently open to all ages and equally accessible to those in suits or jeans. Showing that we are tribal members tells others that we are "cool", technologically alert, musically driven and have discerning taste with, incidentally, the disposable income to purchase tribal membership. It is also possible to use packaging in the creation of tribal brand properties, for example, designing energy drink containers for the urban teenager that are "cool" to be seen with.

To do this successfully, however, designers need to understand these new social groupings and the factors that motivate them. This also applies to brand extensions, where a brand sees an opportunity for diversifying into a new product area while maintaining its tribal band of followers. In the way that the on-line bookseller Amazon advises you that "the people who bought this book also bought the following books", it is helpful in the understanding of target audiences to follow a similar procedure. If, for example, the tribe buys Wrigley's chewing gum, what other products do they buy? Would they also buy Wrigley's toothpaste, if it existed? This type of thinking leads to innovation and represents a way forward for design.

Social trends

Key issues with specific implications for design

Rich/poor gap increasing	creates pressures for those seeking to escape from the poverty trap
Ageing population	segments differ widely, including fit and active/elderly and infirm
Increase in singles	choice of career/money before family—cash rich/time short
Children born later in parents' lives	wealthier parents with higher expectations
Health/fitness gap	lifespan shortens for the poor and extends for the affluent
Increased environmental concern	climate change becomes evident to many
Women in work	less time for family
Lack of life skills	cooking, mending, making—seeking solutions
Fear mentality	disease/disasters/terrorists/litigation/crime

Changing issues

Some contemporary issues affecting design are summarized in the list above, but it is by no means exhaustive. Designers, in addition to being participants in society, must also be observers of it. In particular, we need to observe changes in attitudes and concerns so that we may react to them. Keeping research up to date on such issues is vital if we are to produce fresh designs that are meaningful to today's consumer. Design is for people and, therefore, successful designers must understand the people they design for and the restrictions and opportunities that society provides. Many designers keep scrapbooks into which articles, cartoons and adverts all find their way. It is worth including material that reflects social change into such books. Today, this might be about global warming and energy reduction, religious segregation, the design of affordable, energy-efficient housing, public transport, use of open spaces or access to the countryside. Tomorrow's concerns may have a different slant but, to designers, it is all important. With on-line access providing a wealth of information, it is useful to create your own folders of socio-economic data as a research resource, available to provide depth to any design project.

Technological advances

A time-travelling citizen from our self-imposed base date of 1945, moving directly from then to current times, would be astonished, delighted or possibly horrified by what they would now find. Computers, plasma screen TVs, mobile phones, microwave cooking, GPS navigation and the Internet are all examples of technological advances that were only in the realm of science fiction in 1945.

Many of the changes in technology that underpin packaging remain largely unseen, materials and processes working in the background but making a significant impact on our lives. The pace of change is quickening and so, today, we are on the verge of a new technological revolution that may, as with previous changes in technology, be hidden from consumers but offer designers new and dramatic opportunities.

Microwave cooking

Percy Spencer invented the microwave oven in 1945, paving the way for the first commercial cookers operating in the USA in 1947. It was not, however, until 1967 that dimensions could be reduced to table-top size and, even then, they were cooled by connection to the domestic water supply. The late 1970s and early 1980s saw microwave cookers that were small and affordable enough to become popular, initially in the USA but soon finding interest elsewhere.

Below left Microwave technology allowed the subsequent development of easy-cook ready meals to take place.

Below right The use of PET trays with their stability at high temperatures has allowed ready meals to have a dual oven capability and opened the market for convenient ready prepared food.

PET

In many cases technical innovations create subsequent opportunities that are not fully appreciated at the time of their introduction. Chemists developing polyester, for example, would have been surprised to find that their new compound, in its PET (Polyethylene Terephthalate) form, would become the ideal material for producing lightweight trays to contain food ready for oven and microwave cooking. PET was first introduced as a packaging material for carbonated drinks in 1979, but the characteristics of heat resistance and transparency to microwave radiation also made it ideal for packaging dual-ovenable ready meals. Coinciding with the development of microwave oven technology, PET and particularly in its crystallized form, CPET, made it possible for the ready meal market to develop. Now, microwavable ready meals represent the fastest growing market sector within multiple groceries.

Packaging designers need to keep abreast of new technical developments, even when they seem unconnected with packaging, as they may be able to be harnessed to develop new packaging concepts.

Frozen food—from commodity to ready meal

The USA set the trend in domestic freezer ownership around the mid 1950s. Freezing provides a means of preserving food for a wide range of products without the need to incorporate chemical preservatives, a marketing bonus in today's health-conscious climate. Despite a period of stagnation, the sector is beginning

Below Often criticized for their lack of innovation, frozen food manufacturers are now beginning to develop products to compete with their ambient counterparts. This German product range targets women concerned with diet yet who seek both convenience and more exotic meal solutions.

to grow and expand from commodity items to include convenience products, vegetarian options, children's meals and organics. Frozen products have not been developed to the same extent as their ambient competitors and are only now beginning to show packaging innovation, but there are still opportunities for development. There are, for example, still relatively few meals containing products requiring different cooking times that can be microwaved directly from the freezer, yet this is an area where packaging technology could assist. Imagine a pack that can defrost fruit juice yet keep it cold, provide hot coffee, crisp bacon and brown sausages and potatoes, all from frozen and at the same time—the all-day breakfast in a pack that goes from freezer to microwave to the table! It exists and the technology is already available to expand this concept into further areas. It works on the principle that any metal components swiftly heat up when exposed to microwave energy. By printing or depositing patterns of metal onto carton board or PET, these "susceptors", as they are known, will radiate heat when placed in a microwave oven. If the metallic patterns are distributed in different densities across the pack the microwave energy heats different areas of the pack to different temperatures. By printing patterns in the correct places, temperature is controlled throughout the pack allowing selective cooking of different meal components to take place within the same timeframe.

Modified atmosphere packaging and film technology

A fresh, crisp salad makes an appealing accompaniment to a meal, but many salad components do not stay fresh for long, even in the fridge. The oxygen in the atmosphere soon makes them limp and off-colour. By placing them in a transparent film bag and flushing out the oxygen with nitrogen, the shelf life of the contents is extended. Additionally, this opens opportunities for preparing mixed salads, incorporating other salad leaves and offering a convenient pre-washed and prepared product. In effect, this extends growing seasons and allows salads and many other products to remain available all year. Although this packaging provides greater consumer choice and convenience, the downside is that consumer knowledge of seasonal produce (particularly amongst children, and also many adults) is declining.

RFID

RFID, or Radio Frequency Identification, is destined to replace bar codes. The RFID tag contains a microchip and circuit that is activated by external radio waves or can be powered to provide vast amounts of data. These range from the simple chips embedded in CD cases, clothing etc., which, unless deactivated on purchase causes the store alarm to sound as you walk through the door, to the sophisticated self-powered chip that explains where and what it is. Such "smart" packaging is widely predicted to influence the future of packaging in a way that will be as revolutionary as the bar code it supersedes. RFID tags could monitor the quality of food within a pack or the temperature extremes that the pack has experienced, warning of deterioration or, alternatively, adjusting the sell-by date. The cost of tags and the equipment to read them has, up until now, prevented their widespread adoption for packaging applications. That is about to change

Above Being able to choose speciality salads and serve them instantly meets the needs of those with busy lifestyles. Ready prepared salads are finding acceptance even in areas where traditional cooking is the norm.

Below Incorporating pressure relief valves in the film conveniently allows cooking to take place in the bag when the pack is heated in a conventional or microwave oven.

Above top Scannable bar codes have created a revolution in retailing in terms of automating checkouts, tracking sales, reordering stock and controlling warehouse and shipping movements, while also tracking individual consumer spending patterns.

Above The RFID tag here is being used to detect theft should the product be taken out of the store without the tag being deactivated. Although the components are concealed beneath the label, in this instance consumers are warned of the device. In other applications the RFID tag may be hidden within the pack.

and, at the time of writing, Wal-Mart are conducting trials within their US stores. There are, however, concerns about the environmentally safe disposal of the chip. Despite this, designers should monitor RFID applications in packaging to see what design opportunities it may offer as the technology develops.

Nanotechnology

As this technology is involved with structures smaller than the wavelength of light, we may only imagine what this sub-molecular world might look like. The effects on the properties of materials, however, are likely to be dramatic. The packaging industry is actively engaged in the development of such nano-materials, and plastics with the strength of steel, self-cleaning surfaces and transparent waterproof paper are all anticipated. The implications for packaging design could be profound, offering a new range of previously unknown material options. Further into the future, it is predicted that nano-robotics will be developed, where molecular sized "machines" could carry out, for example, the cleaning of clogged arteries and other medical tasks. The packaging applications of nano-robotics are as yet unknown and, once more, designers should monitor new developments. In the meantime, however, there are real concerns that nano-materials might "escape" and cause environmental damage. Developments continue while the potential hazards are debated by governments.

Paper batteries

Printed miniature batteries suitable for powering visual displays or RFID tags are already in production. The packaging media have heralded the imminent arrival of packaging that contains self-powered electronics enabling packaging to have an audio-visual output. This could provide moving or changing graphic displays on the pack or some form of audio output—the much discussed "talking can". Supermarket shelves containing talking cans and moving graphics is a daunting thought. It, ultimately, may be a concept with great potential for some specialist applications, for example, augmenting instructional text on medicines by audio output or providing graphics that allow selection from a range of language options. Such technology could also be used in a different way, either on-pack or on-shelf, to guide shoppers into other areas within a store. If packs are selected from, for example, a nut-free range of dietary products, moving shelf displays might suggest other similar products to consider, recipe information for nut-free meals or diet-compatible cookery books. Another potential application could be bar codes that automatically delete when the product sell-by date is reached, preventing them being purchased and eliminating a source of food poisoning. Overall, however, it is the marketing potential to persuade shoppers to buy more or the ability to make economic gains in the supply chain, that are likely to be the driving force behind these developments. Of greater significance for now is the underlying battery technology—soon it will be possible for batteries to be cheaply printed onto paper or flexible film, allowing the development of active micro-circuitry to proceed. As with RFID tags, however, some experts have expressed environmental concerns about safe disposal of such batteries and circuitry and, until these are addressed, progress is likely to be slow.

Retailing

We have seen how changes to society and the emergence of new technologies have had a significant impact on packaging design, but it is, perhaps, the way products are sold that has been the most powerful driver, establishing packaging design as a fundamental part of commercial activity.

Sales of packaged products today are dominated by the major multiple retailers. The concept of multiple retailing began in the USA when, in 1859, the Great Atlantic and Pacific Tea company was established. A&P, as it was known, had rolled out a chain of two thousand retail outlets across America by the outbreak of the First World War. Initially, as the name suggests, they sold only tea, but later other groceries were sold as well. In most instances, products were sold at the counter and measured or weighed out and wrapped by the sales assistant. At this time paper wraps were widely used for dry goods and customers often brought their own containers for liquids. A parallel development was seen in Britain when, in 1871, Thomas Lipton opened his first shop in Glasgow, Scotland, importing tea from his own plantations in Ceylon (now Sri Lanka). By 1900, Lipton had established 450 stores throughout Britain, now also stocking butter and bacon from Lipton's farms in Ireland.

Other names we recognize in Britain today became established around this time. The first Sainsbury's store was opened in 1869, in London's Drury Lane, and by 1939 had expanded to a chain of 255 shops across the South of England. Jack Cohen founded Tesco in 1932, which soon developed as a chain of stores offering low prices. As is the case today, the retailers operated on low profit margins, keeping prices low by bulk buying and, wherever possible, growing and processing their own produce. And as these companies expanded their product ranges, some products began to be sold in pre-packed format.

Above left This 1906 Sainsbury's store, UK, has a very different layout to today's stores. Sainsbury's soon became a favoured supplier across the south of England.

Above right Established in 1859, the Great Atlantic and Pacific Tea Company, USA, became the first multiple retailer, with two thousand outlets by 1914.

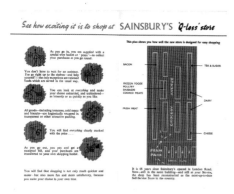

Above top This 1960s leaflet explained how to shop in Sainsbury's new self-service supermarket. Packaging now became the silent salesman for the majority of products, often the only communication between shopper and product.

Above France led the way in Europe, developing vast supermarkets, named hypermarchés, stocking both food and non-food items, such as this early example, Auchan, in the 1960s.

Self-service shopping

Meanwhile, back in the USA, a new and significant event had taken place. Clarence Saunders of Memphis, Tennessee, patented the name "self-serving store" in 1916. Saunders' eccentrically named "Piggly-Wiggly" stores were the first self-service formats and were soon copied. By 1923, San Francisco boasted a 68,000 square-foot self-service grocery store, known as the "Crystal Palace", complete with parking spaces. (This is equivalent to 6317 square metres, slightly larger than the average French hypermarket.) Closer still to the format we know today, the King Kullen "Food Market" opened in 1930 in Jamaica, New York, offering a much wider range of products than groceries alone. The final part of the USA retail revolution was put in place by Albers Super Mkts. of Cincinnati, which registered the name "Supermarket" in 1933. Despite the American public's enthusiasm for the self-service concept, by 1955 supermarkets in the USA represented only 5% of grocery sales although, significantly for the future, they accounted for 50% of food sales. The move towards self-service shopping largely depended on the ability to supply pre-packed products, leading to the establishment of a strong packaging industry in the USA.

Following the Second World War, parallels between events in the USA and elsewhere diverged dramatically. In many parts of the world, nations struggled with bombed-out infrastructures and devastated economies, while America's huge wartime commitment to the manufacture of arms, munitions and equipment remained intact. The factories that had supplied the war effort were modern and massively efficient and were soon employed in producing goods of all types in a post-war boom. By the 1950s, most American households had a telephone, refrigerator, television, washing machine and a car.

In Europe at this time, rationing and shortages were the norm. Shops, both independent stores and the retail multiples, were staffed by sales assistants and, in many instances, goods were purchased as "loose" items, to be weighed and packed into plain brown bags or, where packaged, supplied by the sales assistant from behind the counter. In Britain, experiments with self-service shopping in 1947 were abandoned due to logistical problems in the handling of coupons and ration books. It was not until 1950 that rationing was abandoned for most products (although sugar and sweets continued to be rationed until 1953). This allowed Sainsbury's to introduce their first self-service store in 1950, complete with leaflets explaining to customers what they were expected to do.

Packaging now became the only communication between shopper and product. By the 1960s, austerity in many parts of Europe and Asia was being replaced by expanding economies and full employment. Many women were now working, with less time to spend shopping. They now had refrigerators and freezers, allowing them to do their shopping weekly rather than daily. Car ownership also increased, further enabling shopping in bulk. Commercial television, a novel concept in countries used to state radio and television, introduced advertising for packaged goods, often featuring the pack to reinforce recognition at point of sale.

The self-service supermarket format was rapidly becoming established, joined by the even larger hypermarket format pioneered in France during the 1960s. Across Northern Europe, retailer multiples were increasing their power, both by acquisition of smaller groups and by territorial expansion, pushing south into the Mediterranean regions, east to the emerging ex-Soviet controlled states and west to South America. The success of the retail multiples, in all national arenas, is characterized by the strategies they have adopted:

—Consistently low prices that undercut prices of local small traders
—Highly efficient logistical supply
—Low staff costs
—Own-label products challenging established brands
—Sophisticated marketing techniques such as data mining and consumer tracking
—Low profit margins relying on volume sales
—Ability to drive down supplier costs
—Enforcement of quality standards
—Aggressive acquisition policies such as predator behaviour towards competitors and sites
—Ability to diversify profitably

Below Supermarket layout leaves little to chance. Commonly, freshness is emphasized by having the fresh vegetables and fruits situated at the entrance.

Supermarket design

Little is left to chance in designing supermarkets. Apart from the considerable experience accumulated by the multiple groceries, studies using CCTV and eye-tracking equipment demonstrate shopping behaviour. Aisle widths are adjusted accordingly, wider to encourage browsing for high-margin goods and narrower in low-margin commodity areas. Allocating products to shelf height is important; impulse sales being achieved more readily at eye level. Consideration is even given to which products are to be stacked on the right or left of the aisle, relative to traffic flow, as customers tend to look left but scan right.

The use of bar codes at the checkout allows automated stock replenishment and also provides valuable data on consumer spending patterns. When combined with loyalty card use, it is possible to build an individual purchasing profile correlated with the customer's address and bank details. With so much information available, retailers employ or establish data mining companies, which use supercomputers to manipulate this information to target specific groups with offers.

Global retailing

The multiple retailers now control much of the spend on packaged products and grocery products across Europe. In the UK, multiple retailers now control around 84% of domestic spend on household products. Bear in mind that the bulk of this spend is made with just four companies: Tesco, ASDA Wal-Mart, Sainsbury's and Morrison's, and the power of the multiples becomes clear. The French government has introduced legislation to curb the power of retail multiples, but according to a Euromonitor survey ("Retailing in France", 2004), the market share of combined supermarkets and hypermarkets is still high at 73·9%. While such high proportions of consumer spend, controlled by a handful of retailers, is worrying for governments, it is also of great concern to product manufacturers. Farmers and produce suppliers to the retail giants are under pressure to reduce costs while meeting stringent demands on quality and appearance. Similarly, retailers seek aggressive price deals to stock branded pre-packed products. The result of this has been manufacturers also forming larger groups in response to the economies of scale demanded by retail multiples. Many established brands are now incorporated within the portfolios of larger organizations.

Most of the major European retail companies have been active in cross-border trading for some time, often involving complex alliances and different store names. This has now developed into truly global trading. Carrefour (France), the largest European retailer and number two world wide (Wal-Mart is number one), currently has a presence in the countries listed in the table, left, using a variety of names including Champion, Ed and Dia.

Clearly, the multiple grocery companies control a significant proportion of global retailing, including the sales of many branded and pre-packaged products. Packaging designers should be aware that, in the majority of design tasks, the supermarket environment is where most products compete. Thus it is important to ensure that pack designs are judged by supermarket performance criteria when being evaluated in the studio, an area covered later in Chapter Four.

Retailer global expansion —Carrefour stores

Outlets	Number of stores (2004)
France	5350
Spain	217
Italy	411
Belgium	134
Greece	447
Portugal	293
Poland	87
Switzerland	8
Turkey	251
Czech Republic	10
Slovakia	4
Brazil	360
Argentina	452
Mexico	29
Colombia	15
Taiwan	34
Korea	27
China	226
Thailand	20
Malaysia	8
Indonesia	15
Japan	8
Singapore	2

Source: Euromonitor (2005)

Home shopping

Home shopping, using the Internet to order and pay for goods, has seen slower growth than many experts predicted. While all the major multiples offer an on-line service, they still prefer to get customers into the physical store where it is much easier to create opportunities for sales. Buying bread on-line is not much of an experience compared to smelling hot bread coming out of the oven. It is this "experience" that has proved elusive to create through the electronic media. To have the option of on-line shopping at all requires the shopper to have access to a computer linked to the Internet, and to be in an area served by home shopping services. In addition, shoppers require the technical capability to use the equipment, the financial underpinning to pay for the goods on-line and the flexibility to set up a system for collecting or receiving the products ordered. While these conditions can be fulfilled by an increasing number of the shopping public, it still excludes many, particularly those sectors of society who would benefit most from home shopping, including the elderly and infirm, those who cannot afford personal transport and those who live in isolated rural communities.

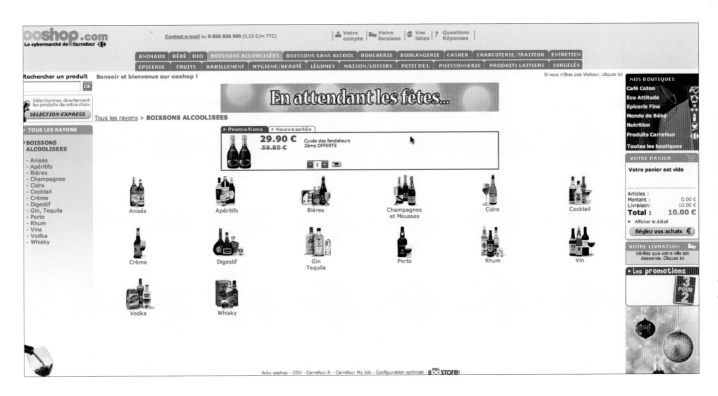

Above Ooshop, the home shopping website of Carrefour's wonderfully named "cyber-marché", presents a screen familiar to most home shoppers, providing click-to-enlarge pack shots.

Most home shopping sites are fairly dull and uninviting, simply providing some special offers and a list of product categories. A home shopping search by category does not present the competitive products next to each other as on shelf, rather presenting a list that the shopper scrolls down. It is a much more analytical process, where price is highlighted and any emotional attraction to products through design, either functional consumer benefit features or aesthetics, is minimized. Images of the packaged product are usually small and even "click-to-enlarge" images are of low resolution, largely due to the amount of information that can be processed by home computers. With much greater penetration of broadband, it should be possible to create much livelier sites with more imaginative graphics.

The debate for designers is whether or not packaging should be designed to sell from the screen as effectively as from the shelf. If so, the pack design would probably need to be adjusted to improve screen recognition. Little research has been conducted into the appearance of packaging as it appears on websites. Most work concerns click-through rates and the effectiveness of banner and pop-up advertising. Drèze and Hussherr (2003) conducted limited trials into how people look at banner adverts on websites, using eye-tracking technology. As a side issue to the main thrust of their work, they found differing behaviour patterns between young and old respondents and between "expert" web surfers and "non-experts". This suggests that there may also be differences in home shopping patterns between different market segments and that the importance of seeing an accurate, enlarged image of the pack may vary between home shopping users. Currently, packaging design is not being developed to meet the needs of the Internet and, until home shopping can create an experience, perhaps drawing on computer games technology, concessions to the on-screen appearance of packaging are unlikely to be made. Consumer motivation is also clearly different, with a deliberate initial choice being made to shop either conventionally, where emotional decisions are more likely, or on-line, where a more analytical approach is adopted.

Diversification

Most European countries are now imposing restrictions on the size and location of retail multiple stores, partly due to the detrimental effect on local communities where small local traders, unable to compete on price, are forced to close. Local authorities now frequently deny further expansion of current sites on the grounds of increased traffic congestion. So, large retailers are seeking to diversify, first by looking at the type of store, and secondly at their product range.

Smaller store formats are being developed to allow mini-stores to be located in high streets and suburban areas. Petrol forecourt sites provide opportunities for fuel cost reduction incentives obtained from shopping in the main stores, together with a further sales platform.

Product ranges are increasing dramatically as more products aimed at niche markets are developed. In the typical edge-of-town supermarket in the UK it is not uncommon for 40,000 different items to be stocked. The range of food has expanded to include many specialist items, fruits, spices and sauces that, just a few years ago, would only have been available in specialist shops. Healthy options, organic and dietary products now find an increased in-store presence but, in the UK, it is the expansion of the ranges of convenience food and ready meals that has been most dramatic. In the non-food area, French hypermarkets have established a lead that others now follow by introducing clothing, cookware, electrical goods, motoring equipment, DVDs, CDs, cameras and other hard goods, together with a range of services including telecoms, ophthalmic and medical clinics, banking, insurance and other financial services. The second largest clothing retailer in the UK is now ASDA Wal-Mart but competition is tough, with Tesco offering its basic jeans for just £3, helping to push its clothing sales figures up by 28% to £700 million in 2004.

Retail future

By 2015, socio-economic changes and technological advances will still be forcing the pace of retail development. Smaller families with less formal meal structures and the growth of the single and elderly populations will continue to fuel the desire for easy-to-prepare, portioned meals, often with the implication of less frequent trips to the supermarket. Retailers will respond to this by trying to make the retail environment more attractive, particularly for (high-spending) families. The average shopping time at an edge-of-town supermarket is around 20 minutes. Retailers recognize that the longer shoppers remain on site, the more they are likely to spend. Because there are often planning restrictions on increasing existing store sizes, the incorporation of radically new in-store features is likely to be limited. Nevertheless, store design will continue to evolve to create an improved shopping experience.

It is likely that RFID tagged packaging will permit scanning of the total trolley content, allowing customers to pack as they shop and eliminating checkout delays, particularly if the loyalty card also develops into a bank card. This would allow shoppers to scan their card at the checkout, automatically deducting the bill from their account and reordering replacement stock, while also gathering information to target packs and future offers to individual customers. Both packs and shelf signage will be able to communicate key information visually and audibly, responding to shopper requests, for example, by providing dietary details and allergy warnings. This type of technology will also be able to guide consumers to other similar products.

The other key issue retailers may seek to address is that of recycling—which will have a major influence on packaging and packaging design. The issue of packaging and waste will increase in significance as the environment and climate change continue to rise in importance. For marketing reasons, and to meet increased environmental packaging obligations, retailers may introduce recycling in a way that engages the public while demonstrating the retail brand's environmental responsibility. It will become as critical an ethical issue as Fairtrade and organic food are now.

Changes in design practice

Packaging design began to be recognized as a design discipline in the booming economy of the USA in the late 1950s. Companies set up packaging engineering departments whose role was to design functional packaging that would stand up to transit conditions, be efficient to fill on production lines and economic to purchase. The emphasis was on protection and cost. A packaging engineer was expected to produce a specification for the pack, which detailed materials, dimensions and style, and made reference to graphics in terms of the number of colours. A packaging standard was also prepared for production departments, showing how many inner packs, labels, outer packs etc. were required for each product. The specification was then used by the purchasing department to obtain competitive quotes. Graphic design was commissioned separately from companies that were beginning to specialize in packaging. As American companies extended their manufacturing operations overseas, they brought their methods with them. One of the first specialist packaging design companies outside the USA was established in 1972 by Richard Head and Ed Siebert. Based in London, SiebertHead drew on Richard's experience in advertising and marketing and Ed's proven track record as a graphic designer with Proctor & Gamble in Cincinatti.

Below left These pages from *The Complete Guide to Illustration and Design*, edited by Terence Dalley, appear in the 1988 edition. Although it is not very long ago, technology has radically changed the way designers work, allowing them to produce artwork without the involvement of artwork specialists.

Below right In the 1980s, preparing artwork often included the use of hand-applied lettering, lines, tints and other effects. Letraset developed a huge range of materials in rubdown transfer format. Their catalogue, shown here, describes how to use the lettering.

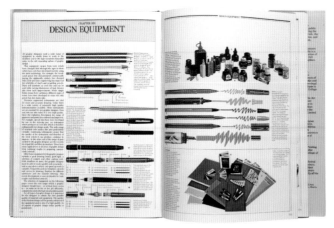

Now there are many packaging design companies, offering a mixture of services including structural and graphic design. It is also common for advertising agencies to incorporate packaging design as part of their portfolio of services.

Technology has transformed the skills required to produce packaging design work. Laborious and time-consuming methods, involving highly developed but mainly manual skills, meant longer lead times in designing packaging than would be the case now. It was the arrival of the Apple Mac, together with design software, that moved studio practice from the drawing board to the screen.

The production of artwork using Letraset and achieved by producing films has been entirely replaced by electronic production, and the latest generation of Apple computers are blisteringly fast (and in colour) compared to their predecessors. Yet the ability to draw remains a fundamental design skill, and there is still a niche for marker rendering and other manual techniques.

While the technology has changed, the conduct of packaging design studies has remained fairly standard across a wide range of organizations. The methods in current use are those described in this book. Many design companies now offer packaging as simply one of many services, often including branding, corporate identity and web design. Indeed, the technology underpinning them has converged, making it entirely possible for animators, illustrators, photographers, structural designers and graphic designers to work together, providing a large portfolio of services.

With electronic communications, companies can have a presence in several countries and relay work to dedicated production groups elsewhere. The increasing power of laptops also means that designers are far more mobile than ever before, working on site, at home and on trains as well as in the studio. The practice of packaging design has become both flexible in its location and multinational in its outlook.

Leading packaging design companies

It is difficult to extract the world's leading packaging design companies from such wide-ranging and diverse company profiles. The following list is, therefore, simply a selection from the award winners featured in The Mobius Awards in 2005, as reported in *Package Design* magazine.

Zunda Design Group
Connecticut, USA for self-promotion
www.zundagroup.com

Wallace Church Inc
New York, USA for 44 Degree North Vodka
(US) www.wallacechurch.com

Liu Wen Originality Team
China, for Century Old Alcohol (China)

Dare!
Leeds, UK for Toro Wine (UK)
www.dareonline.co.uk

Williams Murray Hamm
London, UK for Fortnum & Mason Jellies (UK),
Sainsbury's Organic Line (UK)
www.creatingdifference.com

Pearlfisher
London, UK for Waitrose Soup Line (UK)
www.pearlfisher.com

Ziggurat
London, UK for Jonathan Crisp (UK)
www.zigguratbrands.com

P&W
London, UK for Tesco Finest Suncare (US)
www.p-and-w.com

Design Bridge
London, UK for Lapponia (UK)
www.designbridge.com

Lewis Moberly
London, UK for Mateus Tempranillo (UK),
Icelandic Glacial Water (UK)
www.lewismoberly.com

Amore
Stockholm, Sweden for Bocca Dark Chocolates
(Sweden) www.amore.se

Bloom
London, UK for Unilever, Wall's Ice Cream
Line (UK) www.bloom-design.com

Pure Equator
Nottingham, UK for Label M Hair Product Line
(UK) www.pure-equator.com

Conclusion

Designing exciting and innovative packaging requires more than just good ideas or exceptional keyboard skills. These are valuable attributes but, as this chapter indicates, good packaging design is underpinned by understanding the social, technological and economic factors that motivate and shape the lives of those you are designing for. This, together with knowledge of the marketplace and the environment where products will be bought, helps designers to create compelling packaging that engages the target audience. Chapter Two expands on this theme, assisting you in identifying and understanding a target audience.

Further reading and additional resource list

Xavier Drèze and François-Xavier Hussherr, "Internet Advertising: is anybody watching?" *Journal of Interactive Marketing* 2003 Interesting research into "click-through" rates—how internet users react to online adverts

John Grant, *The New Marketing Manifesto: The 12 Rules for Building Successful Brands in the 21st Century*, London: Texere 2000 Easy-to-read view of how society is changing

Martin Lindstrom and Patricia Seybold, *Brandchild*, London: Kogan Page 2004 Fascinating insight into "tween" behaviour across different countries

Robert Opie, *Sweet Memories*, London: Michael Joseph 1987 A historical look at packaging, with plenty of interesting images, mainly UK products

Andrew Seth & Geoffrey Randall, *The Grocers*, London: Kogan Page 1999 Excellent account of the rise of multiple groceries, mainly UK but includes reference to Wal-Mart and European companies

Reports on-line

www.bma.org.uk/ap.nsf/content/childhoodobesity British Medical Council reports on childhood obesity

www.gmid.euromonitor.co./reports.aspx Euromonitor, "Consumer Lifestyles in [series of countries]"

www.gmid.euromonitor.co./reports.aspx Euromonitor, "Retailing in [series of countries]"

www.ias.org.uk/resources/factsheets/binge_drinking.pdf Institute of Alcohol Studies (August 2006), "Binge Drinking"

reports.mintel.com Mintel (November 2005), "Organics—UK"

Websites

www.apple.com Lifestyle site; indicating Apple strategy

www.carrefour.com Major French retailers, now a global operator

www.delhaize.com European based food retailer but expanding into other territories

www.kitabienmanger.com Gourmet fast food with minimum cooking. Meal kit that French company, A Bien Manger, delivers in the 5th, 6th, 7th, 14th and 15th arrondissements, Paris

www.nike.com Lifestyle site; provides a good indication of their target audience

www.j-sainsbury.co.uk UK retail group; interesting approach to ethical issues

www.sieberthead.com London design consultancy—one of the first to specialize in packaging

www.tesco.com One of the major global retailers

www.walmartstores.com The world's largest retailers show their ethical and green credentials

Understanding the target audience II

From mass to niche markets

At first sight, it may seem desirable to design products and packs that will appeal to a mass market across the broad spectrum of age, gender and lifestyle. By following this route, we might speculate, maximum sales volumes would be obtained and maximum profits gained. As discussed in Chapter One, however, increased competition within markets, expansion of choice and changes in individual lifestyles create a climate where very few products can stimulate such universal appeal. The era of mass marketing has passed. We are now far away from the famous statement made by Henry Ford in his 1922 book *My Life and Work* that "any customer can have a car painted in any colour that he wants so long as it's black." In direct contrast, his concept has been replaced by brands and manufacturers developing products for increasingly smaller, more specialized niche markets. Such "mass customization" is still in its infancy but has the potential to design products for specific individuals. While we may now specify a bicycle or car to be built to meet our personal requirements, the same is not true for pre-packaged products, at least, not yet.

However, that is about to change. The US cosmetics company Lab 21 has already marketed a range of women's cosmetics, individually formulated to match the purchaser's DNA. This is about as personal as it is possible to get. The system works by women providing a mouth swab containing their DNA. The company use this to predict skin ageing characteristics and produce products that can best address the prediction. Lab 21 encountered ethical and financial problems that drove them from the market, but there is little doubt that formulating products to match specific DNA profiles will become a technique to re-emerge in this and other areas. Whether DNA may hold the key to predicting consumer behaviour in addition to personal health remains to be seen.

The example of such a personal approach, even one like Lab 21 that went out of business, serves to underline the need for designers to be able to understand who they are designing for, what motivates them now and what might motivate them in the future. This chapter considers ways of achieving a degree of familiarity with the target market that your pack will need to communicate with and how this can be captured in a visual manner. We start by examining market sectors as they exist at a given point in time through demographics and psychographics, before exploring further by looking at the lifestyle of the target audience through the creation of a virtual consumer. This then leads us to an examination of the aspirations of the target group. To help make all this research relevant and accessible we look at practical ways of undertaking and collating research before discussing the ultimate goal—the creation of an effective mood board.

Defining market sectors

Previously, in Chapter One, we have seen how social and economic changes continue to alter the way we behave and influence our individual needs, wants and desires. A proliferation of individual profiles means that it becomes more difficult for marketing professionals, designers and, crucially, governments, to identify and categorize groups of people. People stubbornly refuse to be placed into any one "box" and frequently move between "boxes". We can, for example, be concerned about the environment at one moment yet still race motorbikes at the weekend. As many individuals demonstrate, it is also possible to acquire all the trappings of wealth and luxury at one life-stage and yet, at another, discard them for the adventure of a transatlantic crossing in the uncomfortable and sometimes hazardous conditions of a small sailing boat, for example. Despite this trend of apparently contradictory, unpredictable and individual behaviour, as designers we do need to find a way of establishing some kind of group characteristics.

Demographics and psychographics

The established technique of defining market sectors used to rely, largely, on demographics. This is still an important marketing tool, providing useful numerical information about categories within any population.

The important word here is "numerical". Demographic information is a measure of categories within populations giving us statistics on sizes, volumes and percentages for almost any area of interest we might have. National governments maintain statistical data, much of which is now available on-line to the public. Market research organizations such as Mintel and Euromonitor also collect and publish demographic data, which is available for a fee, but much of this data can also be accessed free through university libraries and learning centres, providing that copyright conditions are respected. These reports provide valuable information to assist the designer, containing both demographic and some psychographic data, which may be specific to:

—product category *e.g. confectionery, soft drinks etc.*
—business activity *e.g. retailing in Japan*
—subject *e.g. obesity, binge drinking*
—groups *e.g. teenage spending habits in the USA*

Product manufacturers and marketing organizations regularly commission market research to provide information about very specific markets. The major grocery retailers also generate, as we have seen earlier in Chapter One (see p.30), much of their own consumer market research through analysis of sales patterns correlated with loyalty card use.

For designers, however, knowing how many people buy organic chocolate, for example, might be interesting, but unless the data can be used in some way it simply remains as a statistic, apparently unconnected to design activity. Demographic data, usually presented simply as figures or in chart form, frequently fails to inspire designers. It is, however, worth persevering with, as this information, typically, may indicate the importance of the market in terms of value and purchasing trends or, perhaps, it might reveal brand share within the

---

Demographics: numerical count of categories within populations

Typical statistical information available concerns:

Gender
Occupation
Educational standards
Socio-economic status
Religious and ethnic groupings
Geographical location of population
Marital status
Family size

Demographic information is directly linked to the timeframe when the information was obtained, e.g. a particular year or defined period, but is often extrapolated to predict future trends. Such information that may be of direct use to designers would include, for example, the predicted increase in the elderly population.

Psychographics:
group motivation and lifestyle

Psychographics seeks to determine consumer beliefs and opinions and interests through consideration of their lifestyles, thereby providing an argument for finding what motivates groups of like-minded people. Groups are often classified under descriptive names, selected by marketing or design organizations to reflect particular group lifestyle characteristics. This can provide designers with an understanding of what motivates a particular target market. For example, purchasers of four-wheel drive vehicles may, in fact, have very different lifestyles and motivations for purchase.

Group 1 Rural traditionalists
may or may not live in countryside
drives Land Rover
grown-up family
dog owner—retrievers
wears tweeds/country casuals
attends country fairs
brand dismissive

Group 2 Urban adventurers
town/city dweller
drives Porsche/BMW/Mercedes 4x4
no children
rarely drives off-road
into sailing/powerboating/jet skiing
brand aware

Group 3 Safety seekers
town/city dweller
young children
car bought by dad, driven by mum
car used for school run
drives Ford Maverick

Descriptions are often stereotypes but do nevertheless help to create a visual image of target audiences and what is likely to motivate them—important for designers.

sector. It might also reveal the age range, disposable income and other details about organic chocolate consumers, all providing a significant input to a packaging design study. These are important factors to aid our understanding of the market, but we must also supplement them by trying to find out what influences consumers to buy organic chocolate and why they buy a specific brand of organic chocolate. To find this information we may turn to psychographics, the study of group motivations and lifestyles. Here, populations are segregated into categories on the basis of their lifestyles so, although it considers psychological motivations, a degree of measurement remains embedded within the system.

SRI Consulting Business Intelligence (an offshoot of the Stanford Research Institute) pioneered this approach in the USA during the 1970s, leading to the publication of a book *Nine American Lifestyles* by Arnold Mitchell in 1983. The VALS™ system, as it was named, was a useful marketing tool, but it was underpinned by the social values of the time. Recognizing the rapid changes in society, the system was redrawn and launched as VALS™ 2. This has since been modified and, in its latest reincarnation, VALS™ uses psychology to underpin consumer preferences and choice. It suggests three primary motivations that influence people's behaviour: ideals, achievement and self-expression. Personality traits and levels of resources also form part of the VALS™ system, leading to eight consumer groups (within the 18+ age group of English-speaking Americans) with the primary characteristics of each groups being (in brief):

—Innovators *take charge, sophisticated, curious*
—Thinkers *reflective, informed, content*
—Achievers *goal oriented, brand aware, conventional*
—Experiencers *trend setters, impulsive, variety seeking*
—Survivors *nostalgic, constrained, cautious*
—Believers *literal, loyal, moralistic*
—Strivers *contemporary, imitative, style conscious*
—Makers *responsible, practical, self-sufficient*

This system, and others based on it, work by showing respondents a series of statements to which they can indicate their reaction, such as that they "mostly disagree", "somewhat disagree", "somewhat agree" or "mostly agree" with the statement being presented to them. Gender, age and income are added to help in subsequent analysis. In this way populations can be segmented into groups.

Companies and brands use similar market research techniques and often develop their own categories of consumers to suit their particular markets and product offerings. For example, a project that involved marketing to a 50–60-year-old male audience in the UK divided the market sector into the following categories, each category being described by the activities, products and brands associated with their characteristics:

—Hidden Hippies *tattoos, motorbikes, denim, beer, roll-ups, guitars*
—Design Gurus *Hugo Boss, Muji, Calvin Klein, BMW, Audi TT*
—Clean & Greens *organic food, VW Polo, dogs, bikes, vin ordinaire, allotments, camping*
—Happy Hobbyists *Internet, models, old cars, pottery, renovation, homebrew*

The advantage of showing group characteristics in terms of tangible objects rather than behavioural descriptors is that an immediate image is brought to mind; important for designers who are primarily working in a visual language. It enables progression to the next stages, creating a virtual consumer and encapsulating them visually by preparing a mood board.

Creating a virtual consumer

A recent Mintel report into "Snacking on the Go" (April 2004) uses national statistics in the UK to indicate a rise in the number of women in work, many of whom also have children to look after. The data is broken down by the age of their children, yielding some interesting statistics. The report shows, for example, that of those mothers with children under five, more than half are working mums, but this figure rises to 73% when we consider those who have children between five and nine. The implication in the report is that, to feed members of the household at the correct time, ready meals, snacks and lunch-box fillers may need to be purchased and that a sit-down family meal during the working week is often impractical. The report continues to examine issues concerning healthy eating, diet and obesity, all related to snacking on the go.

Clearly, this information has implications for packaging across a broad spectrum of product categories, but to make effective use of the data designers need to create packaging that will find resonance with the target audience. As packaging communicates to consumers principally on a visual level, this means establishing imagery appropriate to the target market, imagery that they can identify with. In this particular instance, depending on the nature of the product, the designer may be looking for ways of visually expressing key consumer requirements, including convenience (to reduce time spent preparing food), trust in the brand (to care for children), healthy eating and, possibly, child appeal if the child is involved in the purchasing decision-making process. To help in the accurate creation of these visual elements—which, we should remember, may also include pack shape in addition to graphics—greater familiarity with the target audience is required than provided by the market report data alone. When the target audience is thoroughly understood, it becomes much easier to understand their motivations, needs and desires, then predict their behaviour and, ultimately, identify how packaging can best interact with their lifestyles. As packaging design output is visual, it helps the subsequent design process to capture our understanding of the market in a visual way. In effect, we are creating a virtual consumer, albeit one fabricated from several images. In practice, designers use mood boards where the virtual consumer is represented by a series of images. Later in this chapter we shall be considering the practical issues in the preparation of mood boards. For now, however, and as a prelude to that, our task is to find ways of understanding the consumer, adding flesh to the bones of marketing data.

Lifestyle profiling chart

Lifestyle issue	Questions to consider	Examples of useful response areas
Relationships	Current/past status?	Married/single/divorced/partners/gay Family—nuclear/dispersed
Finances	Disposable income?	On a tight budget, money to spare
Living	Location—where respondent lives? Type of accommodation? Furnishing/decor?	Country, region, city Flat, town house, dockside apartment, farm Chrome and glass, traditional
Work	Employment/retired/job seeker?	Professional, trade, full-time, part-time
Leisure	Sports: participant/spectator? Hobbies and pastimes? Health and welfare?	Motor racing, football, baseball Painting, photography, chat rooms, dressmaking, guitar playing, clubbing, hanging out, dancing, dating Exercise: gym, walking, cycling, diet
Travel	Package tour/self-organized?	Adventure, sunbathing, Ibiza, Himalayas, whale watching
Transport	Car? Motorcycle? Bicycle?	Ford, Volvo, Chrysler, BMW, SUV, Renault Harley, Suzuki Mountain, folding, racing
Gadget	Most important?	Mobile phone, iPod, MP3, PDA, PC or Mac
Food and drink	Food? Drink?	Organic, TV snacks, wholefood, microwave, ready meals, vegetarian, dinner parties, home cooking Beer, lager, wine, vodka, whisky, binge with mates, cafes, eat at home, restaurants, bistros
Fashion and brands	Fashion brands bought?	Vivienne Westwood, Diesel, Nike, Gucci
Taste	Music? Art? Design?	Classical, folk, jazz, rock'n'roll, rap Impressionist, modern, abstract, pictorial Retro, classic, modern

Lifestyle profiling

Most packaging design projects are conducted over a short timescale, of weeks rather than months, and don't provide enough time for organizing pre-project market research using questionnaires or setting up focus groups. Normally, specific target audience data is provided by the client, and forms part of the brief. Usually there is no need to categorize a whole market sector, as in the 50–60-year-old age range example discussed previously. Where, however, target data is thought to be incomplete, vague or simply not detailed enough, designers may have to fill in the gaps themselves. A quick way of approaching this is to try and judge how the target audience would answer a series of questions about their lifestyle. This process builds a profile of the target, highlighting their likes, dislikes, wants, needs and desires. The chart opposite, which can be called a lifestyle profiling chart, aims to help this process by providing a list of key lifestyle pointers, under which are a series of questions. (This, by the way, is not a definitive list; more points could easily be added to cover more specific areas.) By attempting to predict how the target audience would respond, we begin to understand a little more about their lifestyles. It gets us thinking. The process would, of course, be enriched if we were able to address these questions to a representative sample of the target audience but, as previously mentioned, time constraints often prevent this taking place. To show how the lifestyle profiling chart works, consider the following scenario.

As we saw earlier, the "Snacking on the Go" report indicated the pressures experienced by working mothers with young children. Without actually experiencing what it is like to be a mum with small children, it is difficult to know how we would feel or react. The lifestyle profiling chart helps us to focus on the reality of individual lifestyles and face the issues that are of importance to particular segments of society. It is never going to be perfect, and we have to accept that we might end up with a stereotypical representation and that there will be variations within the sector we are considering. It is, however, probably accurate enough for us to begin informed design. We need imagery that represents our target audience and, in fact, the process of obtaining this will help us think through the parameters involved. A parallel can be drawn here with actors who adopt the "method school" of acting by knowing the character they play well enough to "get inside their head". Designers working in a team have the advantage of being able to tease out target profiles through discussion, but even designers working alone can benefit from addressing the questions shown in the lifestyle profiling chart. The accuracy of the outcome will rely on how thorough our research has been, our knowledge of the world and our individual experiences—reinforcing, incidentally, the requirement for designers to be curious about everything, something we shall return to later in this chapter.

Lifestyle profiling case study

To demonstrate how this process works in greater detail consider the example below. This is based on a live project tackled by a group of undergraduate packaging design students.

The project brief, outlined opposite, concerns frozen organic pizza, where the ideal purchasers will be working women with children. In this brief, the client company has concentrated on two categories of existing customers that it feels are particularly important and who would benefit from the results of this project.

Most of the students working on the project had little experience of the target audience and produced lifestyle profiles in group discussions, using their own judgement. A few did have relatives in the categories outlined in the brief and used this to augment the lifestyle profiles. All of the students visited branches of the client company and observed customers shopping (in addition to researching store layout, product types etc.).

A consensus of the resulting lifestyle profiles is shown opposite. Already, this level of detail allows us to build a mental image of the targets, helping us to understand what motivates these particular groups and, ultimately, to design a product that they will want to buy.

The results of this research suggest that the key to this brief, for both groups, is their home environment and there are similarities in how this might look in both types of household. Because of staggered meals and time constraints, the freezer and fridge are important because reliance is placed on frozen food and ready meals. Accompanying this is a microwave oven for baby bottle sterilization (for young mums), fast defrosting and cooking. Washing is frequent and ongoing for both of these families so the kitchen is home to a washing machine and possibly a drier. The kitchen environment, in these small houses, will be crowded. The freezer is packed, which, as we shall see later, provides a strong design direction. The family eat at different times often while watching TV as there is no eating area in the kitchen and no separate dining room. There are also some differences between the groups that have to be considered. Because the older mum has older children, the two eldest are able to prepare their own meals when they come home from school, at least cooking pizza in the oven. They can also provide food for the youngest. Having a store of pizza and ready meals helps the older mum cope with her busy schedule and allows her to cook "proper" meals from time to time. Because they are fussy eaters, however, several varieties of pizza have to be stored in the freezer. In this group, the children influence purchasing decisions. In the other household, young mum is buying pizza primarily for herself and husband but the three-year-old is now capable of having a slice of pizza too. Unlike the other group, the problem here is not storage of varieties but simply the volume occupied by frozen food.

Project brief

Target market:
24–36-year-old working mothers

A usage and attitude study reveals that, within this market, there are two categories of customer, "young mum" with pre-school aged children and "older mum" with school children. Both these groups are time-pressured by work, school and family schedules. They have limited culinary skills but are keen to ensure that all in the family have an adequate diet. Value for money is important, particularly to "young mum" as there is little spare cash in the household. "Young mum" mainly purchases frozen ready meals while, at the other end of the age spectrum, "older mum" has fussy eaters in the household but she loves to cook and provide a balanced diet at the different eating times dictated by balancing her job, his job, school and budget. She buys some frozen ready meals to help her through the week.

The brand
The brand is well established and sells a range of own label frozen food (and non-frozen groceries) from its own medium-sized high street retail outlets. The brand has a reputation for value and, less well known, has eliminated GM modified contents, reduced fat and salt levels and eliminated artificial colourings and preservatives. It has introduced a kids range, family range and luxury range (of more indulgent products). The brand personality focuses on fun and friendliness balanced by down-to-earth values.

The problem
With increased competition from the ambient and chilled ready meal sectors offered by major grocery retailers, the company perceive that packaging innovations offer the potential to retain and build on their customer base. Research has identified that customers have problems with space in the freezer and become frustrated by packaging that is ineffective or takes up space and is perceived to be a burden on the waste-stream.

The challenge
Using frozen organic pizza as a demonstrator project, design a pack that protects the product but reduces environmental impact and increases customer convenience.

The frozen food market
Target 1—young mum

Lifestyle profile

Age
25

Relationships
Married with children aged 3 and 6 months

Finances
Money is in short supply

Living
First-time home owner with a mortgage—terraced house, edge of town, student area

Work
Does some part-time work in a shop

Leisure
Most of her time is taken up by the children. Gets occasional night off to go out to the pub with 'the girls'. Manages a package holiday in Spain

Transport
Drives an ageing VW Polo

Gadgets
Mobile phone, pay as you go

Food and drink
75% of her food shopping is frozen—mostly convenience meals. Enjoys white wine. Shops at Asda/Wal-Mart

Fashion and brands
Buys clothes from supermarket, toiletries from Boots

Taste
Treats in her life include chocolate and buying *Hello!* magazine

The frozen food market
Target 2—working mum

Lifestyle profile

Age
36

Relationships
Divorced but with new partner, two daughters, aged 14 and 12, son aged 5

Finances
Just manages to keep up, spends on family necessities

Living
Rented semi-detached in housing estate

Work
Works as market researcher, mainly street and in-store surveys

Leisure
Spends much leisure time on-line in chat rooms, enjoys pub music nights

Transport
Drives a three-year-old Nissan

Gadgets
Small lounge contains widescreen multi-channel TV with wrap-around sound system

Food and drink
Enjoys cooking and trying to provide a healthy diet despite fussy eaters in the family. Meals tend to be simple, meat and veg, pasta and a roast on Sunday. 25% of food is frozen—mostly ingredients but some ready meals to help out during the week. Enjoys a glass (or three) of white wine in the evening. Holidays are in a seaside caravan park

Fashion and brands
Does not buy fashion brands but keeps up with style through mail order catalogues

Taste
Treats for her are dining out without the kids, indulgent baths and buying sexy underwear

Visual referencing

Going through this process deepens our understanding and forces judgements to be made, that, ultimately, will influence design directions. Rather than simply retaining a mental profile of the target groups, we need to convert it to a visual representation—usually a mood board. This is important, not only for the designer searching for imagery to incorporate on the pack, but also when we are discussing our design thinking and process with clients, colleagues, tutors or examiners. Visual references always make communicating thought processes to others much faster and easier. We are trying to create a characterization here as an integral part of the design process and so it can help to give the characters names, as many market research organizations do. (In the frozen pizza example, on page 45, the client assigned names to both target groups but, for commercial reasons, they cannot be included here.) We now need to select and collate images that represent the target audience. These images might be from a variety of sources, either as self-generated photography or from found material. The lifestyle profiling results provide clues as to where to look. Particularly useful sources for tear sheets are from catalogues matching the target's shopping choices and from magazines they are likely to read. Tear sheets are quite literally pages of material torn from magazines. These frequently contain images, often slightly aspirational in character, that are perfect for the task.

The catalogue of the Swedish home furnishing store, IKEA, for example, contains images of their products shown with idealized "customers" matching exactly IKEA's desired target audience. So if your lifestyle profile suggests that your target shops at IKEA, or would like to shop at IKEA, get a copy of the brochure.

Below left Design magazines not only keep us up-to-date but provide an insightful source of research. Here, modernist design is featured in *Design Week*, demonstrating its contemporary relevance and the genius of its practitioners.

Below centre This IKEA catalogue features the people that IKEA would like to see as their customers. If your target market is likely to be IKEA shoppers, then sales catalogues like this will include idealized images that also represent your target group.

Below right Here, a packaging designer has collated their desk research into a report. Note how the information is annotated and highlighted, indicating that real conclusions are being made from the research, driving the project forward to a successful outcome.

The same process holds true for other areas too. Consideration of the car they aspire to own (not a dream car but a realistic choice if they had just a little more money) again leads to collecting brochures of that car, which depict the type of person the car manufacturer is targeting. Later in this chapter we will consider how to use these images to prepare mood boards.

Of course, you will have to justify your selection of answers based on the *likelihood* of the target conforming to your choices, as you will not know for sure. Remember, the point of this exercise is getting you to think hard and eventually think your way into constructing a virtual consumer and their environment.

The purpose of this section has been to consider identifying market sectors rather than provide design solutions to the brief we have been looking at, but we need to appreciate how this approach contributed to design success. It has helped us confront, understand and predict the real problems that groups of people encounter and, therefore, provides a firm basis for making design decisions. In this brief one of the many proposed design directions was to make the frozen pizza in separate slices, suitable for different family members at different times. The pack incorporated tear-off portions, reducing in size every time a slice was removed, thus minimizing space in the hard-pressed freezer. This approach was particularly suitable for the older mum whose family members all have different preferences. Additional concepts explored how each pizza slice might have its own tray/sleeve/wrap to ease eating, and the use of paper-based packaging rather than plastic to reduce environmental impact.

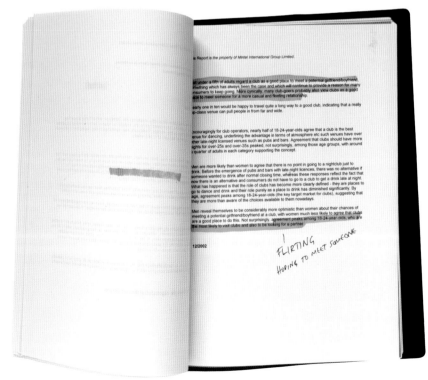

Identifying aspirations

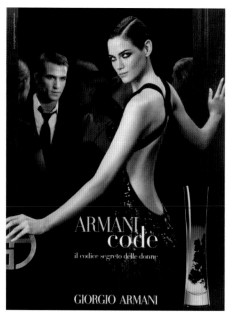  

Above Although we know that we may never achieve the physical perfection of those depicted in these adverts, buying the dream and, of course, the product will make others envy us just as we envy the beautiful people shown. Gucci are blatant about it here with the perfume name "Envy me".

The previous section helped us to identify market sectors using our knowledge supplemented by imagination. The lifestyle profile should have helped in the creation of a virtual consumer whose behaviour is, to some extent, predictable. If the profiling has been thorough, we should know our virtual consumer almost as we know a real person. We will have established their behaviour and needs but, now, the next step in the design process is to find out their wants and desires. To do this we first have to return to the reality of human lifestyles.

We all aspire to something, whether it concerns possessions, wealth, fitness, beauty, youth, fame, creativity, power or love. Some of these things may be impossible, totally the stuff of dreams, while others may lie just within our grasp if we really work at achieving them. Coping with aspirations is an emotional experience and, whenever emotions come into play, so do marketing opportunities. Most of us are unhappy with our personal appearance and aspire to look younger, more radiant, sexier, glowing with health or smouldering with passion, whatever our particular personal aspirations might be. A psychological explanation suggests that we envy those who embody our aspirations and, in turn, by achieving our aspirations we shall become an object of envy to others. John Berger, in his book *Ways of Seeing* (1972), suggests that the spectator-buyer, in viewing aspirational advertising, envies themselves as they will become if they buy the product. We are, according to Berger, meant to imagine ourselves transformed by the product into an object of envy for others—an envy that will justify loving ourselves. The images presented to us by shop displays, adverts and, to a lesser extent, packaging, offer us the envy of others for the price of the product. It is hardly surprising that advertising for toiletries and cosmetics features beautiful people as objects of envy.

If we look at the three adverts for Armani, Gucci and Jean Paul Gaultier, shown opposite, and want others to see how risqué we are (because we aspire to be outrageous), we might be tempted to buy the Jean Paul Gaultier Classique pack. This pack, featuring a female torso said to be modelled on Madonna, draws inspiration from both art and fetishism, providing an unconventional and risqué presentation. While the purchase itself reinforces our aspirations, any opportunity to show or discuss the pack with others justifies the cost of purchase by indicating our unconventionality and, therefore, receiving their admiration.

In each of these examples of fragrances, envy is enhanced by the deliberate sexual tension created by the choice of imagery. The target audiences for these products may be, or may aspire to be, discerning, sophisticated and elegant. The imagery used is sensual but not overtly sexual. Nevertheless, it is implied that by buying these products, our aspirations to possess greater sexual attraction will be achieved. As sexual emotions are innate and so deep-seated within us, advertising frequently features sexual imagery to appeal to our aspirations.

Other personal products are bought to aim for different aspirations. "Sporty" shower gels probably have little to do with sporting prowess but, for those who aspire to be fit, it becomes a less onerous way of buying into fitness than working out, being envied by those who may see the product in our sports bag or bathroom. Sports are also tribal, with sports supporters, rather than sports participants, proclaiming loyalty to their particular sport, club or clan through purchasing particular brands. In this instance, the aspiration is to be acknowledged by others as a member of the tribe, obtained for the price of the product.

Emotional forces

Personal aspirations may take many different directions but it is important for the designer to understand the powerful emotional forces that underpin aspirations and how these provide a compelling reason to buy particular products. If this can be reflected in the pack design, then the pack begins to appeal on an emotional level. Incidentally, critics of packaging and advertising may decry this approach on the grounds of selling poor or inferior products by promising too much. The designer must assess the product fairly. One of the best guides is the selling price and where this positions the product relative to competitors. No matter how client marketing staff may proclaim the superiority of their product, it is simply a waste of time to dress a VW car in Bentley clothing at Bentley prices. Disappointed consumers might buy it once before rejecting the brand for evermore. (VW own Bentley and wisely keep the two brands entirely separate.) When aspirations are involved, what the product is expected to promise, it must deliver. Although emotionally we buy into products that claim to reduce wrinkles, rejuvenate skin or make us unbelievably sexy, the rational side of our brain recognizes that, actually, we expect an improvement but not necessarily a miracle.

Above top This example from the Jean Paul Gaultier Classique fragrances shows just one of the torso bottles featured in the range. The outer pack is also interesting because it takes a commodity item pack and places it out of context. The effect is eccentric, quirky and mildly erotic. Buying this pack for someone special or for ourselves also suggests that we are aspiring to be seen as quirky and sexually liberated.

Above Buying a sports brand, such as this range from Adidas in Germany, allows entry to a club of sports supporters, not necessarily participants. It tells others of our sporting pretensions and supports our view of ourselves as unsung sporting heroes.

Above TV chef Ainsley Harriott lends his brand to this product. By simply adding boiling water the aspiring cook in the kitchen can produce something special enough to receive plaudits from others as they enjoy their couscous, which, promises Ainsley, will be "warmer than a Moroccan sunset".

Creating aspirational packaging

To create aspirational packaging it is therefore first necessary to identify what the target audience aspires to, with particular reference to the product to be packed. Take "gourmet" sauces and instant meal ingredients as an example. Background research indicates that while the time-poor cash-rich trend continues in some nations with reliance being placed on convenience meals, there is also a counter-trend towards recreational cooking. Cookery programmes on television are extremely popular, particularly those featuring celebrity chefs and competitive cooking. The reality is that culinary skill levels, particularly in the UK, are low and would benefit from TV cookery shows that are more about instruction and less about entertainment. Yet the TV programme offerings often demonstrate high skill levels, featuring more elaborate, intricate and imaginative dishes. While this may expand consumer knowledge and expectations, it is not connected with the everyday experience of most, and so cooking sometimes becomes confined to a weekend activity. It is at the weekend when the man in the household aspires to function as a chef and the female aspires to stop being the provider of meals (Kirkham, 1996). A typical scenario is that, after two hours of devoted preparation, the promised mouth-watering morsels, served on a bed of rocket, are burned to a crisp. To avoid such failures and ensure the male ego remains intact, gourmet sauces and accompaniments have been introduced on the market. These are pre-prepared and provide a convenient way of achieving culinary credibility and the subsequent adoration of wife and family—it almost guarantees that on the pack. The design task is to present the gourmet addition to the meal as an essential, precious ingredient and not as a solution to inept cooking. Although this may be just a good product, it must appeal to the aspirations of the "chef". It cannot, therefore, appear to be packed as a commodity. This could be achieved in a number of ways. The container could perhaps reflect the imagery of a professional kitchen, picking up on the stainless steel kitchen equipment. Alternatively, depending on brand, it might adopt a very simple and distinctive approach, perhaps using black and white photography and elegant use of typography. Whatever the design outcome, the packaging has to convey the feeling of being "special" and a suitable "prop" in the kitchen to augment the male ego. Another design route is to use the name and possibly the image of a well-known chef on the pack. Many celebrity chefs, and some celebrities who are not chefs themselves, such as actor Paul Newman, endorse such products, adding a personal dimension to the aspiring cook. The female partner in the household inevitably sees through the whole charade but, nevertheless, provides the applause for the sake of sanity.

Techniques for researching target audiences

Conducting research into identification of target audiences is a fundamental part of a packaging design study but, for students in particular, "research" is often not defined. Worse still, there is often no practical guidance on how this should be done, a point we will address here.

Firstly, we should emphasize that "research" in the context of research for a packaging design study involves seeking, finding and gathering information that is pertinent and will help shape the direction of the study. There always has to be a reason for making design decisions and, frequently, it is a reason that has been revealed through the research. Examiners and clients will be looking for the link between research and design decisions.

As well as making research relevant, there is also a time factor to consider. Many packaging projects have a first stage that, including research and initial concept generation, may require, for example, completion in six weeks. Bearing in mind that other design projects are likely to be running in parallel, some time planning is required. The bulk of the project stage should be design time because that is what, in a commercial arena, the client is paying for. Collecting research material should occupy no more than three to five days in such a project. Junior designers and students sometimes extend the research time, perhaps putting off the dreaded moment of committing pencil to paper and making design decisions. Setting, and keeping to, a realistic schedule of allocated research and design time is a habit worth cultivating.

Most clients commissioning design work will provide ample market data obtained from their own research. In many cases, however, clients are happy to see a design team carry out some additional research and most designers are, by nature, curious to find out more information about products and markets they may not be familiar with. A project that offers a glimpse into a new world is always welcomed and so research, for designers, is actually a natural part of the job. Every new and different project brings with it new research opportunities, and expands and deepens designer knowledge and maturity. This may involve a combination of "desk" research (see p.52) and observational research, both of which can include an element of image gathering.

Collating research material

Before you even begin your research, however, it is useful to set aside some storage systems specifically for collating research material. Packaging design research will involve printed or photocopied text and images. Tear sheets, photographs and images can be stored in a folder or box file ready for use in preparing mood boards. Photocopied text and material printed from the web can be conveniently collated into ring binders and will usually have the website address and date accessed printed on it. This material is so easy to obtain that it tends to mount up. It is worth using a highlighter pen to show the relevant parts of reports and research documents and keep these near the front. Less useful information should be discarded or separated in some way. This is simply to save time when reviewing research. (Examiners, in particular, will not be impressed by having to wade through a mass of documents, much of which may not be relevant.)

Sources of market research

Desk research
—available in libraries and on-line

Because social, economic, political and lifestyle conditions are constantly changing, on-line sources and regular publications provide the latest information.

Market research organizations
  e.g. Mintel, Euromonitor etc.
  Detailed reports available on wide range of subjects
Marketing specialists
  e.g. McKinsey
  Publish insightful articles and reports
Magazines
  Appropriate to the target market
  Look at advert selection appealing to target
Newspapers
  Also check electronic archives
Sales catalogues
  Appropriate to products and services target market buys and uses, e.g. IKEA shows images of their target audience
National statistics
  Government figures are probably the most accurate source of detailed information but may be out of date
Publications
  Annual compilations of statistics, e.g. Marketing Pocket Book, provide convenience for designers
Books
  Essential background reading but be aware of more recent changes

Active research
—conducting interviews

Talk to clients
  They will have great knowledge of market
Talk to advertising agency
  Superb understanding of target audience
Conduct your own survey
  Construct questionnaire and organize market research survey

Observational research

Visit shops and locations where target audience will be—observe and take photographs
Talk to product users in target group—show examples and observe reactions
Use product yourself and make your own observations and assessment

The brief

The brief is always the primary source of information for designers embarking on a packaging design study. Curiously, perhaps, some students apparently choose not to read it and are surprised to find that their resulting work is irrelevant. Read and re-read the brief—use it as a yardstick to assess your design work. It will provide some information about the target consumer you will be designing for. The most basic brief should, at the very least, describe the target audience in terms of: Age range | Gender | Social status | Some lifestyle information.

Be wary of any brief that has a wide age range, or which includes males and females, particularly if this glosses over important stages of lifestyle change. If the brief, for example, suggests an inclusive age range of between six-year-old and twelve-year-old children, then it needs to be questioned. A twelve-year-old girl is unlikely to be motivated by the same things as a six-year-old boy. The brief needs to be tighter to allow meaningful design decisions to be made. This is equally important when students are writing their own briefs. Although, at first sight, a wide brief may be regarded as an easy option, it actually creates problems for the designer who is then unable to clearly focus on the target audience. There is also sometimes a temptation to change a self-written brief mid-way through a project because the work is pushing it towards a particular direction more suited to, perhaps, a different age range, gender or lifestyle. Commercial practice should be the standard to aim at, where it is usual for the brief to be signed off by the client before any design work starts, ensuring that it does not change.

Desk research

By "desk" research, we mean accessing information from the Internet, libraries or other sources to help build a profile of the target audience and provide a background to the project. We have already referred on page 39 to many sources of market surveys and reports obtainable on the Internet and in libraries. The Internet offers an astounding source of information and, as a research tool, it is superb. It should not, however, be the only research source. Books, magazines, newspapers, personal visits and observations are rich sources from which to begin a collection of research information. Tear sheets, photographs and scans are all useful, but fabrics, textures and colours may also be relevant.

You may also wish to conduct some semiotic research. Semiotics is concerned with the cultural conventions initiated by visual "signs" such as colours, shapes and materials. So, for example, if the project is addressing a sophisticated, cash-rich, 45-year-old female target audience, with the proposition of luxury chocolates, you could be considering incorporating gold, long associated with indulgence, into the design. But first, look at other products aimed at this market. The chances are that gold will not feature at all, only re-emerging when a less sophisticated target market appears. As cultural conventions change, gold has lapsed for the sophisticated market targeted above. Now, simpler, more natural colours or simply less colour signify sophistication, elegance and luxury. In Chapter Three, further examples of semiotics will be discussed when the use of colour is considered (see p.79).

Observational research

Observational research involves physically looking, observing and, frequently, recording what is seen. It may take the form of people watching from a strategically located coffee shop or, perhaps, actively photographing the inside of refrigerators, kitchen cupboards or bathrooms, depending on the brief. A fast food project inspired one designer to photograph people eating outside city office blocks. Following his arrest for suspected terrorist activities, he returned with not only some very useful photographs of just how people balance plastic cups, lids, sandwiches, wraps and bagels, but also the obvious struggle they faced in disposing of the soiled packaging. This level of detail led to a radical new pack design, focusing on disposability and environmental performance. Be aware, however, that while the camera is a superb way of collecting information, it has to be used sensitively to avoid offending members of the public, security services or other authorities.

Ethnographic research

If it is appropriate, try using the product yourself or speak to others who do use it. If the project concerns children or elderly people, for example, talk to relatives or friends who are representative of the target audience, share your design thinking with them and obtain their opinions. This type of research is also referred to as ethnographic research, where the researcher can become both an observer and participant in the process of considering how products and packs are used by particular groups of people. The participant technique involves fieldwork where the researcher attempts to become an insider within the group, acting and observing reactions to particular activities. Some studies, for example, have investigated the relationship between pack forms and the elderly by equipping the researcher with simple devices restricting physical movements and special glasses to simulate poor sight. Although this artificial ageing process constructs a scenario whereby some insight to the problems induced by lack of mobility can be observed and appreciated, it has to be acknowledged that it does not give an entirely accurate picture as short-term artificial incapacity does not incorporate the adaptive learning experienced by the target groups themselves.

In some instances video ethnography has been more successful in recording people's behaviour and interaction with packaging. There are ethical issues involved when the camera intrudes into personal behaviour, so, if you are considering using this technique, make sure that all subjects are aware of the research objectives, consent to being filmed and have open access to the resulting footage.

Multiple influences

It is also important to identify the decision makers within the purchasing process. A mother purchasing for a child is a simple example where the child has influence and is the consumer but it is the mother who is the decider and buyer. Supermarkets, in particular, through running their own observational research programmes, understand how purchasing is influenced over a much wider spectrum than just at the point of sale. The initiator may not be the purchaser and,

>> Tip
Consider adverts as these often cleverly focus on the emotional values that contribute towards creating an atmosphere or tone

>> Tip
When considering consumer behaviour, examine the purchasing process and determine who:
Initiates
Influences
Decides
Buys
Uses
It may be one person or several people

indeed, this event may take place outside the supermarket environment. Some shoppers write a list before they visit the store with the aim of purchasing specific products or brands outside the supermarket's control. To encourage such shoppers to purchase different brands, some supermarkets will attempt to extend control into the consumer's home territory, initiating and influencing purchase through mail shots or e-mail. Once in-store, the supermarket will try to provide a shopping experience that influences spending and decision making. Creating a pleasant, relaxed atmosphere encourages browsing and impulse spending.

While product purchase is in-store, the product experience does not really begin until it is unpacked, stored and used. It does not end until the product is consumed and, ultimately, the pack disposed of. In each of these stages, one person or more can be involved. Any market research has to take account of this extended interface between product and, potentially, a multiple target audience.

For some projects, it is possible to conduct your own market research. If you wish to find out information about elderly and infirm people, for instance, you might visit a day-care centre, observing and helping both carers and patients. If you are exploring the concept of altering a chocolate bar to include a spare portion designed to be given away, you might try such an idea out in a city centre.

Many companies also publish consumer-related information, particularly marketing, branding, design and advertising organizations. It is useful to visit such websites periodically to see if new information has been posted. Some, such as McKinsey, encourage registration on the site and will forward regular bulletins, while others offer immediate access to articles and publications.

There is increasing integration between marketing, branding, advertising and design organizations, many of them now encompassing all these activities within one multi-disciplined group. Some of the leading companies involved with global branding and marketing are included in the list on page 58. For students of packaging design it is worthwhile visiting these sites, reading the articles posted within the sites and reviewing the portfolio of work, as they reveal marketing strategies adopted for brand development and changing consumer targets.

When researching target markets there are some final points to consider:
—Accuracy is more important than volume. Collect only the material that defines the target market.
—Don't assume you know. Really make an effort to find out.
—Try and consider what the target audience aspires to, what they would like to own or how they would like to look.
—Are there any "heroes" or role models that you could use to typify the target?
—Experience the product for yourself or make contact with people using it.
—Don't prolong research. It can be an excuse for putting off the design task.

Preparing mood boards that work

Designers often have their own collections of packs, photos, leaflets etc. assembled in scrapbooks, files or on shelves. These are items of interest, collected over time and which may also find their way onto mood boards. A collection of this type not only provides historical reference material that would be difficult to access in any other way but can also reduce research time if the collection contains material applicable to particular projects. Frequently, however, the project will require new or additional research. Once you have collected your research material, sourced images etc., the next stage is to present them—usually in the form of a mood board.

Mood boards are really just visual devices that represent the lifestyle of the target audience and their aspirations. They help the designer to establish the broad direction that the project is going to take and may incorporate specific elements, which, ultimately, become embedded within the design work. Mood boards are also used to convey information to others, primarily to gauge the right tone of voice for the project underway and to portray lifestyle information about the target audience. For example, for a project concerning the repackaging of a sports drink, the mood board might correctly concern itself with the lifestyle and aspirations of the target audience but not, at this stage, address the technical details of pack construction. It might include images of the target audience, their activities, or details of products or brands they are likely to buy. While the collection of research material is the most time-consuming element, the actual assembly of the mood board would probably be under three hours.

Although there are no rules for choosing what to include on mood boards, it is wise to be selective. A mood board needs to be concise, showing encapsulated thinking and real understanding. One board is enough. Too often, students produce pages of "research" material not related to the project, together with mood boards that are too vague. Be selective when assembling material for a board and consider the board as a piece of design. It should convey design competence through the quality of its contents, in addition to their relevance. Take trouble to ensure the boards are accurately trimmed and mounted. Any thoughtful piece of work that may be presented to a client deserves the respect of being competently finished. Finally, try to limit the board to communicating the most important message, to avoid confusion and difficulty in understanding. As with advertising, conveying multiple messages in one communication dilutes their effect.

Boards are visual expressions of designer thinking and are a useful way of setting the tone during client meetings or presentations. They also encourage client participation and subsequent discussions, often a valuable way of understanding some of the more subtle requirements of the project brief. Mood boards do have their limitations, particularly because of the reliance placed on available material. It can be tempting to use what is easily obtainable rather than what accurately reflects the brief. So, assemble board content with care because if you are wrong at this stage, subsequent work will also be off-target.

Left and above The two mood board examples shown here both target a similar audience of young professional women with a high disposable income. The "Elemental" example, above, is drawn from a project to reposition the humble soap bar into the luxury category, while the second board concerns an indulgent dark chocolate. We gain from each of the four sections of the "Elemental" board a sense of serious indulgence with a hint of exhilaration, probably right for this project. The second board, however, is far lighter in mood but seems to contradict its message of relaxation by incorporating an element of party fun, not necessarily appropriate to a dark chocolate moment. It might have been better to try and convey just one message that is more aligned with the product type.

Conclusion

There is little doubt that the trend is set for packaged goods to be directed at smaller, niche markets. This will involve an increase in the number and variety of products available, providing increased choice and, by implication, increased competition. There will also be, however, an increased risk of consumer confusion. In these circumstances, the demands on packaging designers will increase, helping to establish product differentiation and creating packaging that is designed to appeal to specific groups of people. To do so successfully means that designers must be able to develop an understanding of the increased number and complexity of market sectors, even when they have no first-hand experience of the sectors involved. The lifestyle profiling chart, shown on page 42, is one technique that can help. Market reports, now easily accessible on-line, also provide a convenient source of data and students should be encouraged to use them. Whatever the source of data, the information provided ultimately requires interpretation into a visual format—the mood board—understandable to fellow designers, examiners, clients and consumers. The ability to identify key consumer motivators within market sectors and then develop and incorporate these into packaging will become the yardstick by which designers are judged.

Further reading and additional resource list

John Berger, *Ways of Seeing*, London: Penguin Books, 1990 Good explanation of
how advertising images work

Pat Kirkham (ed), *The Gendered Object*, Manchester: Manchester University Press,
1996 Useful insight into gender roles and gendered objects

Arnold Mitchell, *Nine American Lifestyles*, New York: Macmillan, 1983 The origins
of psychometrics and lifestyle profiling

Gillian Rose, *Visual Methodologies*, London: Sage, 2003 Easy-to-understand methods
used to assess art and design, also applicable to packaging

Reports on-line

reports.mintel.com

Mintel (March 2006), "Frozen Ready Meals—UK"

Mintel (April 2004), "Snacking on the Go"

Mintel (July 2002), "Impact of Celebrity Chefs on Cooking Habits"

Mintel (June 2000), "Childhood Obesity—UK"

Websites

www.futurebrand.com Good examples of global branding from this highly respected company

www.interbrand.com Brand specialist group with substantial portfolio

www.landor.com Good case study outlines

www.lovemarks.com Saatchi site considering new approach to defining brands. It has raised
some questions among the design community

www.marketing.haynet.com Brand Republic site—useful articles

www.McKinsey.com Strategic marketing specialists

www.ogilvy.com Ogilvy & Mather, part of WPP, advertising agency with site providing insight
into campaigns

www.saatchi.com Interesting company philosophy on creative issues from this leading ad
agency

www.schiaparelli.com The original female torso perfume bottle, designed with the intention to
shock, similar to the Gaultier bottle (see p.49)

www.sric-bi.com/VALS SRI Consulting Business Intelligence, the originators of psychographic
profiling. Take their on-line test and see what group you fit into

www.wpp.com Parent site for group of advertising and communications companies

The packaging designer's toolbox III

Choosing packaging materials

Packaging design involves both manipulation of three-dimensional shape and two-dimensional graphic elements. Within these elements lies a diverse range of options, many of which influence one another, as we shall see in this chapter. In a structural design project, deciding on shape cannot be separated entirely from the material that the pack will be constructed from and, in turn, the limitations of the processes involved in its manufacture. Even when this becomes clear, there will be other decisions to make concerning surface finish, texture, embossing/debossing, closure styles, surface decoration and the implications of combining different materials. Surface graphics also involve decisions as the options here include colour, typography and the use of photography or illustration.

All of these options reside in the designer's toolbox, to be selected as required in order to create imaginative design solutions that meet the brief. It is at once obvious that, while both analytical and creative skills are required in packaging design, the designer also needs to be able to reach into the toolbox of technical skills if workable design solutions are to be obtained.

The flowchart (opposite above) indicates an idealized view of how a packaging design study is conducted, from the brief to final design recommendations. It, quite deliberately, includes both structural and graphic design elements because, in packaging design, both disciplines are nearly always involved. Even in studies that may appear to focus on graphics alone, there are usually practical implications for any design recommendations made, which inevitably benefit from technical insight. For example, a project apparently biased towards graphics may still need to address what print method is to be used and where in the production cycle print is added to the pack.

Choices may depend on a variety of issues, including the type of substrate material, type sizes needed, run length and cost constraints. Potential options considered might well include in-mould labelling, direct screen printing, on-line labelling or shrink sleeving. Each of these options will influence the graphic possibilities as they impose their own restrictions on type size, number of colours, use of halftones and so on, some of which are described later in the chapter.

Almost by definition a flowchart suggests a smooth linear flow from one activity to the next, whereas in practice it may, as this chart shows, flow back and forth at certain points. The role of the designer is part creative and part analytical. Creative concepts, emanating from imaginative thinking, require analytical probing to establish their validity, while concepts driven by analytical, practical considerations require creative interpretation.

That is why even the most creative packaging designer requires a toolbox in which reside the basic implements to allow design skills to be exercised. In this instance the tools are both physical and knowledge-based, from materials, through print processes, to the use of colour and imagery. While we shall be looking at physical tools in Chapter Four, it is the pots of basic information we are considering here—toolbox essentials.

Typical sequence of events during a packaging design project

Most commercial design work is organized on a stage-by-stage basis with interim client meetings. Further stages would take the selected design concept through to artwork/proofing and production.

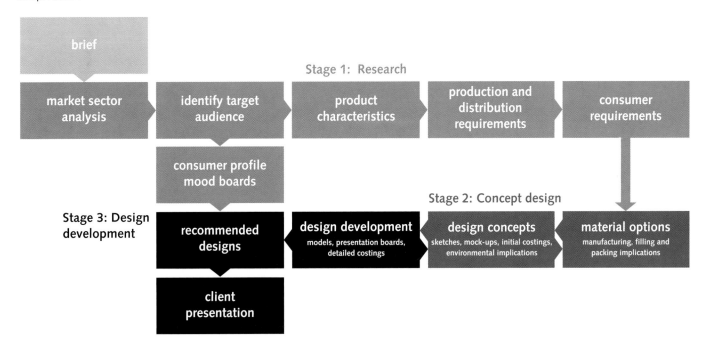

Principal material choices

	Wood	Paper and board		Glass	Metals		Plastics	
type		solid board	corrugated fibreboard		aluminium	steel	flexible	rigid
typical pack forms	crates pallets boxes	rigid boxes sleeves folding cartons trays backing cards	die-cut fittings shipping cases point of sale	jars bottles	foils bottles trays drums tins/cans tubes		bags wraps tubes foams	jars bottles trays blisters tubes
principal properties	strength	display low cost protection versatility print quality	strength protection	gas/liquid barrier clarity quality	gas/liquid barrier strength versatility		versatility cost effective lightweight	

——————————— composites ———————————

Packaging often includes more than one material, e.g. laminates of aluminium foil, plastics and paper

Materials

When beginning a design project that involves the structural design of the pack, designers may select a range of materials to consider as potential candidates. Of course, in many studies, the choice of material may be specified by the client but, even then, there are likely to be technical options that can dramatically influence the design outcome.

The chart on page 61 shows a range of the principal mainstream material types available to packaging designers, together with an indication of the pack forms associated with each material. It also includes a section on the relevant production methods for each material, which has a direct bearing on the pack style. A full, in-depth understanding of all that is contained in the chart, however, is almost impossible. Indeed, to be an expert within the category of plastics alone is beyond the grasp of most professional designers. Rapid advances in technology make the task of assimilating this vast body of knowledge even more unlikely. Yet packaging designers, especially those who wish to exercise their creativity within structural design, need to achieve at least a working knowledge of materials and processes. Even then, they will undoubtedly need to plunder the much deeper toolboxes of suppliers and manufacturers to add detail, but, if they are armed with a basic knowledge of processes, they will at least be talking the same language. This section outlines some of the principle materials and concentrates on the design opportunities and restrictions of each. It is recommended that inexperienced packaging designers should learn more about materials and processes through reading trade magazines, books, attending courses or contacting manufacturers.

Paper and board

Paper-based packaging has an environmental advantage over most other materials as it is produced from sustainable, renewable resources, primarily using fast growing pines and spruce from the northern latitudes of Europe and North America. Being a natural material it is also biodegradable, composting well without polluting the soil or water courses and is suitable for recycling, until the cellulose fibres that provide its strength become shortened by successive reprocessing. Paper on its own has few barrier properties and does not protect products against moisture or gases, but there are many coatings applied to paper that address the problem, from wax to sophisticated plastics and aluminium.

The choice of paper-based packaging is broadly between corrugated fibreboard and solid board, the principle characteristics of each being indicated on the materials chart on page 61. Corrugated fibreboard is usually associated with transit packaging, typically as outer shipping cases, where protection against physical damage in transit is paramount. Solid board, most commonly folding cartonboard, is used to produce practically all the cartons we might expect to find used for fast-moving consumer goods, usually being supplied as flat cut and glued blanks ready for machine erection and filling. Many standard styles are available but, equally, new variations and modifications are continually being developed. There are publications detailing carton styles, some of the most useful being documented at the end of this book. Most carton manufacturers now use software that stores a wide range of carton styles, allowing dimensions to be changed to suit requirements. This is frequently linked to sample-making equipment that allows the carton manufacturer to produce samples quickly for designers to conduct trials and provide amendments or approvals.

When considering packaging, it is important to think about how the empty packs are stored prior to filling and the filling methods that can be used. Rigid boxes occupy space even when empty and don't lend themselves to automatic filling, so they tend to be used for small production runs of high value items where storage is less of a problem and labour costs can be justified. For high volume items, packs need to be delivered flat and be suitable for machine erection and filling as an integral part of the production process. Some "wraparound" pack styles allow carton blanks to be formed around the product while on the production line.

Opposite page Carton board enjoys widespread use for packaging applications. On this Chinese tea pack, the board has been embossed in addition to being litho printed.

Right Rigid boxes demonstrate their heritage as one of the oldest packaging forms by offering exclusivity. The fact that their construction precludes automatic filling and incurs storage problems, and that they are more likely to be reused by consumers, makes them suitable for expensive products. Here, the fashion brand Red or Dead makes a point about their exclusivity by opting for this flamboyant presentation of spectacles.

Folding cartons

When specifying cartons, consider both the filling methods and how consumers will use or re-use the pack before deciding on style and material.

Tuck flap carton (blank)

Carton length and width are always used to specify the carton opening.

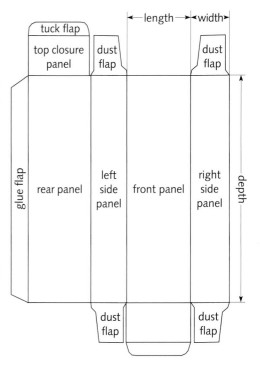

Rigid boxes

Rigid boxes cannot be folded flat and therefore occupy more storage space when empty than folding cartons during delivery and storage. Machine erection and filling are possible but usually at far lower speeds than for folding cartons. They can, however, have many different finishes, making them suitable for high quality items such as fragrances and gifts. Robust construction and removable lids make rigid boxes particularly suited for products that are repeatedly opened and closed, such as children's jigsaw puzzles, games and artists' materials.

Corrugated fibreboard

Corrugated fibreboard is constructed, in its single wall form, from two paper-based liners or facings separated by a corrugated fluting material to which the liners are bonded. Where greater strength is required, further layers can be added to produce doublewall with two fluted plies or triplewall with three fluted plies.

Materials

Liners and fluting media are specified by paper type and mass in grammes per square metre. Natural brown Kraft paper is the strongest liner as the fibre length is long. The use of recycled paper and board is common but shorter fibre lengths reduce strength.

The height of the fluting medium has a direct bearing on fibreboard properties. The largest standard flute is designated as A-flute. As the liners are spaced further apart, A-flute provides good stacking strength, referred to as compression strength, when flutes are vertical, and good cushioning properties when flutes are horizontal. Standard fluting is configured as shown right.

Material specifications are expressed as the board grammage, from the outside. A C-flute case with outer liner of 200gm Kraft, 127gm fluting and 150gm test inner liner is shown as 200K/127C/150T. The dimensions of corrugated fibreboard cases are specified as length x width x depth.

Double corrugated fibreboard

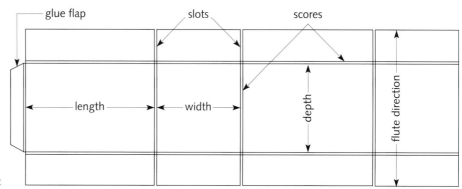

A (coarse)	105 – 125 flutes per metre	4·5 – 4·7 mm height
C (medium)	120 – 145	3·5 – 3·7 mm
B (fine)	150 – 185	2·1 – 2·9 mm
E	290 – 320	1·1 – 1·2 mm
Micro-flute	400 – 440	0·7 – 0·8 mm

Right Micro-flute has been used here to create a robust corrugated fibreboard transit pack. As product weight or fragility increases, larger flute sizes offer greater cushioning and improved stacking properties.

Plastics

Of all the materials available to packaging designers, plastics provide the most variety, both in terms of type and processing methods. In many packaging studies, the choice of container may be made on the basis of rigidity, as in the case of a bottle of mayonnaise, or flexibility as demonstrated by a pouch or sachet of the same mayonnaise. Both pack forms are plastic based and both protect the product, but they offer a different presentation to the user, the bottle being resealable for repeated use and the sachet for a single serving only.

Rigid plastic packaging

Rigid plastic containers include bottles, jars and tubs, with a wide range of different plastic materials being used for each container type. The container, its particular plastic and the manufacturing process involved in its production are interwoven, and affect the overall design and eventual end use of the pack, as the chart below indicates.

 HDPE LDPE PS V PP PET OTHER

Types of rigid plastic

A variety of plastics are used to produce the jars and bottles we encounter on a daily basis. Symbols on the container identify the type of plastic. The list here gives an indication of the most common plastic container types, materials and manufacturing processes. The production processes used, blow moulding and injection moulding, are illustrated separately in this chapter.

HDPE High Density Polyethylene The most common plastic used for containers of shampoo, detergent, milk, motor oil, garden and household chemicals. In natural form, the material is milky white but it is often highly pigmented for packaging applications. It is an excellent barrier to moisture but oils will eventually migrate through the container walls, causing panelling or distortion.

LDPE Low Density Polyethylene Softer material than HDPE, which makes it suitable for squeezee containers such as dishwasher liquids, sauces, jams and honey. The grease-proof qualities decrease with density and containers may suffer from splitting due to environmental stress cracking induced by oily products.

PS Polystyrene The crystal-clear clarity makes this material useful for injection-moulded tubs, boxes, cosmetic jars, tubes and CD cases. Disposable glasses and tableware are other common uses for this material. It is, however, brittle and so is sometimes used in its High Impact grade, HIPS, although at the cost of losing some clarity.

Left This washing-up liquid container is a typical application of rigid plastics. In this instance PET has been chosen because of its clarity and sparkle, which allows the colour of the liquid to be seen clearly.

PVC Polyvinyl Chloride (denoted by the symbol V) As PVC is brittle, plasticizers, lubricants, extenders and other additives are used in container manufacture although their inclusion has raised issues around food contact and recycling. PVC provides good clarity and grease resistance making it suitable for products such as bath oils.

PP Polypropylene This is normally used for injection-moulded containers and closures that utilize the "live hinge" properties of the material, allowing repeated opening and closing and snap closures. Its high temperature resistance makes it suitable for medical products requiring steam sterilization.

PET Polyethylene Terephthalate Extensively used for injection blow-moulded carbonated drinks bottles, where its strength allows light weighting. With a high temperature resistance, it also ideal for ready meal trays.

Other Used for all other plastic resins and multi-materials.

Extrusion blow moulding and injection blow moulding

Extrusion blow moulding and its more sophisticated offspring injection blow moulding are the principle methods of producing bottles and other narrow-mouth containers. The extrusion blow moulding process involves extruding a tube of semi-molten plastic, called the "parison", that is clamped into a mould, as shown in stage 2 of the illustration opposite. This is then inflated, pushing the soft plastic into the mould where it cools before the mould opens and the bottle is ejected. The container is automatically "de-flashed", trimming excess material at the neck and base. When designing plastic bottles produced by this process, there are some considerations that will affect design thinking:

Limitations

—The plastic becomes thin where the parison is stretched furthest, i.e. corners

—Design must ensure the bottle can be removed from the mould

—Decoration is usually done as a secondary process

—Storage problem if bottles are made off-site

—If product contains gas, e.g. fizzy drink, container shapes incorporating flat panels may distort due to internal gas pressure, whereas cylindrical panels distribute the pressure evenly without distortion

—Some plastics are permeable to gases, leading to product deterioration over time

—To assist processing, many plastics incorporate plasticizers, stabilizers and lubricants, some of which are toxic and have been proven to leach into the product

Opportunities

—Design can incorporate integral, hollow handles

—Allows wide variety of shapes, even the introduction of corrugations to provide a "bellows" effect, to allow containers to be squeezed or expanded

In practice, most limitations can be overcome but the designer needs to be aware that not everything on the design board will be easy to manufacture.

Injection blow moulding is essentially similar to the extrusion method, except that a first stage sees the production of an injection moulded "preform", which is inflated in stage two. This technique allows high definition of the neck section and is used, in particular, for PET containers, where the material is difficult to blow and requires close tolerances to maintain thin walls.

Extrusion blow moulding

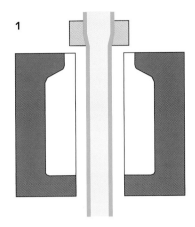
1

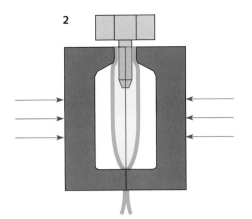
2

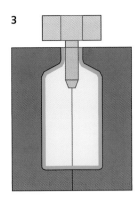
3

Metal moulds are produced, using dimensional detail from design drawings. Size is adjusted to allow for shrinkage of the plastic as it cools and to ensure the correct amount of head-space (ullage) is incorporated. The interior of moulds can be highly polished to give a smooth finish, sand blasted to provide texture or can incorporate design features such as ribs, patterns or text. Often, interchangeable inserts are used at the base of the mould to indicate production date and other variable information.

1. The first stage in the process is the extrusion of a parison or tube of semi-molten plastic material.
2. The mould moves over the parison and closes, trapping the parison.
3. The mould moves down and the parison inflates. The next parison begins to be extruded. Excess plastic or flashing is trimmed from both base and neck. The mould opens and the container is released.

In practice, the parison is often extruded through a programmable die to allow material thickness to be varied during extrusion, helping to direct more material to the outside edges of the mould where the plastic would be stretched thinly. Plastic trim is recycled wherever possible, depending upon colour and grade.

Injection blow moulding

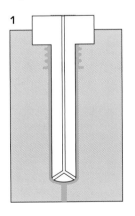
1

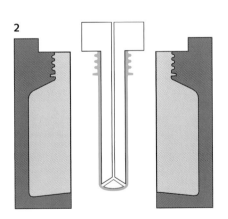
2

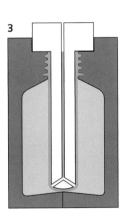
3

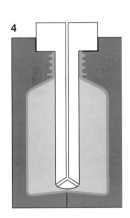
4

1. The first stage in the process uses injection moulding to produce a preform. This is formed around a blowing stick, which is used in subsequent parts of the process. The advantage is that the fine tolerances associated with injection moulding allow precision moulding of the neck section.

2. The subsequent stages are similar to extrusion blow moulding, except that the preform substitutes for the parison. Here the preform is being introduced into the two-part bottle mould.
3. The mould closes around the preform and is inflated by pressurized air. Finally, containers are ejected from the mould.

4. Variations of this method, particularly injection stretch blow moulding, are used to produce carbonated drinks bottles in PET, by mechanically stretching the preform. Preforms are often shipped to drinks bottling plants for subsequent blowing and filling, thereby reducing storage space required by empty bottles.

Flexible plastic packaging

Flexible plastic packaging includes films, foils and laminates in permutations that can be tailored to suit just about every requirement. Some of the most common forms of flexible plastic packaging are shown in the chart on page 68 and it will be immediately apparent that these are made up of complex combinations of different materials. Although such materials often provide cost-effective packaging, they have the disadvantage of being difficult to separate back into individual components for recycling. Also, as a component of domestic waste, flexibles cannot be separated into coherent grades and remain as an unidentifiable mixture. On the other hand, being derived from oil, many flexible plastics have a calorific value when burnt, enabling some of the energy expended in their manufacture to be reclaimed. Using heat and pressure, some flexibles can be recycled to produce semi-rigid waterproof sheeting suitable for use as a building material.

Most flexible plastics are produced in a continuous process that allows them to be stored on reels. It is the ability of films to be processed through form-fill seal operations that has been fundamental to their widespread adoption. Apart from the efficiency of this pack form, which uses very little material, it allows the convenience of in-plant filling/packing lines without the need for storing empty packaging, other than space-efficient reels of film.

Types of flexible packaging

Flexible packaging is a term that is used to describe films and laminates. A film, in the context of flexible packaging, is a thin material that may be constructed from one or more different plastics that can be co-extruded or laminated together. A characteristic of these materials is the ability to combine the properties of different plastics into a single material that then has the required property attributes for the packaging task in hand. This will depend upon the product and the shelf life required. Dried soup, for example, will have very different packaging requirements to cheese. Note that flexible packaging frequently includes aluminium foil and paper as part of the laminate structure.

The choice of extruded or film laminates influences both laminate thickness and its folding characteristics. Aluminium foil is often replaced with vacuum metalized films, using a fine coating of aluminium to achieve barrier properties and metallic appearance.

Packaging attribute	Possible packaging task requirements
physical strength	low/high stretch, easy/difficult to tear, puncture resistance
barrier properties	against/for moisture, gases, odours, UV light
machinability	ability to run on machines, ease of sealing
consumer acceptance	tactile feel, clarity/opacity, ease of disposal

Shampoo sachet

Dried soup sachet

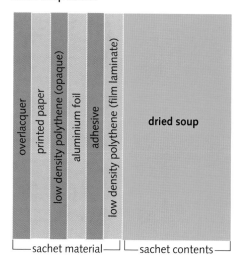

Form/fill/seal

The principle that applies to all form/fill/seal machines is the creation of a pouch from reel-fed stock, into which the product is inserted. The vertical form fill machine, VFFS, uses a vertical hollow tube around which plastic film is formed, with a back and end seal allowing the product to be filled through the tube before the final end seal is made. Horizontal form fill machines, HFFS machines or flow wrappers, use a forming box to create pack shape with a horizontal fin seal, the product being inserted horizontally prior to end sealing. Horizontal sachet machines fold the film, adding side seals to create an open pouch ready for filling before adding the final top seal.

Horizontal sachet machine

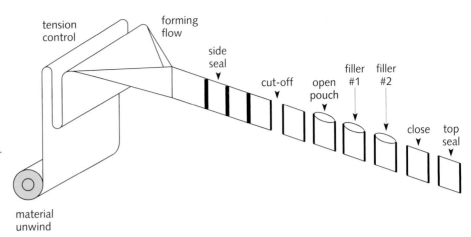

HFFS machine or flow wrapper

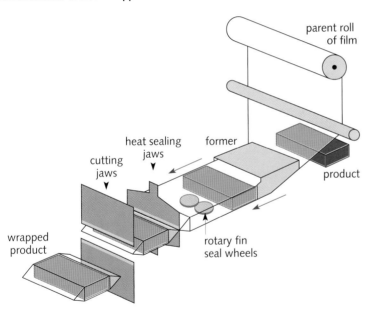

Material and product flow in a VFFS machine

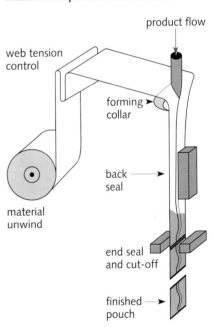

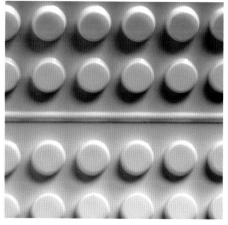

Thermoformed packaging

A further significant use of plastics is in thermoformed packaging. While there are many variations in processing methods, all share the same fundamental principle of heating thermoplastic material until it is soft and then forcing it into moulds through the use of vacuum, pressure or combinations of these. A characteristic of thermoformed packaging is the "draw angle" or taper required to remove the pack from the mould, usually between two to eight degrees.

Blister packs are a typical application of the thermoforming process, often, as in the case of pharmaceutical products, having a flexible foil "lid". Other styles use a blister that is welded or adhesively sealed to board. For environmental performance, packs should be designed to allow the plastic blister component to be easily separated from any dissimilar material, encouraging consumer recycling.

Above The thermoformed pill pack has become the generic style for many drugs in pill format. The in-line process efficiently thermoforms blisters, then fills and lids the pack, often with pre-printed flexible foil.

Thermoforming

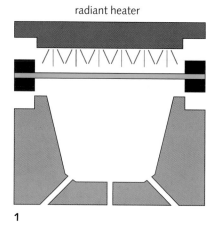

radiant heater

1

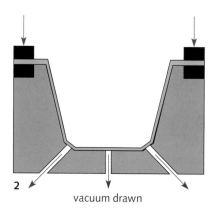

2

vacuum drawn

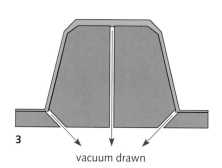

3

vacuum drawn

Simple vacuum forming uses heat-softened plastic sheeting that is drawn into the mould by a vacuum. Using a female or cavity mould, as shown here, produces good thickness control over the flange at the top of the mould—useful for subsequent heat sealing. The material thins, however, as the depth of draw increases and it can create a thin base. As the plastic cools, it shrinks away from the mould, allowing easy extraction of the formed item.

A plug or male mould (above right) provides the opposite effect to using a female mould, giving a thinner flange but thicker base. As the plastic shrinks onto the mould, it can be more difficult to remove. The vacuum is often reversed to create a positive pressure to blow the pack from the mould.

An advantage of thermoforming is that it can be used as an on-line process, creating packs ready for filling. Most pharmaceutical blister packs are created in this way.

Glass

Glass, although rigid, is actually a supercooled liquid that is inert to most materials and therefore able to contain a wide range of materials without contamination and without any permeation of gases through the container walls. This technical performance makes it ideal for protecting products against degradation but it is the sparkle, gloss, weight and feel—the aesthetic qualities—that are often used as design features.

The nature of glass and the distribution of it during the moulding process, restrict the use of sharp angles. When designing glass containers, generous rounding of corners and panels helps to reduce stresses that lead to breakage. Glass does, however, lend itself to embossing and surface texturing. Recycling glass is cost-effective and does not impair the properties of the material. If possible, avoid using colours other than brown or green as these cannot be recycled due to contamination from their pigments. Blue glass, for example, may provide great standout and strong product differentiation but it cannot be recycled conventionally. If the glass container design must have a coloured finish, consider the use of a coloured shrink sleeve. Although this brings its own environmental problems, they may be less significant than using coloured glass.

Above The bottle incorporates embossed panels highlighting the name of this popular Spanish brand, Carbonell. The clarity of glass allows the product to be the star of the show. Note here also how the glass is softly contoured but still allows touch-points on the base and shoulders.

Glass container production

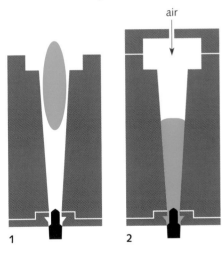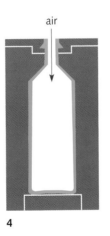

1   2   3   4

The "blow and blow" process

1. Molten "gobs" of glass are delivered into the parison mould.

2. Pressurized air forces the gob into the parison, forming the neck finish.

3. Compressed air is now applied through the preformed neck to complete the parison.

   The parison still has thick walls and is now removed, rotated through 180 degrees and transferred to the final mould.

4. Air pressure forces the still fluid glass into the final container shape before being transferred to an annealing oven or lehr where reheating removes any stresses.

   The blow and blow process is particularly suited to making narrow-necked bottles.

The "press and blow" method

In this process, a plunger is used to create the parison, rather than air pressure as shown above in stage 3. The parison then follows a similar path to the blow and blow method. Using a plunger makes press and blow suitable for wide mouth containers such as jars. The parison shape is removed, inverted and transferred to the blow mould where air pressure creates the final container.

Metal container manufacturing

Draw and wall ironing process (DWI)—used for carbonated drinks cans in both aluminium and steel.

1. Steel or aluminium strip is lubricated with a thin film of oil before being cut and pressed into shallow cups in the cupping press.

1a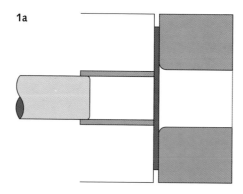

1b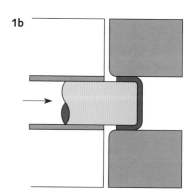

2. Each cup is forced through a series of tungsten carbide rings, drawing and "ironing" the cup to a smaller diameter, thinning the walls and increasing the height.

2a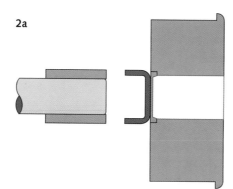

2b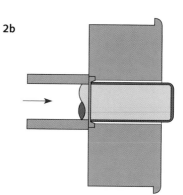

3. Trimmers remove the surplus irregular edge and cut the can body to the required height. Trimmed cans are then washed, dried and lacquered externally before printing. Flanges and beads are added to the neck and the can is lacquered internally before being palletized ready for dispatch to filling plants.

3

Metals

Steel and aluminium are extensively used in packaging applications, mostly in the form of cans for drinks and food. Their 100% barrier properties with respect to the permeation of gases, liquids, solvents and UV light have helped establish metal containers as a viable method of preserving products since the 1880s. The traditional steel three-piece can is still widely used for food. As the name suggests, it is made from two ends and a rolled and welded central body. This type of container can be made from litho printed steel (see p.75), giving the opportunity for superb quality printing. Other production methods for both aluminium and steel containers involve deep-drawn or impact extrusion as shown in the diagram opposite. Here printing is carried out after manufacture, using the dry offset process (as mentioned later on page 75). New manufacturing technologies now allow greater use of shape and the incorporation of embossed/debossed features onto metal containers. If your design calls for this approach, check with a container manufacturer what the limitations are. The engineering feel of metals can be exploited in packaging design. For inspiration in this area look, for example, at car or motorcycle design and, in particular, detailing in engines, grilles, dashboards, etc.

Above Hinged-lid tinplate containers such as this German biscuit tin are robust and attractive, often finding reuse as storage containers.

Speciality packs

In addition to packaging that we may regard as mainstream, there are many instances of special packs. Containing and protecting products, these also fulfil a special role, sometimes making it difficult to distinguish between product and pack. An example is the aerosol inhalers used to administer drugs for asthma sufferers, which is just one application amongst an increasing use for this method of drug delivery. The technology is packaging based, using a metered dose aerosol to dispense the product. Other packs feature dispensing as their critical role, including coffee sweeteners, sweets and air fresheners. In order to achieve the precision required in these applications, many of the pack components and, in the case of sweetener dispensers, the pack itself, use injection-moulded plastics.

It is anticipated that emerging technology will encourage a further convergence between packaging and product. There are already experimental packs, for example, that combine mobile phone technology with packaging technology, enabling critical drug regimes to be monitored. The phone reminds the patient to take their medication. As the medication is dispensed, the phone contacts the medical centre advising a positive response. If the drug is not dispensed, the medical centre will be advised and can track the patient via the phone signal to administer assistance.

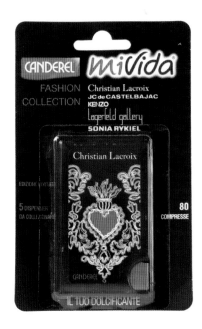

Above Although this injection-moulded sweetener dispenser pack is still packaging, it begins to combine product and pack into one functional unit, giving increased consumer benefit through convenience in product dispensing. This is part of a series of designer dispensers, encouraging collection.

Surface decoration

In packaging design, the term "decoration" is used to indicate that, in addition to printing methods, other techniques are used to create images, graphic devices and text. It is beyond the scope of this book to go into detail about each process but there are some considerations to be taken into account that may have consequences for the overall design. It is, however, worth defining here some of the terms that are referred to in the print processes described below:

—halftone *image created by dots of varying size*
—line-work *solid colour used in text, illustration and diagrams*
—process printing *colour reproduction using three-process colours: cyan, magenta and yellow (black is usually added as a fourth key colour)*

Mainstream printing processes

Relief printing—flexography

Relief printing relies on a raised surface to hold the ink in exactly the same way that a rubber stamp works. Flexography finds widespread use in packaging, using flexible photopolymer plates to carry ink onto non-adsorbent surfaces, such as plastic films and plastic labels. It is also used to print rougher surfaces, typically corrugated fibre-board. Despite improvements in quality, particularly with regard to the reproduction of halftones, flexography can be recognized by a halo effect around letters, where the soft polymer plates "squeegee" the ink.

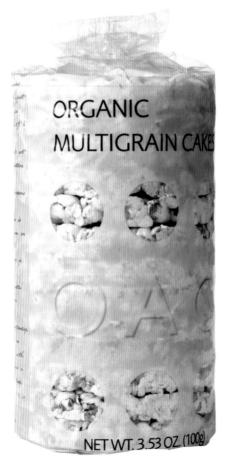

Left (and detail above) Soft polymer plates do not damage the delicate film surface but you can see in the detail from this flexo-printed film from Belgium that the squeegee effect of the plates has left a "halo" effect around letters, characteristic of the process.

Relief printing—offset letterpress (or dry offset)

This is primarily used for printing metal cans but it is also used for plastic tubs and metal or plastic tubes. As, in this method, the separate wet inks do not mix, it is not possible to print process colours. The use of halftones, however, can give the illusion of process work.

Planographic printing—lithography and offset lithography

Here, both print and non-print areas are in the same plane, there being an oil attracting image area, attracting the oily ink, and a water attracting non-image area on each printing plate. Aluminium alloy plates are used with chemically enhanced ink-receptive and water-receptive print areas, achieved through photographic exposure. It is common practice to use a rubber coated offset cylinder (referred to as a blanket) for print transfer onto the substrate. Litho is primarily used for printing paper stock for labels, folding cartons and sheet-fed metal, often using the process colours (cyan, magenta and yellow), black and one or two specials. (Specials are frequently corporate colours, which would not reproduce acurately from process colours or metallic inks.)

The oily nature of ink makes it unsuitable for printing onto many plastics, but litho has to be a front runner in the quality stakes.

Offset letterpress

Dry offset assembles the image on a blanket roll.

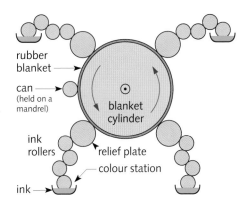

Lithographic printing

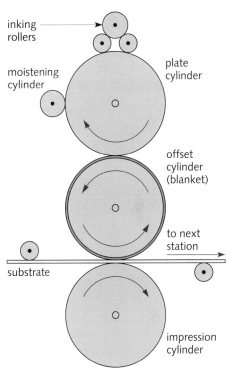

Above The bird of prey featured on this litho-printed pack has all the authority we might associate with a bank—these are obviously serious tuna products. The clean lines of litho are evident here, emphasized by printing onto a coated carton board stock with a heavy overprint varnish.

Gravure printing

A gravure cylinder may have millions of tiny cells or wells whose volume can be controlled to carry different amounts of ink.

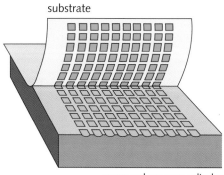

substrate

engraved gravure cylinder

highlight area   shadow area

copper cylinder surface

A gravure station

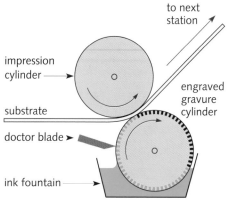

to next station

impression cylinder

substrate

doctor blade

ink fountain

engraved gravure cylinder

Gravure—rotogravure

Gravure printing or, to be more accurate, rotogravure uses print areas in a gravure cylinder—it is always a cylinder process—that are engraved or etched onto the surface in a series of minute cells. Each cell can be engraved deeper into the roller surface to carry more ink where this is required, for example, when the heavy pigments for metallic inks must be laid thickly onto the substrate to obtain the desired effect. Etching can be chemically achieved or laser cut directly from a photographically imposed print pattern onto the cylinder. The results are always laid down as a dot pattern, even for line work, and give gravure a distinctive saw-tooth edge to letters, when examined under a lens. Nevertheless, gravure printing arguably achieves the highest quality results of any process, but it comes at a price. Cylinders are expensive, which means that it is a process reserved for long runs. Typical uses would be printing the plastic wrappers on confectionery "count lines", the industry's term for popular snack bars such as Snickers.

Above (and detail left)
This spicy Japanese seaweed pack indicates the level of hot chillis through a simple graphic device—steam from the ears! The foil laminate is gravure printed. Looking at the enlargement reveals the tell-tale "saw-tooth" pattern around letters and lines and the cell pattern etched onto the cylinders may also be seen. High quality reproduction, however, is always a feature of gravure printing.

Other decoration processes

The mainstream print processes described previously meet many of the requirements for packaging, but there are additional techniques that can be used to good effect.

Foil blocking

Heat transfers of metallic film stamped from reels of material.

Advantages
—Excellent quality
—Achieves real metallic effects

Disadvantages
—Needs heat tolerant surface
—Off-line process

Stretch/shrink sleeving

A pre-printed film sleeve is placed onto the container and shrunk by heat to conform to the container surface. (The stretch version pre-stretches a film prior to placement, where it shrinks onto the container surface.) The technique is widely used for drinks bottles.

Advantages
—Can shrink onto compound curves, e.g. spherical shapes
—Film can be opaque, coloured or clear
—Print carefully controlled off-line

Disadvantages
—Special print origination process to build in distortion for areas that shrink more than others
—Design needs to build in shoulders for positive location of film
—Does not shrink into debossed or recessed areas

Screen printing

Ink is forced through the areas of fine mesh exposed by a photographic development process.

Advantages
—Suitable for plastics, textiles, rigid boards, metals and glass
—Heavy lay-down of ink, great for metallic or pearlescent inks

Disadvantages
—Slow production
—Not brilliant for halftones

Embossing/debossing

Creating a raised/depressed area or relief. In plastic and glass container manufacture (and some metal container manufacturing methods) the mould is machined with the desired pattern, allowing material to flow into the pattern and reproduce it as a raised section on the finished container. Materials capable of deforming and maintaining their deformed state, such as carton board, metals and aluminium foils, can be embossed using an embossing die on one side of the substrate and a resilient pad on the other, creating a raised (embossed) or depressed (debossed) area.

Advantages
—Allows tactile areas to be created
—May remove need for printing

Disadvantages
—May require an additional off-line process for sheet and web based materials
—For moulded containers, the pattern used needs to avoid fine details that might fill-in

Far left L'Oréal foil blocking. Creating real metallic effects provides a way of indicating luxury and opulence, frequently used in the packaging of cosmetics. Metal is thermally transferred from a film web impregnated with metallic particles directly to the pack surface.

Centre left Printed shrink film on moulded plastic Ribena pack. Conventional print techniques cannot be used to print a surface that curves in two directions. By printing onto a clear film and then shrinking this onto the container, the pack can carry all-round graphics.

Centre right Screen printed vodka bottle. The heavy ink deposit can clearly be seen, characteristic of the print process. Printing directly onto the glass, as here, allows maximum product visibility while maintaining a quality appearance not often matched by the alternatives of pre-printed transparent labels or shrink-sleeves.

Right Embossed tinplate, J&B whisky. Tinplate can be embossed to create added personality and interest. Here, as is usual, the print has been laid down prior to embossing.

To help decide which combinations of materials, processes and decoration methods are candidates for meeting the brief, it may be useful to review what the consumer requirements are, what is required to maintain the integrity of the product and if there are any production issues that might affect pack selection. The chart below shows the questions that can be asked to help to narrow down the pack material options.

Identifying packaging restrictions and opportunities

Consumer requirements

When designing packaging, it is essential to establish what benefits can be provided for consumers. Try to determine the relative consumer benefits of the following design options by addressing these questions:

Product visibility
—how important or desirable is it to see the product before buying it?

Specific configurations
—do consumers require any specific pack sizes/weight/volumes?
—are there any established practices in the market sector?

Value for money
—how important is it to be able to see what you are getting before buying?

Ease of carrying
—does it need a handle or finger holes?

Opening/closing/reopening
—can you make it easier?

Storage in the home
—where is it stored?
—if it is in the fridge, does it fit?
—if in a bathroom, will it be stable on a washbasin or shelf?

Safety
—will it be a hazard to users/children/pets?
—can it be designed to be safer?

Product dispensing
—is it useful/essential that it dispenses the product well?
—would a measured quantity be useful?

Disposal
—how does the consumer dispose of the product?
—can it be reusable/recyclable/compostable?

Product requirements

It is not possible to select packaging materials or begin designing until the nature of the product is understood. These are the type of questions you might ask:

Product characteristics
—solid/liquid/gel/cream/tablet etc.?

Compatability
—does the product react with some materials?
—can the product be affected by contact with some materials?

Product shelf life
—what conditions will it be stored at: frozen/chilled/ambient/hot?
—what shelf life period is required?

Product degradation
—what is it that degrades the product: moisture/temperature/light?
—can the product spoil because of odour/taste/contamination?

Physical damage
—how fragile is it?

Sizes/weights/volume
—what is the anticipated pack size?
—is this the same as in the consumer requirement table?

Dispensing
—how is the product used/dispensed?

Production limitations (if any)

How the product is going to be packed and the processes involved all have implications for packaging design. Most new packs will have to fit into current product production facilities, and the following list suggests the type of information packaging designers should know before considering material selection:

Project product sales
—how many containers are required per annum/batch?

Sterilization
—if required, what conditions must the pack withstand?

Filling/weighing
—how are packs filled?

Closing and sealing
—how will this be achieved?

Checkweighing
—what is the method of checking that filled containers meet standards?

On-line print and labelling
—will this be handled on-line or as a separate, off-line activity?

Quality control
—what will this involve?

Pack collation
—how many primary packs per secondary pack?

Storage
—methods/stack heights/time in store?

Distribution
—road/rail/air/sea?

Colour

Designers often work in pencil, ink or other single colour media in the initial stages of a project. This has the advantage of allowing design work to be developed without introducing any further variables from colour choice. It is a recognized and recommended way of working. Inevitably, however, there will come a point where colour decisions have to be made. In some cases, decisions may be imposed, such as the use of corporate colours, while in other cases there will be a greater degree of freedom. In order to use that freedom to best effect, it is important to understand that colours are "read" much faster than text, communicating immediate information to the viewer. Specific colours may identify a brand, tell us something about the nature of the product, have meaningful cultural associations or invoke some innate emotional reaction. These messages can be contradictory and the problem with this powerful tool, and therefore a challenge for designers, is to balance these frequently opposing design parameters. The sections below attempt to separate these elements and explain some of the semiotic colour associations—areas where colour has cultural and emotional signifiers, as mentioned in Chapter One.

	emotional	cultural	product categories
	passion heat love energy	revolution communism stop/danger	beef chilli
	joy creativity	sectarian associations in Ireland danger	orange flavour
	happiness	warning cowardice in USA and UK nobility in Japan	chicken banana flavour
	freshness natural fertility	Islamic colour go/on sectarian associations in Ireland	vegetable/organic lime menthol spearmint
	cool calm male trustworthy	mourning in Iran immortality in China	fish low calorie peppermint
	luxury wealth fantasy romance	death in Latin America	luxury products

Colour chart

In packaging, colours are often used to denote product categories, cultural meanings and emotional associations. Of all the tools in the design toolbox, colour is perhaps the easiest to get wrong.

Corporate requirements

Established brands often have strict policies on the use of colour that you, the designer, cannot challenge. If the logo is specified as being in Pantone 185, do not be tempted to suggest an alternative. There may be aspects of a brief that can be challenged but this is definitely not one of them. Instead, ensure that you obtain full specifications of any corporate identity requirements from the client, which should provide detailed information on the permitted use of colour and any restrictions that might apply.

Some brands have embraced colour, using it as a brand property. Red, for example, is a brand property for both Coca-Cola and Marlboro. While brands benefit from ease of recognition through the use of colour, there are also potential problems, particularly when brand extensions are involved. Coca-Cola found that the introduction of Diet Coke required a design that would maintain the brand values of the original product but also be perceived as a sugar-free variety. Coca-Cola could, perhaps, have used the waisted bottle shape or their distinctive typography as powerful brand identifiers, both strategies that would work independently of colour. Instead, they opted to retain the corporate red, using it for text that was displayed on a silver and white background rather than the white type on a red background used on the original product. The product name "Coke", running vertically on the can, is short enough to justify the use of large lettering, allowing a substantial area of red to appear on-pack. The resulting design effectively balances corporate colour use with a lighter feel appropriate to the diet drinks sector.

Below Using less colour suggests fewer calories. Here, Coca-Cola have cleverly retained their corporate red but, rather than reverse the logo out of it, have chosen to print "Coke" positively in red on a metallic/white background to give a lighter feel for the Diet can.

Marlboro also uses red as a corporate colour. Due to legal restrictions in some countries, the use of company logos is not permitted trackside when tobacco companies sponsor sporting events. It is interesting to observe that, in these circumstances, the Marlboro chevron, a powerful graphic device, and red colour appear without any text and yet are still instantly recognizable. To continue with this example, the corporate red and chevron work together strongly enough to allow brand recognition even when the colour is changed to green on a packet of menthol cigarettes.

While colour is used extensively on packs as a brand property, it can present problems for later product diversification. The examples above, however, give clues as to how designers may retain brand colour but still distinguish product varieties. Among the favoured strategies for consideration by the designer are: printing familiar type in the negative as opposed to the positive; incorporating graphic devices that provide strong links to the brand; or using graphic devices that have become part of the logo, as in the case of "Virgin", for example. Here the stylized text "Virgin" remains constant, in either positive or reversed out format, but is accompanied by different graphic devices for the many sub-brands in the Branson empire. Visit www.virgin.com to see how this works.

Category conventions

The use of colour to denote product categories and product variants is at its most important within the self-service retail area, where products are located by category and displayed by brand, allowing competition between brands adjacent to one another on-shelf. In most instances where colour is used as a product category code, it is the brand leader that originates the convention which competitors are, ultimately, forced to adopt. However, in the last five years, the range of product variants has expanded vastly, so now is perhaps the right time to challenge the wisdom of continuing to consider colour coding as a means of assistance to consumers. As an example, we may review the stock cube sector where we are likely to find Oxo and Knorr competing as major brands with Bovril and Kallo.

Below Traditionally, the colour convention for vegetable stock cube packaging has been green. The introduction of new and increasingly complex products, and a diversification in the market, has led to a breakdown in the convention. A wider range of colours is now used, with the addition of images.

Oxo, the brand leader, originated the colour convention with a rationale that is clearly understandable, using red for beef (red meat), yellow for chicken (it is a yellowish colour) and green for vegetable stock. Now we find additional varieties: Oxo lamb (purple), Oxo Italian herbs and spices (green) and Oxo Chinese (also green). The rationale for colour choice is, therefore, becoming less convincing and Knorr, who have a wider range and, plainly, have decided not to follow the colour coded route, use one pack colour (yellow), together with a photograph of prepared food for each variety: ham, lamb, fish and pork. As the trend for introducing new and more complex products continues, colour coding becomes less relevant and, ultimately, more confusing.

Using less colour on packs can signify new meanings. On diet packs, for example, there can appear to be a correlation between colour reduction and diet, almost suggesting that by stripping out colour, or using a tint of the parent product colour, calories are also removed. Using less colour, particularly confining it to white and a single colour, also suggests basic, value-for-money products, where little of the cost is spent on the packaging. In reality, there is very little cost advantage involved but the illusion of value created by simple one-colour or two-colour work is often used by supermarkets for own label basic commodity items. In complete contrast, minimal colour use can also create exclusivity. The use of black and white photography and simple but minimal text can be striking, providing that, as with all simple things, each element is beautifully crafted.

Typically, colours carry different meanings in different sectors so that, for example, while green in the toothpaste sector denotes spearmint, it may, as we have seen, indicate vegetable in the stock cube sector or salt 'n' vinegar in the snack foods sector. It is also used extensively to denote "organic" across a wide spectrum of products. For every packaging project, it is necessary for the designer to become familiar with the market and its colour conventions. Client marketing staff can help but it is still important to see the point of sale conditions and analyse the use of colour.

Cultural meanings

Colour also has cultural significance that designers should be aware of, particularly when designing for markets outside their territories, or multi-cultural markets where some colours may have an unexpected meaning within some sectors. Black and white, although strictly not colours, also have cultural associations:
—Black *death in the West*
—White *death in the Middle East, China, Japan and India*

It is, however, useful sometimes to deliberately adopt colours because of their cultural associations. Red, for example, is associated with revolution, particularly communist revolutionary movements and has frequently been used to good effect on packs that aim to invoke a sense of rebellion. On a cautionary note, however, it is important to remember that it is often the local perception of cultural associations that is significant rather than the actual associations themselves. A Russian vodka, with red used as a graphic element, may appeal to an 18–25-year-old male audience in the UK, who are likely to have little in-depth knowledge about the

» Tip
If possible, take photographs of the point of sale and review this later, specifically focusing on colour.

» Tip
When designing for markets other than those that you are familiar with, it is essential to conduct some colour research. As a general guide in these circumstances, find out and avoid the national flag colours (and associated graphic devices), unless you are intending to make a particular appeal to national identity.

Soviet era but, perhaps, perceive the connection between red and Russia in terms of romantic, possibly heroic, rebellion and hard drinking. The local perception here, in other words, is largely emotional rather than analytical, embracing the passion and finding no desire for further explanation. In this instance, colour associations are being used as a pastiche of cultural values and, therefore, must be considered carefully in relation to the target audience. The same pack may find a different reception in the Czech Republic, for example, or within modern Russia itself, where memories of the Soviet era have different cultural values.

Emotional associations

One of the most powerful uses of colour is in appealing to emotional values and associations. As these appear to be deeply rooted within our brains, our reaction to specific colours is frequently innate and not reasoned. We simply respond. It becomes clear that when packaging incorporates such colour signifiers, it can communicate at an unconscious, intuitive level in addition to a conscious, analytical visual level.

The terminology we use to describe colours frequently indicates their emotional associations. We refer to "rich" purples and "fresh" greens, acknowledging an assignment of human values to colour. Not surprisingly, therefore, packaging frequently draws on these emotional values to set the tone for products. While reds are concerned with passion and fire, blues are analytical and cool. Frequently designers will also describe colours in terms of their "temperature". It is a useful way of referring to colour intensity and tone. A "hot pink", "warm yellow" or "cool grey" become descriptors that are full of meaning. The temperatures of colours become hotter as yellow diminishes and red increases, whereas they become colder as blue increases. This is where our visual and spoken languages meet, both governed by a deeper subconscious interpretation of colour.

Above Blue is a colour that inspires trust and efficacy, making it a favourite for pharmaceutical products and financial services where packs must adopt a serious, responsible and authoritative tone of voice.

Below The rich dark colours used on this chocolate packaging, combined with gold text, are associated with luxury and indulgence.

Gender associations

The origins of adopting a colour convention to identify gender are obscure but the evidence suggests it was introduced during Victorian times. Certainly pink has found a new lease of life with Barbie dolls and Hello Kitty products for girls. Studies on colour preferences do indicate a female preference for pastel colours—pinks and warm reds, while men prefer stronger colours—silvers and blacks. There is even some evidence to suggest that cultural values deepen this colour divide. For example, a manufacturer of power drill products used dark blue for product colour in the UK but black in Italy, where a more macho imagery found favour. Where products are gendered, designers need to avoid patronizing their target audience with clichéd colour choices. It can be useful to analyse the colour ways used by other, successful gendered products already in the market and to talk any design proposals through with those of the relevant gender before making any firm recommendations.

Vignettes

Many packaging designs incorporate a solid background colour into which images, text and graphic devices are embedded. On occasions, however, it can provide an interesting effect when one colour is faded into another. Producing vignettes of this type used to involve mastery of the air-brush but now, with graphic design software, it is a simple task. As with many print effects incorporated into software, they can be overused. Just because you can do it does not mean that you should do it; there has to be a sound reason to justify their use. Kleenex, as shown here, have used a vignette intelligently. There is a feeling of the balm-impregnated tissues offering relief, indicated by the colour change. Vignettes offer this dynamic colour shift technique that visually represents change. Where there is a before-and-after story, there is a potential role for vignettes. It is, however, still an effect and, like most effects, not a replacement for good design.

» Tip
When working on a gendered product, seek opinions on the use of colour from those representing the gender who will purchase the product, in addition to those who will use the product. An example is women buying electric razors as gifts for men—where there may be significant differences in colour perception between purchaser and user. (Blackwell, Engel and Miniard, 2005)

Above This French razor pack uses pink as a gender identifier. Some products, such as tampons, are gender specific yet continue to use male/female colour coding when, in fact, no possible confusion can exist.

Right Just because technology now makes it easy to create colour gradients, it does not mean that you should always do so. Here there is a justifiable reason for using a vignette to show the efficacy of the product.

Typography

No designer's toolbox would be complete without the means to understand and select typefaces that will fit the requirements of the brief. With every PC or Mac equipped with around two hundred typefaces as standard, it is hardly surprising that many take the view that selecting typefaces requires no further thought, other than individual taste. In fact, the effective use of typography is fundamental to achieving great packaging layouts.

In this book, there is only room to take a very brief overview of typography as it such a large and important part of graphic design. For packaging applications, the information shown below is only the mere basics that you will need. All design students are recommended to research, read and learn about typography, practising the manipulation of type and space at every opportunity. Apart from being a fascinating subject in itself, it will also help your design work. Phil Baines and Andrew Haslam's book, *Type and Typography* (2002) would make a good starting point.

The ease of producing new typefaces using digital technology has led to a proliferation of new fonts supplementing the classic fonts that have been in use for many years. The chart on the right indicates some of the most relevant terms that are used to describe letterforms.

Choosing typefaces

There are two broad categories of type. The first are those typefaces designed for text that is intended to be read, historically for books. Here it is important that the eye is led smoothly along the text, moving from line to line without interruption, in order that the reader has the best chance of understanding the text and does not become fatigued by the effort of reading. Clearly, this was the aim of many early typographers, and arguments still rage about the comparative virtues of particular typefaces in this respect. This group of classic (or Old Style) fonts includes Garamond, Bembo and Caslon, all of which are serif typefaces. It is argued that the serifs help link letters visually and therefore aid reading. Nowadays, there are many who would dismiss such claims and point to new evidence that suggests that once familiarity is achieved with non-serif faces, there is little difference in reading ability. The arrival of hot metal printing led to the introduction of new Roman faces during the 1930s, of which Times New Roman is an example. Modern, or Transitional, serif typefaces, such as Bodoni and Baskerville, are more geometric and less influenced by calligraphy, yet still suited to books.

For most packaging applications, however, there is little need to read large blocks of text. At most there may be some instructional or explanatory text, and so many of the typographical criteria that apply to books are not entirely valid for packaging. It is the second category of type, known as display type, which has greater relevance for packaging designers. Originally introduced in the nineteenth century for advertising and public notices, display type is characterized by bold, slab letters where the letters are design elements rather than text. Today, designers often use sans serif typefaces as a basis for developing display faces.

Letterform descriptors

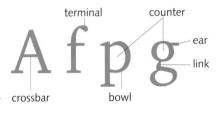

Serif types

Sans serif types

Letterform measurements

III: The packaging designer's toolbox   85

The voices of type

Maybe there is something classically English in

Baskerville.

There is a hint of Montmartre and the left bank of

Paris in Garamond.

On the other hand, the USA provides us with

Goudy.

But we might make this our choice for Italian fashion

in Rome, Bodoni.

For clear text on packaging, sans serif

Helvetica is often used where

a clean and simple effect is required.

For other effects and minimal blocks of text we
could consider,

Comic Sans, just for a joke, **Book Antiqua** for something traditional; GILL SANS FOR AN ANNOUNCE- MENT; *MISTRAL* *for something a little less formal and hand crafted;* **Fette Fraktur** for a hint of **Gothic darkness;** Futura provides geometric precision; LITHOS HAS A

DISTINCTLY GREEK FEEL.

Sans serif typefaces achieved widespread popularity in the 1920s, being seen as clean, uncluttered and "modern", in line with the design revolution typified by the Bauhaus school of design, where functionality was paramount and "stream-lining" was regarded as futuristic. Gill Sans, Helvetica and Avant Garde are examples of sans serif typefaces that remain popular today.

In deciding which typeface to use on a packaging design, there are several criteria to consider:
—Sympathy with product
—Typesize required (consider this also for any language translations)
—Substrate being printed
—Print process
—Design features *tints, reversing out*
—Measure *line length (usually small on packaging)*

The most important consideration regarding choice of typeface is the nature of the product and its appeal to the target market, where these factors are to be translated into an appropriate typographical language. When trying to give a particular national flavour to the design, it can be useful to know that, for example, a classical English typeface is Baskerville, whereas Garamond is French and Goudy represents the USA. In the same way, the use of own-language type, such as Gaelic, Greek or Cyrillic styles, for example, provide recognizable clues about national identity that may be significant to the aims of a packaging design project. Similarly, typefaces can be chosen to convey powerful emotional meaning, whether this is concerned with authority, humour, fun, prestige or any other attribute that reflects the intended product nature and its target audience. Remember, however, that text on packaging has to be read quickly, so restraint in using complex typefaces is sometimes required to ensure that standout, impact and readability are maintained.

The remainder of the criteria on the above list are practical considerations concerning print quality. If typesize is to be small, the substrate is porous or the design calls for type to be reversed out of another colour, for example, then a sans serif typeface may be more appropriate to avoid loss of letter detail in the print process. If there are any doubts, it is worth showing design proposals to the printer or the client's technical staff.

Measure, or line length, in packaging is usually not a problem because there is usually little need for blocks of text over which the reader's eye passes back and forth frequently. Instead, where there is extensive text, perhaps of instructional text running onto several lines, the optimum number of characters per line is around 60 to 72. Less than this interrupts the flow of reading and more makes it difficult to pick up the next line. As, however, most pack forms are slim and vertical, or portrait, in order to maximize the number of packs per linear measure of shelf, it is more likely that 30–35 characters per line will be the achievable maximum.

Spacing—kerning and leading

Another factor influencing readability is leading, the term used to describe spacing between the lines. If there is insufficient leading, the lines will be close together and difficult to read, an effect that is exaggerated if the typeface is condensed, a serif face or one that has large x- heights with reduced ascenders and descenders. In packaging work, where there is little copy, the need to meet objectives of effective instant recognition, communication and emotional appeal are probably more important than ease of text readability. Kerning, the space between letters, is frequently adjusted for display type (headings) used in packaging applications as, for example, product descriptors. Increasing kerning can make reading more difficult but can be used purposely as a design element.

Rather than follow set rules about which typeface, size, measure, kerning and leading to use in packaging designs, it is better to develop "the design eye" to see what layout works best. Here the designer has more scope to use typography as an element of the pack design than in book or magazine applications. Remember, however, that this must be the one that also meets the brief. As with all design, there must also be a typographical rationale that underpins decisions. This should spring from the product itself and the target audience.

If the end user is not the purchaser, as with children's cereals, for example, the design must work on both parent and child levels. In this instance, for example, the design may incorporate "childish" type but, possibly, use a more serious typeface for dietary information. Mixing styles, typefaces and sizes should, however, be avoided wherever possible for most packaged products, particularly where the product is regarded as a "sensible" one. On the other hand, greater freedoms with typography might be entirely in line with the aims of some design projects, deliberately using typography and letterforms to create graphic effects. Only the brief, your imagination and practised design skills will let you use typography as a really effective design tool.

Left Packaging design often combines different typefaces to distinguish between messages. Here, one typeface is used to provide health information, another to declare "organic".

Photography and illustration

Nearly all packaging projects will require the use of images or illustration as an integral part of the design. Packs, in the all-important supermarket environment, have to communicate information quickly without the need for detailed reading. Images have the ability to convey sometimes complex information instantly in a way that text cannot. Although packaging is sometimes considered to be a "mini-advert", it is this need for immediacy that sets packaging design apart from other sales media. Most magazine adverts and moving images on television advertising allow time for the eye to detect the image and then to consider it, picking up more subtle information as it does so. We have much less initial engagement with packaging, tending to scan it rather than read it. This explains why packaging designers frequently reduce the on-pack design elements, compared to those used in printed adverts, to allow fast recognition of brand and product. Later, having achieved the purchaser's attention, other information on the pack can be read systematically. Simplifying information, however, to allow the essential

Below Effective use of images gives this pack an immediate fresh, outdoor feel. The tea-picker's broad brimmed hat suggests warmth from the sun while incorporating a sense of ethnicity appropriate to a Fairtrade tea.

communication messages to be conveyed, is, as with many simple things, concerned with detail and by no means an easy option. It is here that the ability to handle images and illustration becomes important.

To begin, packaging designers need to be able to know how to create their own images, where existing images can be sourced and understand the alternative strategies between using photography or illustration.

Photography

At the initial concept stage of a design study, most visual information can be sketched or obtained as tear sheets to indicate the designer's thinking. So, for example, the designer might want to indicate the use of photography for a food product by using an illustration or photograph from a cookery magazine. It probably won't be exactly right but it will suffice to convey the design concept. Similarly, image banks offer stock photographs that can be accessed on-line. These are a very useful source of professionally generated images that can be freely downloaded for trial purposes. If the designer registers with the company, watermarks on the "comp" image can sometimes be removed. Take care, however, in using images sourced from image banks as their business income depends on selling images. Before an image becomes incorporated into any final design, costs must be investigated. The level of cost and royalty agreement will depend on a number of factors, such as image size, purpose, circulation and positioning. It can be extremely expensive. Alternatively, a royalty free image may be found, which may be financially attractive but there is no guarantee that another product or brand might not use the same image.

Sometimes, however, there is no alternative but to carry out experimental photography, where suitable images just cannot be located. The term "experimental" is used to denote that its purpose is for trials and is not to be confused

Above left Food photography is always difficult. Here, the bread looks better than the pâté and the overall effect lacks freshness. However, this is representative of the normal standard of food photography on packaging.

Above right It is particularly difficult to photograph hot food and make it look appetizing. The situation is complicated where there are sauces that often appear congealed, as here. Shots like this are time-consuming to set up, usually requiring a cook to prepare the food and a specialized food photographer.

with carefully controlled photography for production use. While film cameras can (and do) provide superb results, digital photography provides images that can be downloaded within minutes into photo-manipulation software programmes and printed out just as quickly. Designers will already be familiar with Photoshop and should have no problem in adjusting their own images.

Using photography as a design tool helps to create believable concepts but it should be remembered that, if the client accepts a design incorporating photography, professional photographers are likely to become involved at a later stage. This will be expensive and costs will vary depending on the nature of the assignment, location, use of models, props etc. If the project looks as though it is likely to go this way, make sure that the client is alerted to the potential costs of a photographic shoot. Food photography, a common area for packaging design, is particularly difficult, requiring specialist skills and the assistance of cookery experts to ensure that the food looks appealing. In addition, as the law in some countries requires that any image on the pack must reflect the actual product itself, there are limitations on any creative embellishments. The image on a frozen ready meal, for example, depicts the contents in a "serving suggestion" where the food is cooked and attractively laid out. In many instances, it still looks fairly grim. (Think about how you might shoot porridge, rice or mashed potatoes and the problem becomes apparent.) This is why illustration is often preferred in place of photography for some product types.

Below Illustration and photography have been combined on this Thai packaging. The illustration represents a young woman in the highly stylized manner frequently used in Thailand to portray cool youth. The designer has chosen to use a photographic image of the product, where its reality contrasts with the fantasy of the illustration.

Illustration

As with photography, image banks also include illustrations that can be downloaded and used to create packaging design concepts. Illustrators, like photographers, also specialize in particular areas and genres of illustration. One illustrator, for example, might spend his entire professional life drawing and painting realistic illustrations of domestic cats and dogs, mainly for pet-care product manufacturers, including packaging, brochures, calendars and promotions. Although the work might be almost photographic in its detailing, the illustrator can still build in personality to his illustrations in a way photography would find difficult to do. Illustration styles vary widely and are, therefore, adaptable to many packaging applications to reflect the product nature and brand personality. The materials used depend upon the style required. Watercolours, pen and ink, gouache, crayons or pencils all produce distinctly different effects and their choice will depend upon the nature of the product and what you are trying to achieve. Illustrations can be fresh and unconstrained. Even naive and rudimentary sketches often have a vibrancy that photography struggles to capture. It is worth remembering, however, that professional illustrators, like photographers, also charge high fees for their skills, which need to be factored into budgets.

For initial concepts, designers may choose to create their own illustrations, using the appropriate media for the project in hand to develop an illustration style and sketches to show the positioning on pack. This can then be scanned into a drawing programme, such as Illustrator or Freehand, before being worked up on-screen. As technology converges, photographers may also work in this way and, to some extent, both can produce hybrid results that encompass both photographic and illustrative techniques.

However the illustration or photographic image is derived, the important thing is to be clear about what you are trying to achieve. If images or illustrations are being sourced from a library, understand the style you want as well as the content, always making sure that these are in line with client requirements and brand values. A cartoon style of illustration may be fun to do but is it right for the brand? We are all becoming used to slick visuals produced by computer, and certainly clients see this high standard of presentation from designers as the norm. It can be refreshing, in these circumstances, for clients to see packs that incorporate hand-produced illustrations. A delicate watercolour or bold pen-and-ink drawing can have a quality that reminds the client of the design skills they are buying into. It is not unknown for clients to keep and treasure the hand-produced original artwork.

Even if the project does not require professional photography or illustration, it is well worth looking through the directories of both photographers and illustrators (available in libraries or on-line), just to become familiar with the huge range of styles available.

Above The concept here relies on using a real sardine tin for chocolate fish. It would be difficult to use photography as effectively as the illustrations used here. They provide a clear visual explanation of the product and the chocolate surprise within, while incorporating the fishy theme in a simple, yet amusing way.

Below On this Malaysian coconut milk can, photography is offset by an illustrated background to provide a romantic portrait of tropical shores. Combining techniques can provide interesting solutions to design problems, particularly where foods are portrayed.

Conclusion

It can be seen from this chapter that the packaging designer's toolbox contains a diverse range of tools and techniques that can be used to create packaging design work. As with all tools, it takes practice to use them wisely and time to build experience. It is worth reflecting, however, that even with a dazzling array of technical effects, many packaging design classics feature simplicity and restraint.

Further reading and additional resource list

Phil Baines & Andrew Haslam, *Type and Typography*, London: Laurence King 2002 Clear guide to typography

Contact—Illustration and Photography, Elfande Catalogue of creative illustrators showing their styles, updated annually

Edward de Bono, Beryl McAlhone and David Stuart, *A Smile in the Mind: Witty Thinking in Graphic Design*, London: Phaidon 1998

John Ingledew, *Photography*, London: Laurence King 2005 Practical information on all aspects of photography

Robert Mason, *A Digital Dolly?: A Subjective Survey of British Illustration in the 1990s*, Norwich Gallery, Norwich School of Art & Design, 30 March 2000

Quentin Newark, *What is Graphic Design?* Hove: Rotovision 2002 Well-illustrated examples of graphic design

Walter Soroka, *Fundamentals of Packaging Technology* (Revised UK Edition), Melton Mowbray: Institute of Packaging 1996 Covers most packaging technology subjects with some limited information on design and marketing

Websites

www.britglass.org.uk Glass manufacturers

www.cancentral.com Cans

www.fefco.org Corrugated board

www.fujiseal.com/fsi_en Shrink/stretch film

www.mpma.org.uk Metal

www.pantone.com Colour

www.plasticseurope.org Plastics

www.procarton.com/home Carton board

Creating design concepts IV

Planning a packaging design project

Faced with a blank sheet of paper, where do you start? This chapter is for any designer at the start of a project. This is the time when all distractions seem preferable to actually making a mark on paper or screen. Breaking through this barrier and making measurable progress requires understanding of the design problem and the stimuli that allow creative thinking to take place. In this chapter we will start by looking at the brief before examining techniques to focus research by considering appropriate directions. We will then look at sources of inspiration before exploring techniques to realize design concepts.

Understanding the brief

It is good practice for design students to follow their commercial counterparts in responding to a brief. All design briefs should be documented as they form the yardstick against which all work will be directed and, ultimately, assessed. Some briefs are delivered entirely verbally by clients or, following a verbal presentation by the client, accompanied by a written brief. On occasion, the client may not have a formal brief and it will be necessary to tease this out during discussions. In all cases, it is a good plan to produce your own document encompassing your understanding of the brief and receive approval from the client on this. The reasoning here is that, almost certainly, the verbal presentation will contain additional information not indicated in the written version and this needs to be recorded. Also, when clients present the brief, there is likely to be an opportunity to ask questions that may add more information to the brief. A document such as this is standard practice for commercial design studios and is an essential precursor to any design work. As the brief is going to be the yardstick against which success or failure is measured, it is vital that there is complete understanding between client and designer. Having the document signed by both parties minimizes the chance of misunderstandings later, particularly when invoices start popping through letterboxes.

When working for a client, the brief is also going to form the basis for deciding how to tackle the job, scheduling and costing. Design studios normally respond to a brief by preparing a document, which, in addition to including their understanding of the brief as discussed above, will also describe how the study is going to be conducted on a stage-by-stage basis, the proposed dates of interim meetings and the final presentation. The cost of the study would also be provided by the design studio, broken down into fees, with likely costs and expenses. For complex studies, accurate costings might be given for the first stage only, accompanied by an indication of likely overall budget.

The first step in the design process is to fully understand the brief. Read and re-read it, taking in every detail. If there is some aspect that you are unsure about, ask the client to explain.

Once agreed, a brief cannot be changed. There are occasions when design studios will write their own brief, perhaps to produce promotional material or create a project that will demonstrate their skills. Students also may have the opportunity to produce a self-written brief, often to enable design areas of particular personal interest to be developed. In both instances, once written, the brief should not be changed. The rigour required to meet a design challenge is pointless if the challenge itself is changed. If, for example, you are working on vitamin supplements for five-year-old children, don't be tempted to modify the age range stated in the brief just because, on reflection, you realize that your design work is actually more suitable for twelve year olds.

>> Tip

Use a highlighter pen to mark the parts of the brief you feel are particularly significant

Always keep the brief with your work so that you can easily refer to it

Really read the brief—don't skim it

Keep re-reading the brief as your project progresses

Project stages

If there has been a verbal presentation that brings new information to the written document, you may wish to record this in some way. Although you may not have to cost the job, you should plan it, in the same way studios do. There will probably be certain dates to meet, so produce a schedule showing key dates and activities. This becomes even more important if several projects are being tackled at the same time. There really are no typical projects but most can be defined by a model frequently used by design studios, as shown below:

—Research

—Stage 1 | Conceptual design *This stage is the most important. It is where research is analysed and idea generation takes place. Mood boards are prepared. Design directions begin to emerge.*

—Interim meeting *To check that design thinking is on the right track and show design directions with recommendations for further work.*

—Stage 2 | Design progression *Agreed design directions from interim meeting now developed. Mock-ups produced.*

—Interim presentation *To show progress and narrow down options to preferred designs.*

—Stage 3 | Design refinement *Graphic and structural designs integrated. Models made.*

—Final presentation

—Stage 4 | Production of artwork, container specifications and drawings, and/or presentation boards.

A time schedule also needs to be prepared, showing critical dates (meetings and presentations) to help the designer keep on track and to gain the clients' confidence that they will be kept informed of progress. As with the brief, in commercial practice this plan would be agreed with deadlines firmly fixed, which is why, so often, the ink is hardly dry on the paper when it comes to deadline time.

Remember that the brief is also the template to use when assessing your own design work or the work of others. The question that should be asked throughout the design process is "Does it meet the brief?" As there is never just one design solution to any brief, the answers you get will probably indicate that some designs are closer to meeting parts of the brief than others. Chapter Five expands on this by looking at how designs are selected or discarded.

Making research relevant

Having considered the brief, the next stage is research. There are designers who love research and will continue to produce volumes of material, carefully mounted and arranged in expensive notebooks. It is a process that can extend well into the time that, actually, designing should be taking place in. There are also those who have little time for research and plunge directly into sketch work, discarding the brief along the way. To benefit both extremes and to comfort those moderates in the middle who have not received a mention here, this section looks at how to get the best out of research without it eating into design time.

Earlier, in Chapter Two, we considered market research and a technique of lifestyle profiling that would allow us to construct a virtual consumer (see p.42). It is vital that this is done because if you are not familiar with the target group that you are designing for at this point, then further research may be misdirected. As a rough guide, be prepared to spend half the research time considering the product user and achieving a consumer profile. Assuming then, that Chapter Two has yielded information on the market and the consumer, it is now time to find out more information about the product, the pack, where it is sold, how it is used, the competition and branding and sales strategy.

Product

Packaging and product work together but it is the product itself that must be considered first. To take tinned chickpeas as an example, we probably already know something about the product from experience. It is a fairly inexpensive product, a commodity rather than a luxury and, because it is in a tin, it will have a long shelf life. We know that the product is unlikely to suffer from the effects of modest mechanical damage, although shoppers avoid dented cans. In a commercial packaging study, we would probably want to visit the production site and see how the cans are made, filled, labelled, stored and transported. This has relevance for selecting alternative pack types. We could, however, speculate at this stage whether there is a better way to pack these chickpeas. Could we reduce costs or, for example, build in consumer benefits? Some suggestions to consider might be:

—Square can *more effective use of space, better for transport and storage*
—Thermoformed tray and lid *microwaveable, lighter than steel, saves transport costs*
—Tetrapack carton *square as above, could be resealed, microwaveable*
—Sachet/bag *cheap but difficult to handle*
—Glass jar *often used for chickpeas, resealable, adds weight but pushes product upmarket*

Considering the product's characteristics stimulates thought about the opportunities and restrictions across a spectrum of alternative pack forms.

Below In all packaging projects, the fundamental principles of effectively containing and protecting the product must be addressed. The three-piece metal can, like the one shown here, has a long track record of being suitable for products like these chickpeas, protecting them and providing a long shelf life.

Right Where and how packaged products are displayed at the point of sale is an important consideration for the packaging designer. This is particularly important within the supermarket environment where competition between products, varieties and brands is intense. Time-pressed consumers quickly scan shelves seeking their favourite brands or product inspiration. As the only communication is between pack and consumer, packaging design plays a vital role.

Opposite When designing for a powdered detergent, the designer could concentrate the design elements on the front panel, relegating the end panels to bar code and product information. The reality is that a high proportion of packs have their end panel on display, making it essential for the designer to use this area for branding.

Point of sale

Here, we consider where the product is sold, which will involve looking at the point of sale conditions in the most important types of sales outlet. This will vary depending on product type, but the most common sales outlet is likely to be a supermarket. In Chapter One, mention was made of the strategic design of the store to encourage spending, particularly on items with high profit margins (see p.30). For packaging design purposes, we need to ask the following questions:
—Is the product displayed at eye level, above or below?
—What are the other brands that surround it?
—What other product areas are directly adjacent to it (e.g. is it competing for consumer attention with tinned soups on adjacent shelves)?
—What are the lighting levels?

Photography is a good way of recording this information, but many stores are unhappy about photographs being taken without permission. A covert mission where flash is not used has been the preferred approach for many designers as obtaining permission is not always straightforward and is often time consuming. If photographs are a problem, however, it is acceptable to draw up a grid and indicate the information on it.

Photographs or a drawn representation of shelves reveal what is actually taking place in stores and helps you to avoid problems that might otherwise be overlooked if the design study was confined to the studio alone. For example, a product might be found in store displayed in corrugated fibreboard trays where the lip of the tray obscured the bottom portion of the product label, which you would not be aware of if you had not done your research. Canned products may be displayed on the bottom shelves, presenting blank can ends to the shopper looking down, thus losing a valuable opportunity to carry branding.

Store surveys

Proximity: What product categories and/or brands are beside, above and below the target brand? Packs may not only have to stand out against other brands in the same product sector but may also have to compete with other product sectors. For example, when the target brand is a tea, it may also have to stand out against coffee on the adjacent shelf.

Brand name front facing	Brand name front facing	Brand name front facing	
Brand name front facing	Target brand front facing	Brand name front facing	Eye level
Brand name front facing	Brand name front facing	Brand name front facing	
Brand name top facing	Brand name top facing	Brand name top facing	

Facings: The ideal way of recording the number of facings (pack fronts or surfaces visible to the shopper) is by photography. This is not always possible but they can be physically counted for each brand and recorded using this type of chart:

Brand	Facings

It is important to check where the target brand appears on shelf, relative to eye level. If it is on low shelves, branding on the top surface may be vital, as this, effectively, becomes the main panel communicating with the shopper.

Location: When conducting a store survey, remember to record the location of the store and its classification. For example, Carrefour hypermarket, Amiens, France. Stores in provincial towns may carry slightly different ranges to those near cities. The difference is much greater when the same multiple grocery company is trading in different countries, e.g. Tesco in Prague, Czech Republic is very different to Tesco in Watford, UK.

Above The olive oil bottle shown here is fitted with a useful pouring device that helps to dispense the oil. The appearance of the pack is also important—by making it good looking enough to remain on display, rather than be confined to a cupboard, the brand is reinforced at every opportunity.

Below Redesigning packs that usually remain out of sight, such as margarine packs, for example, could encourage the product—and brand—to be removed from the fridge and placed on the table and so help to reinforce brand awareness.

Product usage

Observational research reveals how the product is used, once it has been bought, and can be carried out either by experiencing the product yourself or by watching others. The pack should be used in the appropriate environment rather than the studio. The information we are concerned with here is:

—How effective is the product/pack at opening, dispensing product, re-closing?

—How easy is it to dispose of and recycle?

—Where is the product stored?

—Can the product be stored where it is always on display?

—Are tools needed to gain access?

—How would people who are disadvantaged by mobility, visual or muscle impairments cope?

This kind of research is fundamental to the sales performance of any packaged product yet, from the number of complaints about packaging, it seems that it is seldom carried out. Many accidents in the home result from attempts to open packs with knives and scissors. In addition to highlighting functional problems requiring design solutions, there may be opportunities to reinforce branding through product display on breakfast bars or tables.

Competitor activity

Standout is the ability to be readily seen or recognized and is a critical area for packaging designers to address. Many briefs will identify competitor products and brands or, at least, those that the client considers to be competitors. What may not be recognized by clients is that their product and brand may also be competing, in terms of standout, against other product categories on adjacent shelves in a supermarket environment. For example, tea and coffee are often displayed on adjacent shelves so that, in a visual sense, they compete for our attention. The relevance for this form of research is the need to establish what visual language is used in both tea and coffee categories. The relevance for the designer, then, is to ensure that "your" product either conforms to the appropriate visual language or is entirely different to both. Tea is generally sold in cartons and coffee in flexible film/foil pouches. Tea in a pouch or coffee in a carton might cause enough confusion for the shopper to simply move on, whereas teabags in a glass jar, for example, might create standout and excite the shopper's curiosity.

It is essential to examine competitor products and establish what they are doing well and what they are doing badly. At the very least, this might mean photographing products on shelf but it is far better to buy the products, if possible, and experience the packs for yourself. Clients can usually provide a market analysis that indicates market share for each competitor, showing the market leader, the up-and-coming challengers and who is gaining or losing market share.

Using the market data, try and see why leading brands are ahead. It could be due to the power of the brand and associated advertising, price, clever strategic positioning of the product within the market sector, accurately meeting consumer expectations, or the fact that it is simply a really good product. What contribution is the packaging making to this success? Is it offering any tangible consumer benefit? If not, then there may be an opportunity to use this to lever "your" brand into a better position on the sales league table. The most effective consumer benefits, in terms of product sales, are those that can be seen prior to sale. Such benefits must perform positively in a technical sense but being seen and understood at the point of sale is a positive advantage, differentiating the product from others and encouraging purchase. Highly visible pouring spouts or in-built measuring devices are examples that are immediately obvious and can provide additional reasons to purchase.

Branding strategy

Branding is a critical area for design, and is considered in detail in Chapter Six. Here, at the research stage, the concern is to find out what the brand stands for and if there is any deliberate corporate strategy to move its positioning. Brand values are usually expressed in human terms, so we might describe the Chanel brand in terms such as, "quality", "upmarket", "serious" and "expensive", whereas other brands may be described as "fun" or, in the case of some pharmaceutical brands, "effective", "caring" or "clinical". The client will advise how they want the brand to be perceived, and you can judge how effectively they are doing it. Be careful though, as companies are often sensitive to any brand criticism.

Some companies also have a corporate positioning statement that runs across all their activities helping to position the brand. Audi's "Vorsprung durch Technik" ("progress through technology") underpins the company's commitment to technology. If a project concerned the design of a container for Audi branded motor oil, we might imagine that the container would be highly technical in its design. In brand value terms, Audi is "technical", "safe", "serious", "classy" and "mechanical". Although they manufacture some fast and sporty cars, somehow their brand values are not "fun", "exciting" or "cheeky" and it would be inappropriate to design packs based on these values. By researching brand strategy, you can then keep checking that your design work is in line with the appropriate brand values.

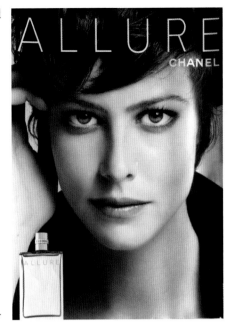

Above The Chanel brand represents high fashion and, as can be seen here for Allure, this is conveyed by the simplicity of the shot, using black and white photography, carried over to the pack design, which retains the classic rectangular glass bottle and minimal text associated with the Chanel brand. Designers working with brands must be sensitive to what the brand stands for and any strategy for change that may be in place.

Below The Innocent brand name reflects the product nature, aimed as it is at the healthy food sector. There is clearly humour involved in everything this brand does, so we could fairly describe its brand value as "fun".

hello

We're innocent and we make smoothies. We thought we'd send you this little recipe book, so you can find out more about us and perhaps try making some smoothies at home. And there's a coupon at the back, so you can get some money off our drinks, and some nice pictures too.

We hope you enjoy it.

recipes

1 strawberries and bananas
2 pomegranates and blueberries
3 kiwi and apple
4 cantaloupe and peach
5 avocado and pear

And then there's some stuff about our family and the money off coupon too.

Husten?

Lindert
Hustenreiz – ganz
ohne Chemie.

Emser Pastillen®

- befeuchten und beruhigen
  die angegriffene Mund- und
  Rachenschleimhaut
- befreien von Hustenreiz
- unterstützen die natürliche
  Selbstheilung
- lindern schnell Halsschmerzen
  und Heiserkeit

NEU – mit Lakritz!

In Ihrer Apotheke!

www.emser.de

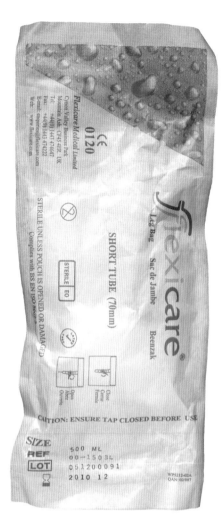

Far left Many pharmaceutical products can be purchased directly by consumers. In this example from Germany, the brand, product name and description are key visual elements in product selection.

Left Packaging plays a critical role in keeping products such as this medical device sterile, while making access to the product easy. The text is simple, and provides important information. Here, branding gives assurance of product quality and clinical integrity, the main concerns of medical workers.

Below Although this is a prescribed drug and not available over the counter (in the UK), it carries both the Amoxil brand and the parent, GlaxoSmithKline logos. The presentation is sober, serious and informative. GSK seek to communicate about the product in a direct manner and use their logo as a reassurance of quality, dependability and product efficacy. For this type of product, brand values are still important, even when patients, in this instance, cannot exercise brand choice.

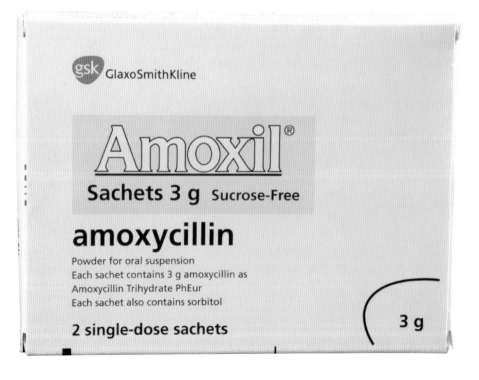

Advertising strategy

In contrast to the example of Audi, in the 1980s the Czech car manufacturer Skoda had some seriously negative brand values to contend with that were associated with issues of declining quality and outdated design. When it was acquired by Volkswagen in 1991, the new owners immediately embarked on a major re-engineering programme and even considered replacing the Skoda brand with the VW brand. Today, Skoda represents high quality and good value, adopting the strapline "Simply Clever" to signify a new set of brand values. The earlier quality problems required engineering solutions to be put in place but it was an advertising strategy that changed public perception of the brand.

The advertising agency turned jokes about Skoda on their heads, using humour as a vehicle for getting the quality message across. As this example shows, advertising strategies are powerful tools in creating, maintaining and repositioning brands.

The advertising strategy of many companies is to feature packaging, often accompanied by advertising copy, reinforcing the visual appearance of the pack and stimulating memory at the point of sale. Adverts are a rich source of research material as they reveal brand values, so ensure they feature in your collection of tear sheets.

Below left Health is the message here. The seascape in the background provides a sense of freshness, augmented by the fruit. The products specifically claim to lower cholesterol, which appeals both to those with cholesterol-related health problems and to those who see the product as a way to avoid them.

Below Bonne Maman is demonstrating a clear set of brand values in this ad, reinforcing its home-made, country goodness image—just as grandmother used to make it. The pack is glass with a traditional feel to it, helped by an almost handwritten label and a gingham patterned lid, replacing the fabric that may have been used originally. The design team have left nothing to chance; even the spoon and tray evoke the heritage of the brand.

Sources of inspiration

One of the most fascinating aspects of being a designer is that each project brings with it the need to learn about fresh topics. Repackaging a skincare product, for example, is likely to involve a quite different set of parameters to the design of a container for plant food. Both, however, require the designer to be curious and inquisitive about these new markets, the people who use the products and what the products are intended to do. Having read and reread the brief, and conducted some research, the designer may now be waiting for the "big idea" to arrive, or maybe any idea, however modest. Sometimes, it can be a very long wait. Better, by far, in these circumstances, is to take some action to push things along and stimulate thinking. Inspiration is required, but how can it be found?

The Collins dictionary definition (above left) implies that stimulation of the mind is the precursor to inspiration but, as we are all individuals with different minds and, it is suspected, different stimuli, what works for one individual may not work for another. The practical suggestions outlined here are derived from working with a range of designers and design students, so it may be worth trying them all to see what pushes your creative buttons.

Brainstorming

A classic technique to stimulate the mind is brainstorming. This works best when a design team can participate, particularly if it is made up of people of different ages, gender and disciplines. It also requires one person to control the session and note ideas as they occur. The concept is for everyone to come up with answers to a question, for example, "How many ways can we pack a soft drink?" Rather than be analytical, the group is encouraged to throw out ideas, even frivolous ones, while every thought is noted down on a chart. Having exhausted the idea generation, the team then reviews the ideas generated and begins making sketches of those with most potential.

Right A Marks & Spencer sandwich pack that opens into a useful tray—a concept developed by the Design Futures group at Sheffield Hallam University, UK.

To take a specific example, Sheffield Hallam University in the UK operate their own commercial design consultancy under the "Design Futures" banner. With access to a wide base of staff, researchers and students, it specializes in offering a platform for companies seeking new ideas and conducts brainstorming sessions as part of the creative process. One such session brainstormed ways of packaging sandwiches leading directly to a pack that folds out to form a tray. It seems obvious now, but the session generated thoughts about ways of eating and not just packaging.

Where a team is not an option, a modified technique can be used where you use a large sheet of paper to record your answers. Using the sandwich example above, ask yourself who eats sandwiches? When? Where? How? How do you get rid of the pack? Have you also bought crisps or coffee? How do you balance multiple items? Can it be recycled? Do you need to see the contents? The objective is to prompt ideas without analytical thought so it should be fast moving, recording your first ideas. When analysing answers, don't be too quick to dismiss the crazy ones—they may contain a germ of an idea that can be developed later. Better to start sketching and exploring before rejecting.

Product history

Sometimes the inspiration stems from the product itself, as it is right there in front of you. It is not a bad place to start. Most products and brands have a history, many extending back over long periods of time. It is often worth checking to see what the product history has been, particularly if it can be reviewed in a visual way. Many companies have a historical section on their websites where early photos of factories, people, products or packs might become a source of inspiration that still maintains a link to the current project in hand. For example, when designing a new whisky bottle for Glenrothes, the packaging designers assigned to the project looked back at such old historical records. They found a bottle that was actually used to sample whisky in the distillery as a part of the production process. It was simple and elegant yet quite different to anything else on the market. This provided the inspiration and the basis for their new design, still in production today (see above right).

Product origin

Sometimes the product ingredients may provide the inspiration. These might be from exotic locations or be particularly pure. Have a look at the ingredients list and perhaps find out more from the client. Designing a label for orange marmalade, for example, might find inspiration in the fact that the oranges come from Seville. This immediately provides a Spanish/Moorish feel that could be interpreted graphically. Seeking inspiration in cultural or ethnic imagery is entirely valid but requires a degree of care in order to avoid clichés. Images of cactus and large sombreros, for example, are not the only way of depicting Mexican products, a country particularly well endowed with other more original and interesting characteristics.

Above An elegant packaging solution, based on a whisky sample bottle, designed by Blackburns for Glenrothes.

Below Both of these packs feature easily recognizable national symbols. The Caesar dressing is shown to originate from the US by the small flag, but it also carries Italian colours to represent its Italian-American heritage. HP sauce incorporates London landmark buildings familiar to people within and beyond the UK. To underline each product's heritage, it has been thought necessary to include the words "The Original" as part of the product offering.

It is, however, important to be aware of the geographical location of product sales, as it will be consumer perception at point of sale that is important for product success. Consumer understanding about what constitutes a cultural or historical association in the country of purchase may be inaccurate and might not correspond to those in the country of production. In this situation, the design must still communicate its provenance, providing that this is an important strategy for marketing the product. As an example, a successful Chinese manufacturer of oriental cooking sauces for professional use, wishing to expand sales into the domestic, non-restaurant markets of Europe and North America, found that the pack did not sell well and approached a UK-based design consultancy for help. The pack was found to be "too Chinese" for European and North American consumers. The solution was found by introducing a vertical red banner carrying the brand name. The pack still communicated its Chinese origins, while presenting a contemporary appearance more closely attuned to the target market. It is a delicate and demanding design task to balance the desire of avoiding stereotypical images, while still also communicating ethnic heritage to a wider audience.

Below This type of biscuit is a Swedish speciality and shows pride in its heritage by displaying the Swedish flag.

Right The Italian imagery used here is obvious and designed to be easily understood as a product of Italy by a non-Italian audience. Despite this rather literal use of imagery, the result does stand out amongst other bottles on-shelf.

Far right Most supermarket shoppers are unlikely to have a clear knowledge of Argentinian culture and probably will fail to identify the country of origin from scanning the graphics used on this bottle alone.The design, however, is fresh and striking, making it stand out against competitors.

Art and design influences

Art has been an inspiration for many designers. In fact, the border between art and design is frequently blurred, with many artists and designers producing work that could equally be represented in either camp. In 1979, for example, the Catalan artist Joan Miró was commissioned by Landor Associates to create a tapestry from which a new corporate identity for the Bank "La Caixa" would emerge. It was a bold, if unusual, strategy that resulted in a distinctive design featuring a star and Mediterranean colours, now a familiar sight throughout Cataluña.

Closer to packaging design, Andy Warhol's famous Campbell's soup can and, more recently, Damien Hirst's ironic portrayal of pharmaceutical packaging, "The Last Supper", are examples of artists deliberately using packaging imagery to express their artistic viewpoint. Packaging designers, too, have borrowed images and styles from art. For example, L'Oréal has, in the past, based packaging designs on the rectangular coloured panels of the artist Piet Mondrian. Not only does Mondrian's work provide a distinctive and attractive use of colour, but the separate panels provide a ready-made graphic design grid, helping to organize the position of type. Often it is the artistic style, rather than specific content, that can provide the inspiration for packaging design work, and here, it is important to have a rationale in place for considering particular artists. If, for example, the pack is for a hair gel aimed at 18–25-year-old men, it could be argued that a retro look might work. You might, for example, consider the work of Peter Blake

Above It is not immediately clear what a plastic chain contributes to the aesthetic design of this pack. The classical style of the bather being anointed by a servant while listening to pipes seems strangely at odds with the use of a modern plastic tube with a plastic flip lid. It reinforces the need to ensure that any influence from art should harmonize with both graphic and structural design.

Far left Art has frequently featured as a design element on chocolate boxes, to the extent of "chocolate box art" becoming an expression of kitsch design. In this Russian example, the romantic portrait is even accompanied by a picture frame.

Left The style of the illustration here has been borrowed from Andy Warhol, although the application is to portray a stamp, making a visual pun on Terence Stamp's name. The result is striking and stands out well against other organic chocolate bars.

Above The work shown here by the Sheffield-based artist, Kid Acne, may be interpreted as art, design or vandalism, but it clearly has impact. Graffiti styles are often anarchic, cynical or politically inspired, yet few mainstream packs have thus far used it effectively to communicate with the street culture sector of the young adult market.

Right Although not exactly copying a style of graffiti illustration, the influence is clear. It is interesting to speculate on who this pack might be targeting as, at two litres, the pack is family sized and not likely to be bought by streetwise teenagers. Perhaps the strategy is for mum to buy the product, attracted by the healthier claims that it makes, thus getting the brand into the household. Its cool style may then find resonance with teenagers, who go on to purchase smaller containers themselves.

(famous for the Beatles' "Sergeant Pepper" album cover) or the comic-book style of Roy Lichtenstein for a graphic style associated with the period. Consider too the use of historical photography to create moods. The photographs of Robert Capa and Henri Cartier-Bresson, amongst others, provide thought-provoking and powerful images encapsulating the feelings of past times. Typographical styles and design movements, such as the Bauhaus, provide their own distinctive references and are a rewarding source of inspiration for design today.

The gritty, yet vibrant reality of street life offers another window of inspiration. This is less about aspirations but more about the here and now. On occasion it can be edgy, even intimidating, but also strangely compelling, where images of urban degradation and graffiti create a feeling of tension, reflecting the rebellious aspect of youth culture. Drawing on this imagery might, for example, be a perfect source of inspiration for designing packaging and products that look cool but have "attitude", such as hair gels, drinks and snacks.

Nature

Nature has always provided inspiration for artists and designers, often in a very direct and literal way and, sometimes, in a subtle adoption of natural forms, colours and harmonies. Many products make direct reference to geographic locations, animals or plants and, not surprisingly, feature these prominently on the pack. Mineral waters, whiskys and "natural" food products are examples of categories that frequently do this. Although this technique is widely used, it is still a valid way for designers to communicate natural product benefits in a highly visual and, therefore, quick-to-read manner. As the Tŷ Nant bottle, pictured below, dramatically shows, it is possible to translate natural forms into a three-dimensional packaging format, here capturing the flow of water. Many designers have found inspiration from the shapes of pebbles on the beach, leaves, fish scales, trees, ripples in ponds, waves in the sea and many other natural forms, abstracting form, colour, texture and patterns to create fresh new designs.

If none of the suggestions discussed here work for you, then consider some of the areas shown below. Remember that actively working on a design brings its own fresh thinking and so it is often better to be positive and work on an idea, even when you know it is not perfect, than to simply sit and wait for inspiration.

Further, rich sources of inspiration can be found by considering the following:
—Art *galleries, books, photography, exhibitions*
—Architecture *cities, buildings old and new, visits, photography, books*
—History *eras such as Prohibition, the Swinging Sixties, Flower Power, books, videos, film*
—Music *sounds, rhythms, jazz, soul, rock, blues, dance, instruments, record sleeves, CDs, fliers*
—Nature *natural forms, colours, seasons, plants, animals*
—Fashion *trends, colourways, magazines, books, websites*
—Advertising *TV, print, magazines, books*
—Signage *"found" typography, photographs, books*
—Street life *graffiti, cafés, urban degradation, skateboarding, visits, books, photography, lifestyle magazines, websites*

Below Evian portray the mountain source of their mineral water to evoke purity. This is represented graphically on the label and also embossed in relief on the bottle surface.

Below bottom Designed in the UK by Ross Lovegrove to invoke the fluidity of water, this is a challenging shape to mould in PET. It has been worthwhile Tŷ Nant persevering in overcoming production difficulties to present this unique container that, as can be seen, needs little further graphic identification.

Ways of working—concept generation

Although the French philosopher, Alain, was referring to religion when he made the comment shown on the left, in the "religion" of design, one idea is equally dangerous. We have to acknowledge that there is always more than one design solution to a design problem. The initial stages of a design project, therefore, are concerned with thinking widely and generating a range of design concepts, each of which needs to be recorded, usually in sketch format. Later, these will be reviewed and some, inevitably, will be discarded for a variety of reasons, including difficulties in manufacture, opening, closing, storage etc. Others might appear more promising and justify exploration in greater detail with the production of more accurate drawings, mock-ups or computer-generated images.

Perhaps unsurprisingly, many design students consider research and concept generation as separate entities. Although it is convenient to separate the two activities, in practice, the rationale that supports design work should be found in its research roots. Frequently, this is not immediately apparent to the casual observer—not, in itself, always a bad thing as it might avoid the connection between research and design being too literal. Take, for example, a designer who designed a pack for a male toiletry product featuring moulded details and a black and brushed aluminium finish. The designer had used imagery inspired by the styling used in sports car design, in particular, the detailing of dashboard instruments. Had the finished pack design closely copied the originals, the design would have been compromised by becoming a cliché. Instead, only the elements of colour, texture and style that make these cars so appealing to men had been incorporated into the pack design, capturing the imagery without the source of inspiration being too obvious. During a presentation of the work, the designer was able to explain the rationale that lay behind the final design concept. It is important, especially for students, to realize that examiners (or clients) will be looking for this rationale and so clear reference to it needs to be made. One way of doing so is to annotate sketch work, making reference to earlier research or, alternatively, include sketches or images of the source objects adjacent to the pack concept drawings.

Before practical design work begins, however, it is worth reflecting on two key issues that make packaging design rather special and, in addition to the requirements of the brief, require consideration in every packaging design study:

—Packaging is three-dimensional providing a fascinating design challenge to create three-dimensional forms where shape and graphics work together. This significantly affects the way projects are approached

—Standout is arguably the most important target that packaging designers must address particularly in the supermarket environment, on the basis of "If you don't see it, you won't buy it". Bear in mind that the average supermarket shopper scans a row of packs in around half a second and it becomes evident how hard individual packs must work if they are going to be seen.

Above In the first illustration we can see that although each tree is different in detail, no single tree stands out from the rest. The second illustration indicates the standout that packaging should achieve, providing immediate recognition of an individual pack through the use of shape and graphics.

Shape

Where a project involves both structural and graphic design, it is usual to develop concepts of shape first. Without an indication of shape, it becomes difficult to consider how graphics might be used. However, graphics and structural design should still be considered as one entity. To resolve this apparent dilemma, each structural concept should be accompanied by an indication of what graphic possibilities could be considered—an indication of print area would probably suffice at this stage.

Sketches

Initially, designers tend to use sketches. These allow thoughts to be explored in a quick and highly visual way in a format suitable for capturing ideas (and sharing them with other members of the design team if it is a team project). Simple sketches are usually adequate at this stage, and any additional features or information should accompany them and be annotated directly onto the sketchbook pages.

Make sure that sketches, however rough:
—Conform to the brief
—Relate to the initial research *design concepts must be underpinned by a rationale*
—Are annotated with your comments about features, opportunities, problems etc.
—Consider how graphics might work *for each proposed concept*
—Explore different design directions

If the above is a list of "do's", the following list is one of "don'ts". Design students or junior designers seeking to make their work more professional should avoid the following:
—Heading design sheets with the word "ideas" or labelling concepts with "idea 1" etc.
—Being precious about your work *be prolific, share, discuss*
—Drawing borders round pages *it is time to start looking professional*
—Sketching primary shapes to no purpose *we know what a box looks like*
—Justifying design decisions by stating "I like it" *Will the client like it? Does it meet the brief?*

>> **Tip**
To give a rough indication of graphic concepts on each container shape, produce graphics on tracing paper and overlay on each container design.

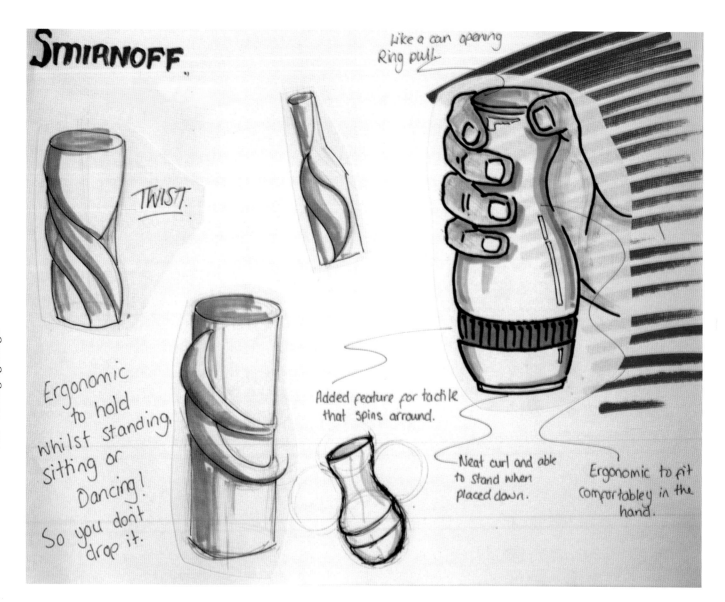

SMIRNOFF

TWIST.

like a can opening
Ring pull

Ergonomic
to hold
whilst standing.
sitting or
Dancing!
So you don't
drop it.

Added feature for tactile
that spins arround.

Neat curl and able
to stand when
placed down.

Ergonomic to fit
comfortabley in the
hand.

Above and opposite Sketches allow the development of ideas and design thinking. In this case, one of the projects involved the design of a PET bottle for a carbonated fruit juice. The first sketches capture some initial thoughts while the second sheet (opposite) begins to explore how these might be developed.

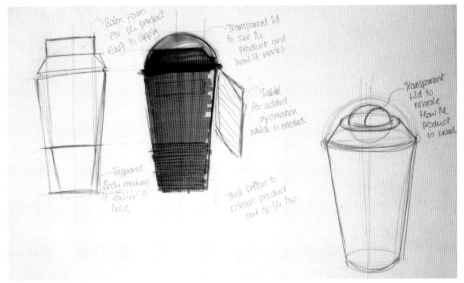

» Tip
To give a rough indication of graphic concepts on each container shape, produce graphics on tracing paper and overlay them on each container design.

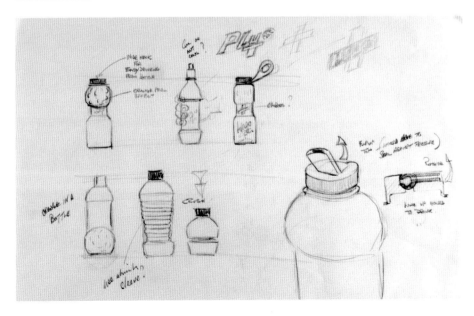

IV: Creating design concepts   113

Visibility of graphics

Before any graphic development takes place, even at this early sketch phase, it is often worthwhile considering which panel of the pack is going to be the main panel, i.e. the one that purchasers will normally see. How packs are displayed is largely beyond the designer's control and it is necessary to consider point of sale conditions. Note that the pet food container on below is branded on the top of the tin because, in-store, pet food tins were seen to be stacked on lower shelves, where only the tops of the tins are visible.

In the case of cylindrical containers, bottles, tubes and cans, for example, check the amount of panel visibility. The front panel size for a 75 mm-diameter can is probably little more than 55 mm, to allow text to be read on shelf without rotating the can. This becomes particularly relevant when considering text sizes and working with sub-brands or product names. Often, in order to maintain a type size that will be legible yet fit on the visible portion of a can label, other options need to be considered, such as vertical or diagonal type or, perhaps, some distinctive holding device. If the designer is choosing product names or sub-brands that will appear on a cylindrical container, this is also a good argument for keeping them short! Four or five letters are much easier to accommodate at a legible type size than seven and, incidentally, are probably more memorable. It is worth while considering if there is any possibility for multiple packs working together through shape and/or graphics to enhance standout and create greater impact. A "block" of integrated shapes and graphics can be a very effective method of increasing a brand's presence on-shelf. Developing pack shapes and graphics together harmonizes the two design elements and avoids the pitfall of trying to force the two together later in the design development.

Right Designers have little control over how packs are displayed. If these packs were displayed as shown, only the bar codes would be seen and a branding opportunity lost.

Far right The designers of the frozen food carton have made sure that the pack is branded and contents identified on all panels, as the pack may be displayed in either vertical cabinets or horizontal chest freezers.

Right Tinned products often overlook the ease of extending branding to end panels where it provides brand reinforcement on-shelf and in the home.

Middle Some pack forms, like this Tetra-pak carton, allow high quality decoration over their entire surface.

Far right Although surface decoration on this cylindrical metal "bottle" extends around the container, on-shelf, only a portion of the front panel can be read. With a long brand name like this one, the designers have maximized typesize by running the brand at an angle.

Mock-ups

When three-dimensional designs are involved, making mock-ups provides a quick and efficient way of visualizing design concepts. In some instances, particularly in the design of containers with complex curves, mock-ups allow exploration of the effects of changing curves as they progress around the container in a way that can be difficult to do through sketches alone. Indeed, using mock-ups in the design of carton board structures is almost the only way of working. It helps here to join panels with masking tape until the design is resolved. The "carton" can then be laid out flat and the "net" or, more accurately, the "cutter guide" drawn (this is a plan showing the location of panels, creases, folds, slots etc.) It is a process that will probably be repeated several times until the concept can be made to work. Mock-ups should be regarded both as a way of designing and also resolving design problems. Moving between sketched concepts to mock-ups and then returning to sketches once more, having resolved some issues in the process, is a perfectly satisfactory way of working. Although the design process involves moving from concepts to recommendations, interim stages are frequently non-linear, with the flexibility to move between media and to revisit earlier work.

Below left These mock-ups made from foamed plastics explore different design directions for a range of indulgent bath oils and scrubs. Foamed plastics provide freedom to explore shapes, particularly how curves interact with one another. These mock-ups include ideas for how an outer carton might form part of the consumer experience.

Bottom These quickly made mock-ups explore different design directions for the same range of indulgent bath oils and scrubs. Using "found" containers and closures as a basis, then adding simple constructions in a variety of materials, helps to resolve issues of proportions, sizes, material choices and surface finishes in an immediate way that is difficult to do through sketches alone. It quickly becomes evident how the glass jar, for example, through weight and appearance, provides a different "tone" to the metal container or plastic bottle. Handling and using existing containers in this way also has a benefit through increasing familiarity with standard pack forms.

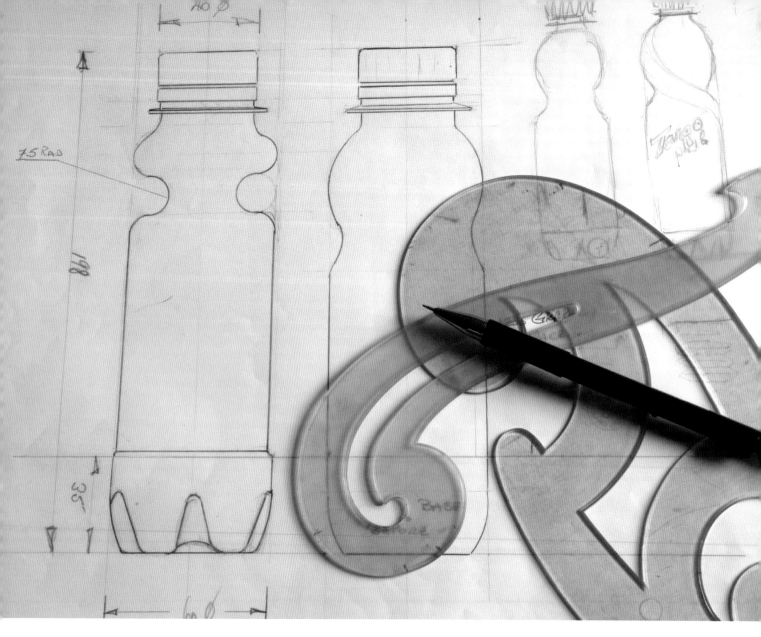

Above Further detail can now be added to consider dimensions and closure sizes. The sketched concept becomes more realistic at this stage. Container design often involves subtle changes in curves, which can only be appreciated when working at actual size and drawing accurately.

Opposite As shown here, adding colour through marker rendering helps to create visuals that represent the design rationale and are suitable for discussion, interim presentation and assessment of designs.

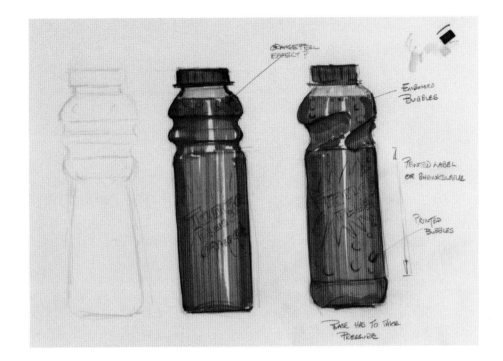

Presenting concepts

As the conceptual design phase draws to a conclusion, we need to be in a position to recommend those design candidates we intend to progress to the next stage and to eliminate others. Although we are still some way from a final design, the design contenders should be produced to a sufficient standard for comparisons to be made. In commercial design work, it would be usual to present interim progress to the client at this point, again requiring a quality of finish that conveys design thinking. For most container designs, especially bottles and jars, a front elevation, drawn at approximately actual size, showing the main panel is probably sufficient. (Later, containers will have to be accurately dimensioned and checked for volume—see Chapter Five.) To this may be added a base "footprint" or cross-section where stacking or stability is an issue and to indicate container curvature.

Drawings become much more believable (and a lot more useful) if they incorporate realistic features. For example, the blow moulded plastic bottle shown in the photograph opposite will have radii around the base. Adding these details and indicating an appropriate neck finish will help bring drawings to life. If you are unfamiliar with the technical aspects that constrain design, examine a similar existing pack. This will usually provide clues on what is possible. If there is still some doubt, contact a supplier of the type of packaging you are working on and seek guidance from them. Draw curves accurately using a French curve template, as shown opposite, to capture the subtle features you desire. It is surprising how slight alterations to curves affect the overall appearance of a container, so it is worthwhile being as accurate as possible in drawings. If you wish to make minor changes or modifications, use photocopies of the original to work on. Graphics can be overlaid on tracing paper (allowing manipulation between design variants) or simply indicated on the panel.

Details can be sketched in using pencil or markers, both being quick to add. Designs at this point can be annotated with notes explaining any particular features, selling points or questions to the client. Colours might be added or colour swatches pasted alongside the drawings.

Where flat surface areas and structures are involved, such as labels and many standard carton styles, graphic design alone is involved. Although it is usual to begin the design process with sketches, computer-based drawing programmes are frequently used from an early stage and provide high quality printouts, which can be pasted onto mock-ups or actual packs. We shall return to this method of working in Chapter Five.

At the completion of this stage there should be a range of design concepts carrying sufficient detail to enable design decisions to be made about which design candidates to progress and which to discard. That will be the subject of the next chapter.

Conclusion

There is an ever-changing source of inspiration within every supermarket, with thousands of packaged products to consider. Take the opportunity to browse and examine packs, finding those that are unusual, well designed or those that, for one reason or another, do not perform. Other designers' mistakes may provide you with opportunities to make improvements. Extend your browsing to specialist stores, paper suppliers, craft shops and food halls. In short, take every opportunity to look at design, particularly packaging design, both in your own territory and, if possible, abroad.

Further reading and additional resource list

Edward de Bono, *Lateral thinking: A Textbook of Creativity*, Penguin, 1990
   A classic on creative thinking
Alan Fletcher, *The Art of Looking Sideways*, Phaidon, 2001 Thoughts from one of the
   most outstanding designers of our time
Christoph Grunenberg and Max Hollein (eds), *Shopping: A Century of Art and
   Consumer Culture*, Ostfildern-Ruit: Hatje Cantz, 2002 Visual record of Tate
   exhibition featuring "packaging" by Damien Hirst, Mike Bidlo, Tom Sachs, Haim Steinbach,
   Sylvie Fleury etc.
The Mind Gym, *The Mind Gym: Wake Your Mind Up*, Time Warner, 2005
   Training your mind
Roger Von Oech, *A Whack on the Side of the Head*, Atlantic Books, 1992
   Ways to stimulate thinking and induce creativity

Websites

www.kidacne.com Graffiti artist with work featured in this chapter
www.phlegmcomics.com Graffiti site
www.portal1.lacaixa.es The story of how Joan Miró designed the logo for La Caixa bank in
   Cataluñya
www.theaoi.com/index.html The Association of Illustrators
www.warholfoundation.org Information about the artist and his work

Design development

Developing a packaging design

The previous chapter described how conceptual design takes place, resulting in several design directions being identified. This chapter considers what steps to take in order to turn those early ideas into real packaging propositions, and how to communicate your design process and conclusions to others. Firstly, though, it is often necessary to decide which concepts are worthy of development and which are going to be rejected.

Brief – NPD in the boxed chocolate confectionery market

Background
Company A is a well-established brand in the UK boxed chocolate market, noted for the quality of their products which rival Belgian imports. Product and packaging innovation are perceived, as key elements to success in this market and The company are keen to extend their range into new areas.

A market sector has been identified which has not been clearly addressed by any of the major companies operating in the boxed chocolate market. It represents an opportunity for developing a new product/packaging concept aimed at a niche target audience but one which is substantial in itself and has the ability to draw in peripheral participants.

Concept rationale
Within the UK, there is a continuing trend for short-term relationships with around one third of live-in relationships now lasting for less than a year. This is particularly evident in the Young, Free and Single sector (under 35's). This trend is set to continue, according to government statistics, in both under 35 year old and 35-54 year old categories. (See appendix).

With this background and media influences to spice up our sex lives in both short and long term relationships and at all life stages, there are market opportunities for products which may assist the initiation and maintenance of relationships.

Chocolates, flowers and wine, purchased by men for women have long become a cliché. They are regarded either as a distress purchase to redress an oversight or as an opening gambit which displays little imagination. We can classify male purchasers in this scenario as 'Hopeful's' or 'Regretful's', who are struggling to convey the following sentiments.

'Hopeful's'
'I really love you and to prove it, I have bought you chocolates'
'Sleep with me – I am sincere enough to have bought you chocolates'
' These chocolates show how much I care about you – now can we have sex'

'Regretful's'
'Sorry – can we get back together again'?
'I will try harder, honestly – these chocolates are just a token of my commitment'
'Lets make up and have a good time again'
'Forget the past – these chocolates show I am a thoughtful, loving guy'

There is also, in the male psyche at least, a correlation between the amount spent on the chocolates, flowers or wine to the level of sincerity or desperation intended. This extends to the quality and presentation of the chocolates themselves. A box of Milk Tray is perhaps too everyday. We may move up to Brand A's Continental rangeor perhaps Belgian Chocolates – the more exclusive, the better.

None of these, however, offer a specific proposition of sharing. We know that in other areas, sharing is important. The two highest ranking boxed chocolate brands; Celebrations and Miniature Heroes have their success rooted in sharing, albeit in family sharing.

The concept, therefore, is to develop a product that is specifically designed for two to share, as lovers or partners. It must, in its presentation, clearly demonstrate it's positioning and become, in use, a shared experience.

Target market
The target market is 24-35's, but should have aspirational appeal to an older audience. Predominately male, the social group will be aimed at ABC1's. Women purchasing to provide partners with a 'clue' should also be considered.

The product should be suitable for all year round purchase and not just for Valentines Day.

Right A packaging design brief for new product development for boxed chocolates. The brief is the starting point for all design work and should be referred to throughout the project.

Selecting and discarding design candidates

Design studios make judgements on their work (and the work of others) on an everyday basis simply because they are responding to commercial pressures, which insist that the project moves forward. Project timeframes are usually tight and decisions concerning which designs should be further developed have to be made. Inexperienced designers sometimes find difficulty with this and may be reluctant to say farewell to a piece of their design work and may, instead, attempt to force it onto the next stage when, in reality, it ought to be discarded. So, how is packaging design work evaluated and how can you choose which concepts to develop and which to discard?

The process of selecting and discarding design candidates described here broadly follows that adopted in commercial practice. Firstly, however, it is important to state that it is not valid for the designer or student to select their preferred design candidates on the basis of "because I like it". The overriding criterion should be deciding which design candidate comes closest to answering the brief. In practice, this inevitably results in more than one design being selected for further development, as some designs will meet different aspects of the brief with differing degrees of success. So, for example, design A may provide the best standout but design B might be judged to have greater resonance with the target audience. For these different reasons both might be worth developing further and there may be a further option of cross-fertilizing designs A and B to achieve a compromise. In this instance, there may now be three designs to develop, which in addition to deciding how to choose designs raises the additional questions: How many different concepts should continue to be developed? At what point should development stop and a final design candidate be selected?

Because each project is different, there are no absolute answers and, if there were, every selected design would be a competition winner or a design classic. It is a matter of judgement, sometimes instinct and a degree of luck. There are, however, some guidelines that can be given to help you make informed decisions.

For an individual designer or design student working on a typical six-week project, there is unlikely to be enough time to develop more than two or possibly a maximum of three concepts. This means rejecting early ideas, typically, down from about twelve to two. There can be no exact numbers here, but even with design groups where perhaps six designers are involved, they would need to reduce a broader spread of early concepts down to about two or three.

To achieve this, experienced designers may make design assessments informally, either as individuals assessing their own work or as part of a design team looking at the team's design output. One way of tackling the problem can be to use a chart as a more formal reference, particularly for students and, at least, as an aide-mémoire for more experienced designers. One advantage of this is that it clearly separates the functions of creativity and analysis, helping to prevent any potential interference between the two conflicting thought processes. In addition, it brings an element of objectivity to the process and also focuses attention on issues important to the brief.

Design development

Selecting and discarding design concepts

Developing concepts
Structural and graphic

Mock-ups
Working with materials and on-screen

Models
Creating visual representations
of finished pack

Presenting design recommendations

Design candidate assessment

Standout

Which candidate provides greatest standout
—against other design candidates?
—against competitor products within the same product sector?
—against surrounding products in adjacent sectors?

Imagery and tone

Which candidate provides
—the right voice (serious, fun, healthy, conveying authority, etc.)?
—resonance with the target audience, evoking a potentially positive response?

Branding

Which candidate
—best promotes the brand?
—best represents the brand properties?

Believability

Which design is most believable
—fits comfortably within the product sector?
—looks the part?
—does not look out of place?

Graphic layout

Which design candidate follows design "rules" in terms of
—appropriate use of typography, type sizes?
—alignment of text and graphic devices?
—legibility and readability?
—providing focus on important elements yet balances the visual elements?
—effective use of colour?
—effective use of photography/illustration?

Aesthetics

Which design looks the most
—elegant?
—balanced in its use of elements of communication?
—integrated as a total visual representation?
—exciting?
—space effective?

Practical and technical issues

Which designs
—are the most cost-effective to produce?
—are transferable to other products?
—allow space for promotional messages?
—are highly visible under store lighting conditions?
—are legible and easy to read?
—meet legal obligations?
—meet environmental targets?

Such a chart would list some of the key packaging design attributes that apply to both structure and graphics, and would prompt the designer to answer the criteria questions set against each attribute. Assuming that there are two or more design concepts on the table, a score can be given to each design candidate: zero, perhaps, being poor and five good. The most important attributes, such as stand-out, branding and imagery, might be placed first on the chart, and a further refinement could be to "weight" the scores in these areas. In theory, the design with the highest score would win through to the next round.

In practice, technical and practical issues are likely to swiftly exclude some design candidates, leaving the design evaluation based on more aesthetic values to be conducted by what is often termed the "design eye". This is where the designer, or design team, uses knowledge of the world, design experience and familiarity with the issues to assess the design work subjectively. Although the design attributes shown in the chart on the left should assist here, getting into the habit of critically analysing your own designs and the designs of others helps to develop your design eye. That design eye, in the case of packaging, however, should include an awareness that the ultimate judgement of design success will be made by consumers buying the packed product, so it is important that visual evaluation takes this into account and that designers do not become distracted by self-indulgent work that simply appeals to their peer group. A prime example of this is the use of a small type size that may win design plaudits but irritate consumers who struggle to read it. Selecting and discarding designs, therefore, is about considering both the merits of the work presented and aligning this to anticipated target group reaction.

In a commercial design studio, a further level of evaluation would typically take place during studio meetings where individual designers show their work and explain the rationale behind their thinking to team members. A number of voices can then contribute to a critique of all work in progress. It is a technique also widely adopted by universities and colleges teaching design, and although a "crit" might sometimes be thought of as an ordeal by individuals presenting their work, it should be remembered that it is valuable in sharpening design focus and in overcoming any tendency for designers to be "precious" about their work.

If the "crit", studio meeting, "design eye" or chart have now left you with two candidates for development, these can progress in parallel through the stages that follow in this section. Ultimately, however, the designer or studio team cannot sit on the fence and must make a recommendation on which single design is the favoured option. Usually, this takes place prior to model making, to avoid time and cost implications. Once again the chart used left can be employed to help decide which design is going to be recommended as a final choice.

Developing concepts

Having gone through the process of deciding which, out of a wide range of concepts, will meet the brief and needs to be developed (probably more than one concept), it is now time to replace wide-range thinking with in-depth thinking. Effectively, the wide-angle lens has been replaced by the telephoto, concentrating much more on the detail to turn that early original creative thinking into a practical output. This does not mean that creative thinking stops. One of the fascinating aspects of design is that we "learn through making", a concept first documented by the Arts and Crafts Movement between 1870 and 1900, but still a widely held view within the design community. Designer-artists such as William Morris and John Ruskin railed against mass-produced goods and celebrated the involvement of simplicity, craftsmanship and design. The principle was established that we, as designers, learn by exercising our craftsmanship and not simply by contemplative reflection. In other words, get designing rather than just thinking about it.

Drawing up an outline packaging specification

Where any structural design work is an integral part of a design study, it is important to consider the cost implications for each design, at least in enough detail to allow designs to be ranked in terms of cost. This will allow some limited design judgements to be made between design candidates, cost clearly being an important criterion in any commercial project. To do this may not require, at this stage, a full packaging specification to be drawn up, but it will be necessary to identify all materials to be used in the pack and to replace concept sketches with more accurately drawn versions that include dimensions. Addressing these requirements is helpful as it forces decisions and commitments to be made and often highlights further issues to be investigated. If we take an outline specification for a plastic fruit juice bottle design, for example, at concept development stage it might include:

—Container description: Injection blow moulded 500ml carbonated fruit juice container
—Material: PET
—Principle dimensions: See drawing
—Decoration: PVC shrink sleeve, printed four colours
—Closure: LDPE screw cap

This exercise for the plastic fruit juice bottle identifies the type of production method (injection blow moulded) and also that there are three different components: container, closure and shrink sleeve, which need to be purchased separately.

>> **Tip**
Inexperienced designers who may not yet have the level of technical knowledge to specify packaging accurately might need to conduct some basic research about production techniques. It also helps to consider existing competitor packs where contents, sizes, dimensions and materials might be similar. Materials can often be identified by recycling symbols on the pack (Chapter Seven expands on this).

To obtain any true indication of costs, the annual container production quantities would need to be known. This, in turn, would be affected by production methods, filling line speeds and other factors, such as the consideration of in-plant moulding capability (where the container is made within the fruit juice factory site to avoid transport and storage of bulky, empty containers). For many packaging designers and, particularly, design students, obtaining information at this technical and commercial level presents a daunting task and might seem a long way from the more familiar design tasks.

This degree of detail requires learning about the bottle-making processes, which, for those who may be unfamiliar with packaging technology, would need to be included as part of the research process. Packaging technology encompasses a vast spectrum of materials, processes and methods, most of which are the subject of continuing change. For this reason, it is unlikely that many true packaging "experts" with the ability to span both the depth and breadth of the subject (as we have seen in Chapter Three) actually exist. Most tend to know "a little about a lot" and have resources that they can draw on for specialist, up-to-date assistance. In the example mentioned here, a simple web search into plastic bottle production would be a good start.

In the commercial arena, one option open to designers is to seek help from the client company's purchasing, production and technical staff. Generally, in this scenario there is a possibility of the designer losing control over some design decisions, typically where practical considerations and cost implications may outweigh aesthetic qualities. Frequently, it becomes a trade-off between protecting the essential design elements and compromising on detail.

With simpler projects, the designer may choose to approach a supplier directly to obtain more information and costs, either for individual benefit or on behalf of a client. This is usually the most useful route to follow for a student project, although some companies are reluctant to deal with students, knowing that there will be no commercial benefit for them. More enlightened companies take the view that assisting a student may be an investment for the future when the student moves to commercial employment. It should be realized, however, that the costs quoted to a student, individual designer or studio are likely to be higher than those quoted to a client or potential client, where client companies might become customers, but it may be sufficiently accurate to allow approximations to be made.

Drawing up this outline specification helpfully prompts additional design queries. Should the PET plastic be clear, tinted or opaque? A shrink sleeve has been selected to carry graphics, perhaps because the designer recognized that printing or labelling might be difficult on a container with compound curves, but are there any other options? From the drawing, will the container be stable on a high speed filling line? (This is an important consideration to ensure fast container filling.)

Incorporating graphic design

Graphic design development at this stage normally involves moving from sketch work to more accurate development on screen. Most packaging designers use Photoshop for image manipulation and either Freehand or Illustrator for line work and text layout. A good starting point for developing sketch-based graphic work is to create a grid to the correct dimensions, indicating where images and illustrations should be placed and where text should appear.

As mentioned earlier in Chapter Four, when working with cylindrical containers, make sure that text does not extend beyond the line of sight. This can be done by making a paper cylinder to the correct size and marking the limits of vision directly onto the paper, then measuring and transferring this to the grid.

Design development may involve the main panel only, but as it is likely that the same style will be applied to other panels, experiment with adapting the main panel layout to other, different-sized panels. When working with cartons, the grid should be based around a cutter guide. The cutter guide is the drawing plan of the carton when it is opened out in its flat form, showing all panels, cuts, creases, etc. Some students refer to this as a net, but "cutter guide" or "carton blank" are the preferred terms.

>> Tip
For carton designs, it is easy to get panels the wrong way up and while, in some designs, such mistakes are easy to correct, in others it may be more difficult, particularly where colour changes take place across the pack surface. To avoid errors, make a rough mock-up in paper or board and mark up the orientation of the text for each panel. This can then be laid out flat alongside the cutter guide, showing the text orientation for each panel.

Left Here, the designer has struggled with two problems typical to placing graphic elements onto a cylindrical container. Firstly, long text that, at a size selected for ease of reading, wraps around the tin and out of view. Secondly, vertical alignment of the textual elements and brand name. Neither issue is satisfactorily resolved in this example.

Packaging design project
—integrating structure and graphics

1 Structural design concepts
Mock-ups help decision-making when selecting design candidates for further work. Here, although the sliding pillar design provided an intriguing opening mechanism, which could engage consumers, it was a complicated mechanism to produce. The more conventional hinged lid carton is more suited to carton production techniques.

2 Hinged lid carton mock-up
Using masking tape, panels can quickly be added, removed or modified without constantly remaking the carton blank.

3 Graphic design concepts
Until structural designs are finalized and panel sizes established, graphic design development can only explore directions. These examples have been produced from initial ideas in sketch format, representing themes using images and the generation of product names—an integral part of the brief.

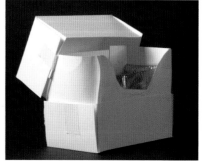

1

2

3

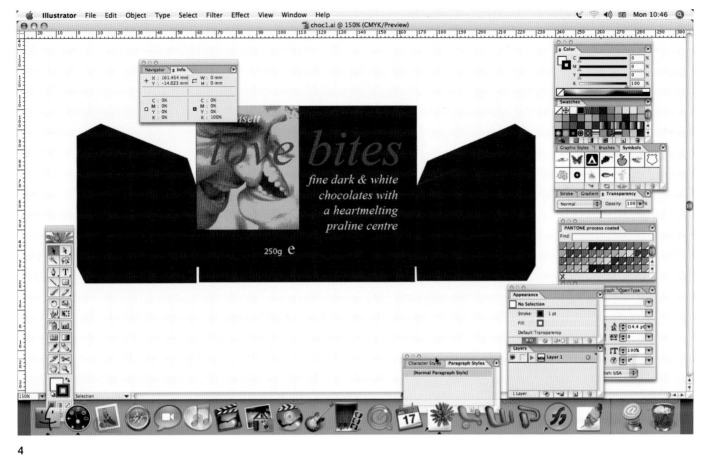

4

5

4 On-screen graphic development
The designer has chosen to separate the constructional elements for the base and lid of the carton in order to obtain printouts for application to mock-ups. Here, work is taking place on the lower half of the hinged lid carton.

5 Mock-ups with graphics applied
Printouts have been applied to the carton using Spraymount. Double-sided tape is used to join board to board but is not so effective when applied to paper printout surfaces, tending to lift the paper from the board to which it is applied. While not yet a model, the results are sufficient to allow design decisions to be made and further development to continue if required.

Mock-ups and models

There is frequent confusion about the distinction between models and mock-ups, the two terms sometimes being used indiscriminately. To put the record straight, at least as far as this book is concerned, mock-ups are physical constructions to allow designers to explore thinking and resolve problems that would be complex to do by sketches alone. As indicated in Chapter Four, mock-ups are a useful way of developing conceptual thinking but they also have a role in helping to develop and refine concepts, which is why we return to them here. Most of them, probably, will not be shown to a client, although some clients do like to see all the work they have paid for. Certainly, in colleges and universities, tutors will want to see mock-ups and judge the part they have played in the design project. Models, however, are far more highly finished than a mock-up, incorporating detailed features, accurate colours, textures and graphics. They are likely to be shown to clients as part of a final presentation and should be close to "the real thing".

The following sections consider some simple techniques that will enable the production of mock-ups to play an informed part in design decisions.

Mock-ups

Carton board is a common material for pack construction, lending itself to a wide range of carton styles and finishes, and so is the obvious choice for making carton pack mock-ups. Some design projects may simply require the use of a standard carton. In this case it is a simple matter to acquire an existing carton and modify it, by covering it with paper, foil, graphic printout or whatever the project requires. In this way, "found" packs can be a fast way of exploring possibilities in a new project. It might be a matter of taking a "found" pack, undoing glued panels and opening it flat. For a folding carton, you can now see how the panels are arranged and where creases are placed, from which a cutter guide (or net) can be drawn up by tracing the outline and marking in creases. In effect, this is a reverse engineering process, which brings you back to the original carton design and the cutter guide drawing used to produce it.

Sooner or later, however, you may wish to change dimensions and incorporate new features—flaps, cut-outs, lids, tabs, closures, etc. If the project calls for a more creative approach to carton design, there are books available that contain carton layouts (cutter guides), providing a resource of different carton constructions. Be aware, however, that some may be unsuitable for machine assembly, which may subsequently eliminate them as serious design candidates. If they follow your design rationale, however, this should not deter you as, later, you may retain the concept but modify the production method.

For making small carton mock-ups up to a size of, say 200 x 150 x 50 mm (8 x 6 x 2 inches) use 200/250gsm board. A production carton at this size might use much heavier board but, for mock-up purposes, a light board is easier to work with. Cutter guides or carton blanks can be scanned or drawn and imported into graphic programmes, allowing graphic design development to be carried out on some or all panels. Computer-generated printouts can then be spray-mounted onto carton blanks, before assembly.

Above The best way to crease board is to stick two strips of carton board to a surface using double-sided tape, allowing a gap between the strips equivalent to the thickness of the board. Line up the required crease with the gap and, using the back of a scalpel (with blade removed), or some other suitable tool, carefully score the board.

Carton board need not be restricted to producing carton mock-ups and flat surfaces; it can also be an effective medium for simulating a range of container shapes and materials. Applying the same techniques described above allows cylinders, for example, to be made in carton board representing metal cans, plastic tubs and tubes. Carton board can be used to create some curves, but this is when it reaches its limitations and it is here that foam and wood become useful.

Because foamed plastic is so quick and easy to work with, it has a role to play early in the design process, allowing three-dimensional design experiments to take place within an acceptable timeframe. "Blue foam" is often used by model makers and is a dense extruded polystyrene foam. As stated before, it is an invaluable tool when designing containers that incorporate compound curves, allowing the designer to see how such curves work as they travel around the container. This type of investigation may take place at concept stage or, equally, as part of a development process. There are, however, limitations. Firstly, when hand-forming foam or using a sanding belt, it can quickly be sanded down and, unless care is exercised, the results can be a shapeless blob with accompanying dust. Secondly, foam is not a dense enough medium to hold accurate curves. The exception here is when the foam is machine-turned, but even then the surface finish can often be rough.

For making mock-ups that incorporate complex curves, wood is a better alternative, as it "holds" a sharper curve than foam. Jelutong wood is the preferred choice because of its close grain and fine, even texture. This straight grain, non-durable Malaysian hardwood has been used in patternmaking for many years and is therefore perfect for producing mock-ups. It is usually shaped by sanding on a disc or band sander, or by hand using a sanding block.

Vacuum forming is useful for some applications where multiples of a shape are required—for example, to explore the effects of different colours. Here half-shells can quickly be made from a wooden block or, more correctly, wooden "tool" sprayed in the appropriate colours.

The techniques for making mock-ups described above require fairly simple equipment and resources, available from specialist model-making shops or material suppliers, but, unless working with board, you would usually need a dedicated workshop environment where dust/fume extraction is installed. National health and safety requirements may vary but it is obvious that basic workshop skills are required for safe operation of equipment. Because some packaging design studios are unable to install workshops and also because some designers would rather avoid working in them, computer-based solutions have proved to be a popular alternative (see pp.131–4). Two-dimensional mock-ups produced by software are increasingly being used as a replacement for three-dimensional mock-ups. They have the advantage of being studio-compatible but they do, however, lack the hands-on, tactile information that a mock-up can provide and are also often slower to produce. For many, product designers and packaging designers alike, the actions involved in physically constructing mock-ups are a crucial part of the design development process.

›› Tip
When creating a new carton design, to begin with, instead of producing it out of one sheet of board, cut individual panels and join with masking tape. If you make a mistake, or want to make modifications, just make a new panel and replace the old one. When the tape and board "lash-up" works, trace round it and then produce the mock-up from one sheet of board.

›› Tip
To create bottle shapes, start with a correctly sized rectangular block of jelutong wood. Your bottle drawings should be produced on a 1:1 scale and consist of front and side elevations with a base and top profile. Photocopy these drawings and spray-mount the photocopies, in their correct positions, directly onto the block. This then provides a visual guide as the block is sanded.

Model making

Highly realistic representations of the final pack are primarily used in client presentations, where a design studio is presenting its recommended design solutions, usually at the completion stage of the project. As mentioned earlier, this usually involves the recommended design being modelled. More complex projects might require several models of different designs or design variants—for example, a design concept followed through into 0·5-litre and 1-litre size containers. When presenting recommendations, it can be useful to display models next to the "old" pack (if there was one) and, as a comparison, alongside competitor products.

Right These models were vacuum-formed in two halves over wooden moulds before being glued together and spray painted. They represent realistically sized 0.5-litre containers for different grades of motor-scooter oil. Labels were produced separately using Freehand and Photoshop. The project was a prizewinning entry in a student competition.

Far right This solid wooden model represents a 400g catfood container concept, cleverly designed to be distinctly cat shaped. The model has been sprayed and graphics applied by transfer. The lid and foil seal form the container base.

As part of their packaging design course, many students are taught workshop skills and have extensive workshop facilities to use. They are, therefore, expected to produce highly finished models themselves. Many commercial design companies also have their own workshops, often staffed by technicians, or rely on outsourcing model making to specialist companies. In both these instances, the designers will be required to communicate their design thinking to the model maker. In practice this can be a problem as the designer, who may have a mental

Right Here, printed board has been used to create models representing Tetra Pak containers as part of a student project to reposition Ribena. Graphics were produced using Freehand and Photoshop.

Far right This lathe-turned solid wood model represents a steel bottle, and has been spray-painted with graphics applied by transfer. The design used a separate magnetic insert in the base containing frozen gel to maintain a low temperature.

picture of the pack design, now has to define it fairly precisely to a model maker who may be unfamiliar with the project and who requires sufficient details to make it. In effect, the model maker needs almost the same level of information as that required by the manufacturer of the final pack. For designers, therefore, briefing a model maker is not always an easy option.

Model makers require accurate technical drawings to work from, showing all the principal dimensions. For a typical container, drawings would include front, side and top elevations, base "footprint", closure and details of all curves and profiles. Specifying the materials and details of any surface finish required for the actual pack allows the model maker to suggest the options available to best represent the pack.

Sometimes models are used for market research purposes, which may require working versions produced in sufficient quantity to allow multiple location focus-group trials. Usually this is considered (and, in commercial practice, billed) as a separate project stage, the pack models being sourced from specialist suppliers.

Computer-generated two-dimensional visuals

While three-dimensional models provide a realistic representation of packaging designs, and allow designers and clients to obtain a tactile feedback through handling models, a highly finished two-dimensional representation can be entirely satisfactory in itself or be the precursor to model making. Producing models is both expensive and time consuming and, in commercial practice, it often features in the project costing as a separate, optional stage. Packaging design students may also encounter the same constraints or have difficulty in achieving the level of finish required. In this case, being able to produce a slick two-dimensional visual is a vital skill to acquire and one that will stand designers in good stead throughout their careers. The sophistication of drawing software now means that slick results are almost guaranteed. There is, however, still a place for hand-produced drawings which, if well executed, often have a freshness and vibrancy lacking in their computer-produced counterparts.

Most designers now opt for computer-generated drawings. Both Adobe Illustrator and Macromedia Freehand offer superb drawing capabilities with a wide range of tools and effects. These two programmes are competing for the same market, with a designer's choice often based on software license costs as much as on software features. Both are vector-based programmes, where lines are mathematically generated, allowing enclosed areas to be filled with colour. Type fonts can be imported or selected from the wide choice included with the software and accurately placed, sized and manipulated. An advantage with vector programmes is their ability to be rescaled and printed at any size without loss of quality, unlike raster programmes such as Photoshop, where image pixelation can occur when enlarged. Illustrator and Freehand allow importation of images, frequently from Photoshop. It is worth emphasizing that Photoshop should be considered as a superb image manipulation programme, but one that feeds the vector-based drawing programmes that handle typography, layout, line and colour. Developing graphics in Photoshop alone can be a source of problems later when printed output pixelates.

For packaging applications, Freehand and Illustrator software can be considered in two ways. Firstly, they can produce printed output that is applied directly to a model as a label or as the surface of a pack. Typically, the printed output would be spray-mounted onto carton board before cutting and creasing. Secondly, they can be used to draw the pack through the use of perspective, shading, "painting" and other software tools, replicating conventional manual techniques of illustration. In this instance, the output is likely to be a visual representation of the pack of sufficient quality to be used at a client presentation, or for digitally placing on shelf alongside photographs of other packs.

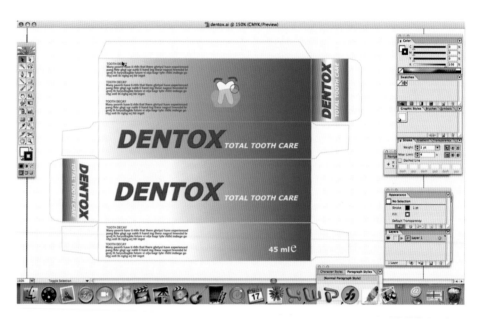

Above The carton design here has been created in Illustrator, allowing printouts of sufficient quality to be made into technically accurate models carrying accurate graphic design elements.

Right Here, Freehand has been used to create a computer-rendered container, which can then be used to explore graphic developments.

Solid modelling software

Students, designers and packaging manufacturers often use solid modelling software when working on structural designs. Early software had its origins in engineering applications where the mathematical approach adopted was not immediately compatible with a more intuitive approach favoured by designers. Even now, despite vastly improved software, it can still be a slower option than producing conventional sketches, particularly for early conceptual work. Most designers could probably originate several sketches in the time taken to produce one solid computer-generated version. It is probably wise, therefore, to think of

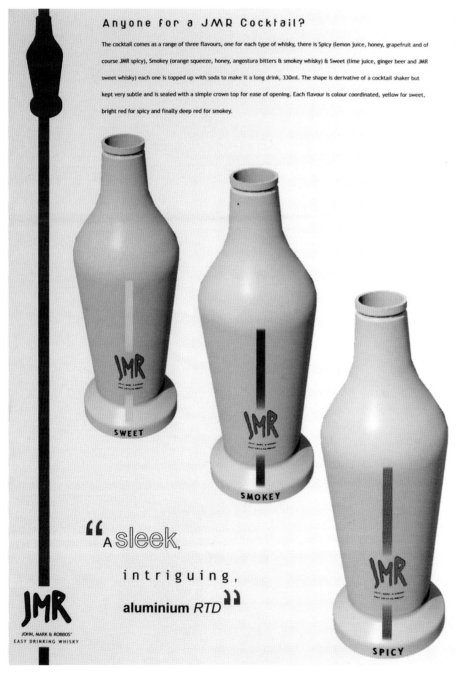

Anyone for a JMR Cocktail?

The cocktail comes as a range of three flavours, one for each type of whisky, there is Spicy (lemon juice, honey, grapefruit and of course JMR spicy), Smokey (orange squeeze, honey, angostura bitters & smokey whisky) & Sweet (lime juice, ginger beer and JMR sweet whisky) each one is topped up with soda to make it a long drink, 330ml. The shape is derivative of a cocktail shaker but kept very subtle and is sealed with a simple crown top for ease of opening. Each flavour is colour coordinated, yellow for sweet, bright red for spicy and finally deep red for smokey.

SWEET

SMOKEY

SPICY

" A sleek,

intriguing,

aluminium *RTD* "

JMR

JOHN, MARK & ROBBOS'
EASY DRINKING WHISKY

Above Container manufacturers use sophisticated software to create highly realistic visuals. Here, Rockware Glass trial a new concept for a client, using Autodesk Alias software.

Left The containers shown here were modelled on Rhinoceros software. Such programmes offer an alternative to workshop-based modelling, although, as shown with these aluminium containers, there are often some limitations in accurately portraying the material type.

using modelling software as a tool to develop and present ideas rather than as a way of originating them. The other benefit of drawing is its speed and flexibility, unhindered as it is by technology that can sometimes influence the direction of work—there is an unfortunate but understandable desire to be driven by what the software can achieve rather than what the designer actually wants. Solid modelling on-screen really scores, however, in its ability to rival conventional model making in terms of cost and speed, and it also has a significant advantage in allowing direct computer-aided manufacture to subsequently take place. Commercially, this is an important benefit for companies involved in the manufacture of moulded packaging, where tooling—the metal moulds used to create the pack form—can be produced directly from the electronically-generated design files. It is important for students too, where colleges and universities have suitable equipment for CAD/CAM manufacture.

Other outputs from computer-generated design work are rapid prototypes. Rapid prototyping, once the preserve of high-end commercial projects, has now become far more accessible, both within the packaging industry and colleges. There are several methods used but stereo-lithography is frequently used for packaging applications as it can produce hollow containers. Here, liquid resin is hardened through UV radiation controlled by computer-operated light sources working in three dimensions. Design colleges and universities routinely use this type of equipment to produce accurate models of design concepts. The stereo-lithography system can accurately prototype bottles and injection-moulded containers to a working prototype standard. Other systems cut and collate "slices" of three-dimensional designs to achieve a solid corresponding to the external dimensions of the container.

When using solid modelling software, you may find some container shapes are more difficult to produce, particularly designs that are asymmetrical or incorporate "sculptural" features. In these cases, there is a temptation to modify the design concept for ease of modelling. Remember that such temptations should be avoided; design "tools" should not form the basis of design decision making. Additionally, solid modelling programmes are able to carry out most of the modelling tasks required for packaging applications, including the incorporation of graphics and simple embossing/debossing.

In the commercial arena, many container manufacturers were early entrants into CAD/CAM systems, spurred on by the economic advantages in producing design work in one operation with a tool-making capability. These powerful computer systems also provide a means of optimizing the manufacturing processes, analysing technical details such as melt flow index in plastic container manufacture and conducting performance/weight calculations. Now, as computer technology converges, there is a greater role for design to play within manufacturing organizations. Packaging manufacturers are able to offer their design services directly to clients or to work alongside packaging design studios. The output from these high-end systems is stunning, creating virtual models that are indistinguishable from the real thing, including textures, finishes and graphics.

Presenting recommended designs

The culmination of a design project is the final presentation of work, whether this is to a client, as a final project at university or for a design competition. This is the opportunity to sell your creativity, thinking and your design, but to do so you will need to put a strategy in place. The starting point for this, as always, is the brief. Before getting carried away with the design recommendations, check that they actually answer the brief.

The presentation of design work usually takes place at a studio-client meeting and involves a verbal explanation of how the project has progressed, the "big idea" behind your thinking and the design rationale, accompanied by visual references in the form of design boards, a PowerPoint slide show or models. Most design studios would probably opt to feature all three options if the client were agreeable. It is essential that you allow sufficient time to plan your presentation because if the design is presented poorly, it will not be given a fair chance to impress the client, no matter how good the design work is. So, even though your efforts may be concentrated on completing the design work, make sure that there is enough time allocated for presentation preparation and rehearsal.

Before beginning to put a presentation together, there are some points that will be critical to the format of the presentation and need to be addressed. As a presentation involves communicating your design work to an audience, it is important to understand who this audience is and to structure the presentation material specifically for them. It is, therefore, useful to try and find out as much of the following information as possible:
—How many people will be there? This may determine the type of presentation
—What are their individual levels in terms of seniority and knowledge about the project? This helps establish the level and detail of presentation information
—What tone will be appropriate? e.g. formal, informal

It may be, for example, that the client who has been a regular contact throughout the project has invited more senior staff to sit in on the presentation. Here, the regular contact will want to demonstrate control of the project and to justify the choice of design team. A senior executive, however, may want to find out if their employee is performing well and value being obtained for the agreed project budget. The level of audience knowledge about the project may influence how much background needs to be covered, while their level of technical knowledge may decide the depth of detail required. Some presentations demand a formal approach, while others encourage a more relaxed, informal atmosphere. If there is any doubt, err on the side of formality with presentation preparations. It is much easier to verbally "relax" a formal presentation than recover from the shock of finding that what you thought was going to be a cosy chat, is in fact a formal presentation to the company president. Most successful design presentations are formally structured but allow the presenter to adjust the tone, frequently making it more informal but appropriate to the audience.

Other questions you might ask concern practical issues and these will dictate what type of and how much material will be required to collate and present. As most senior executives are busy people, timing might be an issue. In any case, presentations should be concise and address specific issues of the brief:

—How long will you have? If you can choose, twenty minutes would be plenty for a four-week project but allow time for discussion afterwards

—Where will the presentation take place? What size is the room? What facilities does it have? (screens, projectors, Internet, sound)

—Will you have time to set up?

The choice of visual aids will also depend upon these practical considerations but may include: slides | computer projection (PowerPoint) | overhead transparencies | video/film | presentation boards | models.

Visual aids are essential to presenting design as they impart meaning simply and directly in place of a complex verbal explanation. They also provide some respite for the presenter by focusing audience attention away from the presenter and onto the screen, board or model. With the increasing availability of digital equipment, the use of both slides and overhead transparencies has largely been superseded and most professional packaging design presentations now employ computer projection as a favoured method, using PowerPoint. However, there are still occasions where designs must be presented on boards or design sheets for logistical reasons. Although the same design project can be effectively presented in either media, with or without models, there are some significant differences to consider.

Using presentation boards

For portability and as manageable visual aids, boards are effectively restricted in size to A3 or possibly A2. This makes them only suitable for showing to a small audience of perhaps up to eight people. The number of boards may also be restricted for practical reasons to, say, between two and six. Although this may seem restrictive, it does encourage concentration on the key points and means that the boards must be concise enough to communicate design thinking within a few visual "frames" and persuasive enough to sell the final concept. With such a controlled format, each board must make a significant contribution to the design story, showing the rationale from early ideas through to the final design recommendations. At the same time, it would be a mistake to fill each board with too much information. It is better to treat each board as one of a series of posters, highly visual with the minimum of explanatory text.

When planning boards, it can be helpful to consider the following points:

—Does the design solution meet the brief? Demonstrate visually how it does.

—Do the boards communicate to the right target audience?

—Do the boards convey the "big idea"?

—Do the boards highlight any consumer benefits that you have been able to identify and incorporate into the design?

—Do the boards tell the design story?

If the project involves improving an existing design, the final board should show old and new, side-by-side. Make sure the old design is on the left and the new on the right. This has become a design convention, leading the eye from old to new. It is also important, however, to make sure that the presentation adopts

》 Tip

Decide whether boards should be portrait or landscape and keep this orientation throughout. This helps link them together as individual components within one integrated project. It is also more useful to do this if the boards are being used in a portfolio.

Presentation boards for a packaging design competition

The examples of student work shown here illustrate presentation boards submitted as competition entries. In each project, there would be additional boards to explain the design thinking. In competitions of this sort there is no verbal presentation, so the boards have to communicate to the judging panel entirely through visual appeal.

1 The designer has produced and photographed models of his work, creating a sequence that explains visually how the new pack works. With a good use of white space, it is a simple yet effective presentation.

2 Here, too, models have been made, photographed and combined with text to create a clean layout that explains the pack concept.

3 A model has been created and photographed with a sequence illustrating how the pack is used. Perhaps the use of such heavy frames around each illustration detracts from the overall effect. With so much information to communicate about the handle/spoon perhaps a separate board demonstrating this might have been a better option.

4 Again a pack model has been used to highlight the possibilities of a square can. The unusual lid is a significant feature but the reasoning is not explained. Although slickly produced, the text elements probably require redesign, as we see a mixture of typefaces, sizes and styles that do not appear to align with other elements of the design.

5 The computer-generated milk bottles carry graphics that indicate milk type (e.g. semi-skimmed) but the black text on such solid colours renders it almost invisible. This should have been apparent to the designers when preparing the board and corrections made. The text below the Underground map is too small and detailed to be read at a presentation.

6 The concept here is to design a window display for Ted Baker clothing, conveying its English eccentricity. The presentation, however, is not immediately clear to anyone unfamiliar with the project, requiring verbal explanation as the text which features on the board is too small to read.

7 A Photoshopped container model forms the basis for this board. The heavy black text on the left is not consistent with the concept of a light, fruity and refreshing drink. In general, the use of explanatory text should be kept to a minimum, allowing the graphics to explain the design concept.

an appropriate strategy to highlight the old design before the eye moves onto the new one.

Presentation boards are a simple form of visual aid and, as with all simple things, the details must be correct to achieve the maximum effect. If photography is used, ensure that images are not pixelated. Audience attention should concentrate on the design work and not be diverted by spotting imperfections. This applies also to mounting and trimming. When presenting, explain each board and, if possible, place them in order as the presentation is completed. Each board then becomes another component in a bigger picture that the client can re-examine when the verbal presentation finishes.

Using computer projection

PowerPoint presentations are an effective method of showing design progression because of the control they offer in the presentation of text and images. Each vital image or critical piece of text can be singled out and featured, allowing the dialogue to offer explanation of the detail being viewed. This enables a greater number of meaningful images to be used, adding interest and variation. Projection onto a screen also permits a much larger audience to view the presentation than is possible with boards, and frees the presenter to add both emphasis through gesture and pace through movement.

Film and video are usually used as a part of a presentation where the moving image is relevant to the project. Embedding video clips within a PowerPoint presentation can be a convenient way to blend static and moving images into a controllable entity, and the technique is particularly useful for advertising design.

There are, however, some aspects that need to be considered to ensure that the presentation is to a professional design standard:

—Avoid too much text *a few lines per page, maybe twelve lines maximum*

—Do not use WordArt or other display typeface *stick to one simple typeface throughout*

—Avoid multiple type sizes *restrict yourself to around two*

Below With the ability to convey written information and images, PowerPoint presentations have become the standard way of presenting design studies to others. Sound and video can be added but, for packaging design work, the addition of models and back-up work help bring presentations to life. With PowerPoint, try to keep written details to a minimum. The first example shown here contains the background to a study but has a little too much text.

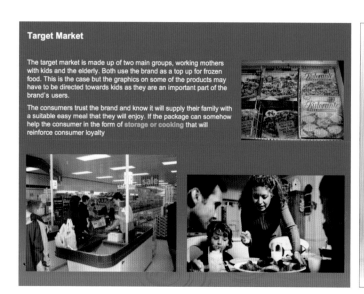

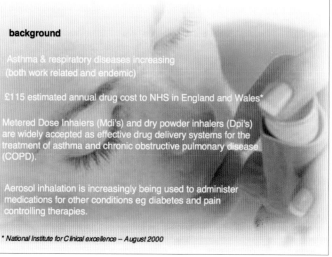

—Avoid too many special effects, entrances, exits and sounds *too many distractions*

—Ensure normal graphic design standards apply regarding layout and alignment

—Consider the PowerPoint presentation to be part of the design project *the presentation showcases your design skills, in addition to your presentation skills*

—Compress images to keep file size within practical limits *96dpi works perfectly well on screen but saves memory used by larger resolution images*

—Test the results *especially if sound or video is embedded*

As the format is electronic, it is easy to e-mail presentations, add them to a website or copy them to disk, making this a convenient format to carry, work on, change, store or send.

Using pack models

Two-dimensional images, whether on boards or on screen, can present an exciting preview of a three-dimensional object. The impact of using highly finished models, however, cannot be underestimated. Not all projects have a three-dimensional outcome but where they do, it is certainly worth considering the use of models. How these are used will depend upon the nature of the design study itself and where it is being presented. In some situations, such as presentations within the design company offices, absolute control can be exercised. Here, pack models can be hidden from view of the client audience until revealed by the presenter, creating a sense of theatre that highlights the design work. Another technique, useful in a number of different situations, is to produce models from a container in the manner in which a magician pulls rabbits from a hat, normally accompanying the final design recommendations. There is little doubt that, having explained the design rationale using PowerPoint, 2D visuals or mock-ups, presenting pack models provides the most dramatic focus for clients. For the first time, they see something that is close to the real thing. It is often an exciting make-or-break moment for the design team.

When things go wrong with presentations

Presentations can go wrong for a wide range of reasons but some of the most common are:

—Technical failure *equipment refuses to work*

—Presenter forgets the script

—Presenter nerves

Your best chance of avoiding technical problems is to rehearse the whole event under simulated conditions and to bring the exact equipment that is going to be used for the presentation. Where any technology is involved, it is absolutely essential to test that everything works. Compatibility between AppleMac, PC platforms and ancillary equipment is a frequent source of problems. The amount of computer memory required for a highly visual presentation may exceed that available on a host system, causing it to run slowly or crash. Either take all your own tried-and-tested equipment or build in time for ensuring that any client-fielded equipment will perform satisfactorily.

More common is the failure of the presenter through nerves. Everyone, no matter how experienced, gets nervous when standing up to present to a critical audience. If this is a real problem, it can be useful to write a list of headings or points you need to make during the presentation. These should be in a large type size and, therefore, easy to read in a darkened room. When presenting boards, notes can be attached to the back of the board to act as a prompt. With PowerPoint, there is less of a problem as the slides themselves can carry text that prompts the presenter.

Conclusion

In developing design work, it may be thought that the creative phase is over and all that is left is the analytical task of deciding which ideas to promote and which to relegate before beginning a process of technical refinement and presentation. As all designers will know, however, the development process brings with it new problems and opportunities, still requiring a creative input. Communicating the process to others through a presentation or demonstration of pack forms should also be considered as a design skill and an essential part of the design process.

Further reading and additional resource list

David Dabner (ed.), *Graphic Design School*, Thames & Hudson 2004 Useful book, providing techniques and describing the design process. Section on packaging design by the author

Mark Gatter, *Software Essentials for Graphic Designers*, Laurence King 2006 Practical guide to using Photoshop, Illustrator, InDesign, QuarkXPress, Dreamweaver, Flash and Acrobat

Bill Stewart, *Packaging Design Strategies*, PIRA International 2004 Explanation of the packaging design process

Websites

www.creative.gettyimages.com Source of stock images, useful for creating mock-ups

www.dandad.org Design and Art Direction; showcase of student work

www.ycnonline.com Site for young creative designers

Working with brands VI

Packaging and branding

The ability to understand the role of branding is critical to packaging design success, with many projects directly concerned with either establishing new brands, or developing existing brands and brand extensions, where the brand is used to develop new products and new markets. Packaging designers are expected to be familiar with branding issues and brand values, working with them to create packaging that establishes, identifies and reinforces brand values at the point of purchase, ensuring that the brand becomes a positive part of the consumer experience. This chapter provides the information needed to develop core brand knowledge and explains how to use it to develop creative and viable brands, sub-brands and brand extensions, with practical advice on how to work with logos—the visual representation of a brand. For those wanting to become professional packaging designers in this brand-aware world, this chapter is essential reading.

Right Branding through shape becomes a way of protecting innovation, as typified by the Coca-Cola bottle shape. The structural design of the pack, as shown in this example, can become a powerful brand property, associated with innovative products and new product sectors, making it difficult for competing brands to be recognized.

What is a brand?

Branding has become a dominating feature of contemporary life across the globe, often with a greater financial and lifestyle influence on people than that attempted by governments. Branding has helped generate unimaginable wealth for some brand owners while other brands have been controversial, on occasion causing violent anti-brand protests. Branding has also become, in some mutated form, bound up with the cult of celebrity, where individuals too have become brands in the eyes of the public and the world's press. Even politicians have become enamoured with branding, some projecting themselves as brand personalities rather than as public servants. Both George W. Bush and Tony Blair have had behind-the-scenes professional marketing help to ensure that their brand values are communicated to the public. It is evident that perceptions of branding are still changing and the consequences of this for the design community are that we must be clear about what branding stands for now, in addition to understanding the directions in which it may be heading in the future. As packaging is a key brand communicator, we have to be aware of the power of the brand and know how to work with it.

What was a brand?

We may therefore choose to start at the beginning and explore the origins of branding, which lay in the need for identification to denote ownership. It is typified by the hot branding of cattle during the early 1800s in the USA, where symbols and letters were used for identification. Shamefully, both before and since, slaves were also branded in the same way and for the same reason: to identify ownership. Branding the slaves also defined their status. It was a permanent reminder to them of where they stood in society and a statement of power by the brand owner that could be seen and acknowledged by others. As we shall see, contemporary branding also incorporates the assertion of ownership, status and power for brand owners and an acknowledgement of that ownership by the buying public.

From being, primarily, a method of identification, branding soon began to develop a new and important function, becoming a device to warn potential imitators against copying.

France was the first country to introduce legislation, in 1857, to protect trademarks that we would now refer to as brand logos. Other countries began to adopt trademark protection legislation during the following 30 years—for example, the USA in 1870, Germany in 1874, England in 1875 and Japan in 1884 (although there were significant national differences when interpreting these laws, which persisted up until the 1990s with the establishment of a Euro-trademark in 1994 and further international agreements).

Before the end of the nineteenth century, many of the world's most prominent and enduring brands began to be established. We tend to think of brands such as Yardley and Gillette as belonging to contemporary times when, in fact, they, along with many others, are over one hundred years old. Many of the early companies simply used the family name of the owners of the business to identify themselves, this later becoming recognizable as the brand.

Established brands

Yardley	1770
Schweppes	1792
Perrier	1863
Colgate	1873
Coca-Cola	1886
Kodak	1888
Shell	1897
Gillette	1902

Johnson's
baby

Kellogg's

Above Both of these established brands inspire trust. In fact, trust is their major brand value—Kellogg's for families and Johnson's for babies.

As it used to be ...
—see me
—trust me
—buy me

As it is now ...
—see me
—trust me
—love me
—buy me
—envy me

In addition to the creation of brands by the manufacturing industries, retailers also began to develop branding strategies. As chains of stores began to spread, the concepts of pre-packaged goods and own label brands were introduced. During the late 1800s and early 1900s chains of stores were developed, by A&P (the Great Atlantic and Pacific Tea Company), Woolworth's and J.C. Penney in the USA, and by W.H. Smith, Thomas Lipton, J. Sainsbury and Tesco in the UK (see Chapter One for more information). In other European countries, similar developments were taking place. Royal Ahold was established in the Netherlands in 1887, expanding to 23 stores by 1897 and introducing its own brand of foodstuffs, Marvelo, by 1911. In Germany, too, Tengelmann grew from a single store in 1893 to 560 stores by 1914 (ultimately, in 1979, going on to take over the founder of chain stores, the American group A&P).

Brands also built a relationship of trust between the brand and the customer, in addition to their identification and legal protection roles. Particularly at a time when product quality and efficacy often varied widely, it was considered worthwhile to pay a little extra for a product with a reputation for consistency. Such consistency was represented on the product or pack by a symbol or stamp guaranteeing quality. Logos, or more correctly, logotypes, were graphic devices that provided the company's signature and, therefore, its seal of approval.

Up until the 1960s, branding was largely concerned with these three functions:
—Identification *of product and manufacturer*
—Protection *against imitation*
—Trust *in product quality and efficacy*

As has been discussed in Chapter One, it was the advent of professional marketing and, in the case of branded packaged products, self-service shopping that led to changes in the role of branding.

What is a brand now?

Since the 1960s markets have become far more competitive and manufacturers have realized that, for survival, their brands have to offer more than just identification, protection and trust. Brands have a role in helping persuade people to want to buy the product for emotional reasons. The disciplines of marketing and advertising have rapidly become much more sophisticated in understanding how emotional persuasion can be used, not only to stimulate purchase but also to create groups of like-minded brand-loyal purchasers who are envied by others. To the functions of identification, protection and trust can now be added a further three functions:
—Persuasion *the emotional involvement with a brand that encourages purchase*
—Disclosure *our emotional desire to reveal to others that we are discerning in our choice*
—Publication *our emotional need to show tribal affiliation*

Emotional brand strategies—persuasion, disclosure, publication

When we look at brands today, our criteria for choice are frequently influenced by emotional responses to a carefully crafted brand strategy rather than rational or practical considerations. As we shall see later, this is particularly important for high-value products.

Kittens and babies have their own natural appeal but this is also reinforced by indicating the love of the baby/kitten by the mother/owner. There are many adverts that use similar strategies, all with the aim of creating an emotional link to the brand to persuade specific target markets to buy the product. To any designer researching a brand they are more revealing as they clearly indicate the brand strategy. Adverts (with their larger canvas, media positioning in magazines or TV and single promotional purpose) are able to convey emotional appeal in a way difficult to reproduce on packaging. The smaller physical size of packaging and its multi-purpose role in protecting and identifying the product, together with its positioning on shelf, make portrayal of emotion more difficult. Nevertheless, many printed adverts also feature the pack within their emotional strategy.

Adverts for beauty products and fragrances make a strong emotional statement by portraying images of beauty and promises of seduction that persuade us to buy them so that we can become like those perfect people shown in the advert. The packaging, frequently also appearing in the advert, should be designed to reflect the personality of the product, reinforcing the emotional bond between user and brand at every opportunity.

Below, left and right The choice of imagery is key to invoking the emotional response associated with the brand. The Swedish company, Tretorn, uses a calm image that portrays the casual, refined and understated values of the brand. In contrast, DKNY brand values are concerned with the vibrancy and energy of New York City life and use dynamic lifestyle imagery to provide emotional appeal that corresponds with their target audience.

Right, above and below Many adverts employ images to encourage an emotional involvement with the brand to stimulate sales. In the first image, the owner gazes adoringly at her healthy kitten, while in the Pampers ad, mum and baby look into one another's eyes—a visual metaphor for shared love.

Above Clearly, Guerlain is appealing to our emotions here, offering seduction for ourselves and admiration from others—a powerful emotional message.

As shown in the examples pictured, the emotional meaning can be varied by the choice of image and, in particular, whether people appear in the image and what part they are playing. A rural landscape, on its own, may invoke a sense of tranquility that becomes more personal if we see someone standing in a river, fly-fishing. The emotional appeal is quite different if the same scene includes a mountain biker splashing through the shallows. When choosing images, therefore, we need to identify clearly the emotional appeal of the brand and be able to express this through selecting appropriate images.

Being persuaded to buy the product is not, however, the end of the story. If an emotional bond can be built between brand and consumers, then the consumers may wish to disclose to others how selective and discerning they have been in their brand choice. Wearing clothing, watches or accessories with logos is an obvious example of purchasers wishing to draw the attention of others, perhaps, to their wealth or "good" taste. Such behaviour can operate on a far more subtle level, as exemplified by women's perfume. The choice of brand is primarily important to the woman. Buying a particular branded fragrance enhances a woman's self-esteem, where she imagines herself being transformed into an object of envy and desire, and hopes that her choice of brand will be acknowledged in this way. While disclosure of this type is frequently associated with high-value, aspirational items and brands, it also can occur with lower-value, fast-moving consumer goods (FMCG). Premium range, organic, low fat, new or special supermarket products and brands all carry an element of disclosure to family and friends. The purchaser may wish, for example, to show how they love their family by purchasing "healthy" brands, or demonstrate their ethical credentials by buying Fairtrade-branded products.

A purchasing decision made on an emotional basis may also involve what we have termed publication. This means that the purchaser is able to join a "clan" that offers companionship, safety or the feeling of belonging. These are some of the most basic of human needs. Buying the brand is the initiation into the tribe, but the important factor here is publishing tribal membership through sight of the brand. Unlike disclosure, mentioned above, where the motive is to impress people by demonstrating individual taste, here it is to demonstrate group loyalty. In effect, individuality is being sacrificed so that the benefits of tribal behaviour can be embraced. Just as sport supporters may choose to wear replicas of their

Left Although both products are beers, they have very different characters. Both are available in supermarkets and the purchasing decision involved tells much about the purchaser. The Peroni drinker might be considered style-conscious, interested in food and the aesthetic qualities of life while the London Pride drinker seeks good no-nonsense London ale—brand values at different ends of the spectrum appealing to different tribes. To complicate things for marketing professionals, our flexible society allows us to be in one clan one day and another the next, making brands work even harder to achieve brand loyalty.

team's sports kit, brands are also selected and displayed to denote membership of a tribe—in this case, a tribe of like-minded people. In this way, the iPod tribe are distinguished from their MP3 player rivals by the distinctive white headphone wires that have become a brand property of the iPod.

Today, then, brands have moved through the practical spectrum of identification, protection and trust to the emotional spectrum where persuasion, disclosure and publication become the main tools for achieving sales. Advertising, film, TV, the Internet and specialist magazines have provided an easily accessible stage where celebrities, stars, personalities and objects of desire are paraded to mass audiences, stimulating the tie between brands and our emotional involvement with them. Packaging, so far, has had a supporting role in this but now is set to become a key player as branding moves towards becoming an experience.

The brand as an experience

Increasingly, we are encouraged to buy into the brand experience, rather than simply purchase a product. As John Grant puts it in his book, *The New Marketing Manifesto* (1999), branding has become "up-close and personal". Grant suggests that this means marketing rejecting the way target audiences were stereotyped in the past, looking beyond consumer research and actually making live contact with customers. He uses phrases such as "walking the market" to express this philosophy of trying to get "inside customers' everyday thoughts and activities" in order to connect brands with people. Some practical ways of doing this are suggested later in this chapter.

In their adverts featuring sporting heroes, Nike is not just offering trainers; its real brand offer is concerned with redemption | vindication | a way out of the ghetto | a voice for sport, personal growth and achievement: "Just do it."

By buying Nike, you are being persuaded to make a personal commitment to moving onward and upward, perhaps against all odds. Grant suggests a parallel here with religion, even down to the use of symbols—drawing a comparison

Below left The Nike Swoosh makes a statement, both to the purchaser and to others who see the logo being worn, that they are part of a brand community who rebels against what is expected of them.

Below right Starbucks' coffee shops are in just about every high street, offering a place to be seen, meet friends, work on the laptop or just relax. It is not about coffee but about providing an experience that we will enjoy and want to repeat. The success of the brand, however, has caused a backlash by those who are against global brand dominance at the expense of local cultural values and independent coffee shops. See Chapter Seven for more.

The best global brands 2006

Brands are ranked by brand value, representing the dollar value of the brand today and projected ahead for the next six years. The financial calculations are complex but explained in more detail on the Interbrand website.

Rank	Brand	Country	% value change
1	Coca-Cola	US	-1
2	Microsoft	US	-5
3	IBM	US	5
4	GE	US	4
5	Intel	US	-9
6	Nokia	Finland	14
7	Toyota	Japan	12
8	Disney	US	5
9	McDonald's	US	6
10	Mercedes-Benz	Germany	7
11	Citi	US	7
12	Marlboro	US	1
13	Hewlett-Packard	US	8
14	American Express	US	6
15	BMW	Germany	15
16	Gillette	US	12
17	Louis Vuitton	France	10
18	Cisco	US	6
19	Honda	Japan	8
20	Samsung	South Korea	8
21	Merrill Lynch	US	8
22	Pepsi	US	2
23	Nescafé	Switzerland	2
24	Google	US	46
25	Dell	US	-7
26	Sony	Japan	9
27	Budweiser	US	-2
28	HSBC	UK	11
29	Oracle	US	5
30	Ford	US	-16
31	Nike	US	8
32	UPS	US	8
33	JPMorgan	US	8
34	SAP	Germany	11
35	Canon	Japan	10
36	Morgan Stanley	US	0
37	Goldman Sachs	US	13
38	Pfizer	US	-4
39	Apple	US	14
40	Kellogg's	US	6
41	IKEA	Sweden	12
42	UBS	Switzerland	15
43	Novartis	Switzerland	2
44	Siemens	Germany	4
45	Harley-Davidson	US	5
46	Gucci	Italy	8
47	eBay	US	18
48	Phillips	Netherlands	14
49	Accenture	Bermuda	10
50	MTV	US	0

Source: Interbrand

between the cross and the Swoosh. Here, however, redemption is being offered for the price of the product. The offer seems primarily to be extended to young people trapped in poverty with little chance of escape except, perhaps, for the chance that sport offers. The same message applies equally to those trying to escape the dull, monotonous routine of an office regime as to those in grinding poverty. It is a clever strategy, using the universal appeal of sport and rebellion against oppression as a way of developing a brand community and, ultimately, increasing sales. It is probably no coincidence that Adidas, the German competitor of Nike, have also used street music to boost their challenge in the same market, as rap and hip-hop, like sport, have found resonance with disenfranchised youth across national boundaries.

Visiting one of Nike's outlandish stores makes shopping a personal experience. Nike also offer a web-based design service where choice of fabrics, styles and colours enable you to customize your own trainers, making them unique to you. While you are a member of the Nike community, you are, at the same time, able to express your individuality within it.

Starbucks positions itself not as a provider of coffee, but as the third place after home and work. So, according to them, we don't go there to drink coffee, but simply to find a refuge. It too offers personal service, experimenting with a system that records customer details and coffee preferences. You enter the shop and your "chipped" card is automatically read, allowing the staff to greet you by name and prepare your favourite coffee just the way you like it. For regular Starbucks customers, the "baristas" already know customers by name and by product preference. Starbucks incorporate a wireless Internet service in some of their cafes so that, while you relax with your coffee, you can access fast broadband Internet services on your laptop. It is not about coffee, it is about experience. To enhance that concept, they also intend to become the most popular music retailer on the high street and have already signed some high-profile artists, notably the Rolling Stones, to exclusive releases. Starbucks now also sell their own branded alcoholic coffee liqueurs, adding yet another element to reinforce the brand offer, making Starbucks a bar to spend time in, relaxing, surrounded by like-minded people and, of course, the place to spend your money.

These examples provide an indication of the strategic thinking that some brand owners are currently developing, making real efforts to create brands that are much more than simply a symbol. We might, therefore, argue that brands that provide a positive experience for consumers in every sphere of their operations are those that are the most likely to be rewarded by success. To see if there is any merit in this argument, we can look at brand winners and losers.

Brand winners and losers

Brand winners are characterized by the ability to form an emotional bond between consumers and the brand and to provide a brand experience. In 2006, the brands that gained most market share in a year all had something special to offer beyond goods and services, according to the "Annual Report on Global Brands", published jointly by *Business Week* magazine and brand specialists, Interbrand. Some of the report's more significant findings are reported opposite.

While the success of brands has traditionally depended on manufacturing products and the supply of services, new types of hybrid businesses are emerging as brands. eBay, a new arrival in the top 100 brands in 2004, where it made an entrance at number 60, continues to be a top performer, now ranking at 47. Interaction between the brand and users characterizes this new approach by creating, in this case, an on-line experience that intrigues and engages users. It becomes more than an on-line auction but a community activity that people can participate in.

Apple could not quite match its dramatic performance over the past two years in 2006, but it turned in a credible increase in brand value. The iPod continues to be successful and Apple demonstrates, through all of its activities, how a brand can create a rapport with its market. Apple has always had a cult following amongst the design fraternity, where AppleMacs are firmly established as the industry norm. Now, with the iPod, a new generation of non-designers and PC users have joined the Apple community. It is cool to be seen with the white wires—revealing to others, from Beijing to Boston, that you are part of the iPod clan. It has become the jewellery of the digital age. The sense of community is something that Apple actively encourages with an almost anarchic, certainly individual, approach. Apple stores offer "genius clinics" where experts will answer any user problems. A lecture theatre, freely available to all, provides workshop sessions on all software applications. Experts will demonstrate how to add a guitar track to drum and base rhythms in GarageBand while the audience follow on their laptops. The programmes are continuous and varied. It is another way of being up-close and personal and of providing a unique brand experience.

By contrast, it is no coincidence that brand losers in 2006 were also the brands showing the least sparkle in their approach to consumers. In most cases, decline can also be attributed to technological changes and company failure to react. Manufacturing brands tended to suffer most. Kodak was slow to respond to digital imaging while both Gap and Ford failed to excite the public. Heinz, too, has been slow to introduce new and innovative products that address changing markets, for example organic convenience foods or healthy children's snacks.

Above, left and right The Apple experience has been brought to the High Street by the introduction of Apple stores, as here in Tokyo. Attention to detail extends from product design and packaging to the store interior, staff training and the ability to try everything in the store. The clever ad for the iPod is simple yet symbolic of urban cool. All of this creates an experience and supports Apple's claim to be "the centre of your digital life".

Brand performance

Winners % change 2005/6		Losers % change 2005/6	
Google	+46	Gap	-22
Starbucks	+20	Ford	-16
eBay	+18	Kodak	-12
Yahoo	+15	Heinz	-10
Apple	+14	Intel	-9

Source: Interbrand, "Global Brands 2006"

Giant brands Microsoft and Coca-Cola have also lost brand value over the year. Perhaps company size and past successes dulled the recognition that consumers have moved on, but now both these companies are reacting. Microsoft is partly a personality brand and Bill Gates's record on charity donations is impressive, which helps to win hearts and minds. On a corporate level, Microsoft is also attempting to bond with consumers by holding mini trade shows in airport lounges. There are, however, technical problems that Microsoft must address in addition to making itself more approachable to consumers. Both Linux and Apple are small but voracious predators, stalking the giant, and both have offbeat brand personalities that currently find resonance with younger consumers. Coca-Cola face a different threat, with obesity concerns encouraging consumers to buy healthier options. Coca-Cola responses include launching Dasani (a bottled water that flopped in the UK through quality problems but is well established in the USA), Poweraid, a Coke energy drink, and low-sugar versions of their other products. Heinz, too, are victims of changing food consumption patterns, perhaps because they have not yet provided credible innovative meal solutions for time-pressed consumers, nor highlighted healthy options for those with health concerns.

It is evident that successful companies interpret branding as being a company philosophy to be integrated into all their activities and that, for them, the brand/consumer interface has become a key communication channel for them to demonstrate their commitment to consumer involvement.

Consumer involvement with brands

Where products are of a high price, we become very involved with the product and its competitors. At the top end of the spectrum, any purchase that involves high expenditure is subject to analytical thinking. Buying a new car, for example, involves comparisons of price, technical specification, trim levels, fuel consumption, insurance rates, colours available, delivery times and other technical details. It also involves emotional issues that may be powerful enough to overcome many of our practical concerns. Our emotions may persuade us to buy a sports coupé when our rational, analytical thinking might suggest a small saloon is actually all we need. High investment implies high risk.

In the supermarket risks are still present but on a very different scale, as price point differences are marginal in real terms. Another fundamental difference between buying groceries and a capital purchase is the timeframe. It is likely that we will buy in the supermarket weekly or even daily. In addition, we are less engaged, both practically and emotionally, with supermarket products themselves. In effect, low price equates with low involvement and low risk. It does not really matter if we make a mistake or experiment by choosing an unfamiliar brand, since the results will not be financially damaging nor have long-term effects.

Packaged products in the supermarket environment compete for our attention on a regular basis with little purchasing risk attached and the brand therefore has to work much harder than it would for BMW, for example. For packaging designers the challenge is to create packaging that consumers recognize, that

Introducing the new S-Class. You've always
looked ahead. Imagine actually being there.

You have foresight. You have intuition. You have a knack of knowing what's
just around the corner. So you expected this. The Mercedes-Benz S-Class with
30 inspired innovations. For people who are hopelessly stuck in the future.

Mercedes-Benz

Visit www.mercedes-benz.co.uk/sclass, call 0800 66 54 38 quoting S-Class 001 or text sclass to 64500.

Left High investment means high involvement
and high risk, typified by the purchase of cars,
cameras and electronics. Here brands need
not shout but merely whisper, so branding is
frequently low-key. Despite practical considerations and trust in the brand, we are buying
the dream to demonstrate our personality as
we would like it to be seen.

effectively promotes the brand, reflects the brand values and creates an emotional bond between brand and consumer. It becomes apparent that to do all this
places a heavy burden on packaging alone and that promoting the brand on a
broader front has a much greater chance of success. Packaging is important but it
is only one element within a branding strategy that also includes advertising and
extends to all company activities.

The brand is often a company's most valuable asset and, in successful companies, what the brand stands for will extend directly to the core of the company.
Brand values will be reflected in every sphere of operation. For brands adopting
this strategy, this means every detail is important. Prestige car manufacturers
spend time and money to ensure that doors close with a reassuring click and
switches feel satisfyingly positive in their operation. Similarly, packaging becomes a key element in expressing the brand philosophy. Here, the way packs
open, close and dispense a product become as critical as how the door closes on
a Mercedes. The thought that has gone into providing other consumer benefits—
ease of storage and environmental performance, for example—impact on the interface between brand and consumer. This applies equally to consumer durable
products, where unpacking the product should reinforce the brand experience
rather than detract from it, which is too often the case. Transit packaging is often
overlooked as a part of the brand yet, particularly for high-value items, it can be
influential in shaping our opinion of the brand. Poorly designed fittings housed in
a shipping case that makes removal of the product difficult becomes a negative
consumer experience. By contrast, presenting the consumer with ease of access
and visible signs of design thought throughout, including environmental considerations, helps to consolidate the positive overall brand experience.

Consumer involvement with brands also includes the way branding is
expressed visually and, to understand this, we need to become more familiar with
the terminology of branding, brand types and values.

Brand attributes

Identification
recognition and familiarity

Distinctiveness
no confusion with other brands or products

Reassurance
trust, consistent quality

Focus
for advertising and communicating at
all levels

Involvement
with our emotions, lifestyle, how we
perceive ourselves and how we are
perceived by others

Philosophy
the brand extends to the core of the
company—it is the company

The lexicon of branding

Brand levels

Parent brand (umbrella brand)
standalone brand or brand supporting sub-brands or brand endorsements
Cadbury's

Sub-brand
registered brand given prominence, with parent brand appearing as signature of approval
Cadbury's Flake

Brand endorsement
parent brand subordinate to registered brand
Obsession (by) Calvin Klein

Personality brand
brand dominated by an individual
Virgin dominated by Richard Branson

Brand values
(what the brand stands for in human terms)

Brand **personality**
fun, sexy, serious, honest

Brand **character**
as above

Brand **essence**
concentration of brand values into one core concept

Brand **soul**
emotional core of the brand

Brand **culture**
the culture it represents

Other brand terms

Brand **identity**
visual presentation of corporate brand—owner, logos, typeface

Brand **extension**
new product offering different benefit or targeting different market

Brand **equity**
financial worth (revenue and goodwill)

Brand types and brand values

Terminology

Branding has developed its own terminology to describe types of brands and brand features but, as yet, with no accepted standard definitions. As with a language, brand terms are constantly evolving but, nevertheless, packaging designers who need to be able to communicate in a meaningful way with marketing staff, advertising agencies and other designers have to understand this new language. The chart here attempts to explain a number of widely used terms but, no doubt, there will be further variations emerging or not included here. Much of the terminology uses the same descriptors we attach to humans, which helps to make sense of the way they are used. For example, when we come to consider brand levels, the term "parent brand" might be used, to refer to a brand that supports "offspring" in the form of sub-brands or brand endorsements.

Most of the terms in the chart are easy to understand and it is simply a matter of becoming familiar with them. Some, however, may benefit from further explanation.

Personality brands

Some brands have evolved from entrepreneurs who have become well-known personalities and it is a useful exercise for designers to see how they have influenced the design of their products in a very personal way. This helps illustrate how designers must first understand the underlying philosophy behind the brand in order to represent it through design. The images opposite show three very different and distinctive characters, all of whom front the business empires that they have created. Their personalities have directed the way each business has developed.

Taking Richard Branson's Virgin brand, we can see that, unlike the others, he has expanded by diversifying his business interests yet he has maintained a unifying set of brand values to underpin each brand extension. He is an entrepreneur and, unlike Bill Gates (Microsoft) and Steve Jobs (Apple), has no technical specialism. His character is that of the respectable rebel, the underdog who dares to challenge convention and succeeds. From challenging the music industry, Branson went on to tackle the state-owned airlines, conducting a bitter campaign against their stranglehold on the airways, exposing some dirty tricks as he did so, and catching the public's imagination. His character infused Virgin Atlantic with a quirky irreverence quite unlike the serious nature of the competition. As this quirkiness came from the core of the business, namely Branson himself, and radiated outwards into every activity, the core brand values were maintained throughout both Virgin Atlantic and the Branson empire.

The relevance of this for packaging design becomes apparent when the amenity kits provided for passengers by Virgin Atlantic are examined. Instead of the normal, predictable contents, we find, for example, a pink toothpaste tube printed with the single word "smile". The Branson brand philosophy is clearly being carried through to packaging. Designing for Virgin means having to encapsulate the Branson philosophy of fun and irreverence.

Brand values

Human descriptors are used to refer to brand values, whether these are categorized as brand character or brand personality. The designer might, for example, assign appropriate brand values for the BMW Mini shown here. These could include: cheeky | sporty | fun | young | trendy | classless.

You may decide which of these is appropriate or substitute them for other terms that describe the Mini as a brand. It is both acceptable and helpful for designers to describe brands in this way. By describing one of the brand values of the Mini as "cheeky", for example, we immediately have the beginnings of a design direction for any sales literature or packed accessories. (You can see how the designers have interpreted the Mini brand values by visiting their website www.mini.com.)

Below Richard Branson (Virgin), Bill Gates (Microsoft), and Steve Jobs (Apple). The brand values of the companies here represent those of their founders. Earlier brands established by individuals often reflected the standards of their original owners, but as the mantle of responsibility passed out of their hands, the brand values often slowly changed over time.

Bottom The brand values of the new BMW Mini can be described in human terms. The car has a personality based on its heritage but brought up-to-date and relevant for today. It is of interest to note that in Mini sales literature, no images include people. Here the cars are driverless. Could this be because the brand wishes to appeal to a wider target audience than the brochure could incorporate?

+++ PUBLIC CONSENSUS REACHED +++ MINI STICKS TO ROAD +·+ PUBLIC CONSENSUS REACHED +++ MINI STICKS TO ROAD +++

Today's main story is the MINI Cooper's wide track and long wheelbase.
Further outbreaks of go-kart feeling are widely expected.

Above The inspiration for this triangular product is said to have originated from the mountains of Switzerland but, by adopting a triangular pack, Toblerone established a brand property through shape. It can be recognized without graphics, which allows Toblerone to move with ease between varieties that differentiate dark, white and milk chocolate through the pack colour while still maintaining the distinctive Toblerone triangular shape. Keen pack observers may spot the white bear cleverly worked into the mountain logo, the symbol of Berne and home to Toblerone.

Below This Tetra Pak container of brown sugar shows how well some products can be transposed into containers commonly used in other sectors. In fact, in this instance the sugar is easily poured, resealed and stored—far more convenient than the more conventional bag.

Branding through shape and sound

We often tend to think of branding as something that is visually represented by a logo or graphic device. While this is frequently the case, for packaging, the manipulation of three-dimensional shapes can create a unique brand property. In some instances the shape becomes so powerful that the brand can be recognized without recourse to graphics, as demonstrated by Toblerone.

The S.C. Johnson product, Toilet Duck, also uses container shape as a brand property in the domestic toilet cleaner sector. Using an angled neck section on the bottle to provide positive cleaning benefits, the flow of the product can be directed inside the toilet rim. It was not long before competitors were forced to follow with similar styles and the toilet cleaner sector soon became identifiable through the domination of angled-neck bottles. The same technique is often used by makers of own-label products, who may deliberately choose to follow shapes created by the brand leaders in particular market sectors, sometimes becoming so close to the original design as to invoke litigation.

It is a problem for brand leaders when their distinctive pack shapes are copied. The good news, for packaging designers, is that brand leaders are then forced to create new concepts as a result. Indeed, the multiple grocery companies expect and encourage brand owners to develop innovative new products. There is, however, a further problem with distinctive shapes. Perrier developed a distinctive shape for their glass mineral-water bottle. When they wished to produce cans of water, the glass bottle shape could not be reproduced in metal. A strong brand shape can force a brand into a corner with little room for manoeuvre.

Developing a unique pack shape, however, is not the only way to create distinctive three-dimensional packaging. Existing pack forms can be successfully moved from one market sector to another where they stand out against competition by presenting a completely different three-dimensional profile. If the effect is dramatic enough, the pack can also become a brand property. The use of a Tetra Pak containing sugar, for example, stands out against the competitor products in bags, creating an association between the pack and the brand—for the shopper it is easy to identify and, of course, to buy. Other successful examples include cosmetics in a paint tin, honey in a tube and cream in an aerosol. At the start of a design project, therefore, do consider pack formats that are more commonly used in other sectors.

As was discussed in Chapter Three, colour is frequently used as a brand identifier. Sound, however, is more often overlooked. Audio logos are usually associated with TV and film advertising, where the final image is accompanied by an audio tag line. It is that little sound or expression, repeated on every ad, that is remembered and associated with the brand. Currently, some packs have a characteristic sound that is associated with a category rather than a brand. The sound of a ring pull opening on a beer can is recognizable as a category of carbonated canned products but is not brand specific. Similarly, the sound of the removal of a cork from a wine bottle is recognizable but this is characteristic of all wines. New technology may change this in the future, allowing packs to "speak" or make noises. The talking pack is almost within grasp but it remains to be seen just how fascinated (or frustrated) consumers will be when it arrives.

Left The Toilet Duck bottle shape identifies the brand, irrespective of language or graphics. This container set a new benchmark for the market sector, forcing competitors to follow in a similar direction.

1868

1938

1966

1988

1995

Above The development of the Nestlé logo illustrates how established brands refresh their logos, ensuring that each change does not alienate their loyal customer base. Here, the design elements have been progressively simplified to create a more contemporary feel and to assist print reproduction in a range of different media.

Working with logos

Sooner or later, packaging designers will be involved in working with logos, either creating new ones or modifying existing ones. A logo is really a symbol or device acting as a visual representation of a company or brand and, therefore, should be distinctive and easily recognized. Logos that work particularly well also create a positive emotional association with the brand, so that when we see it, we instantly acknowledge the principal brand values. In addition, we may also associate the brand with the company's activities.

At Sheffield Hallam University in the UK, a series of experiments were conducted where the logos of well-established companies were flashed onto a screen and the students given a six-second slot to identify the company represented by the logo, provide key words about the company and what business it was in. The three-pointed Mercedes-Benz star, for example, was easily recognized and tagged with words such as prestige, luxury and costly. Most respondents thought that the company business was cars. While it certainly includes cars, Mercedes-Benz is also a major player in trucks, marine engines and motor sport, for example, none of which were mentioned. This helps reveal that a logo can only communicate a limited amount of information and that recognition needs to be reinforced through advertising and brand experience to become familiar. Sight of the logo then prompts us to recall information from our experience. In the experiment described above, most of the group members had no experience of marine engines, commercial vehicles or motor sport.

Most logos have to be capable of growing as the brand evolves through time, presenting a fresh, contemporary face to the world. Sometimes the logo requires modification so that it may react to changes in market conditions or reflect new company activities. Successful, mature brands must do this carefully, making a series of evolutionary changes over time so that their loyal brand followers are not alienated and any risk of declining sales through lack of brand recognition is minimized.

Many older brands have logos that are stylized presentations of the company name. Logos of this type are read rather than recognized as a shape. Nevertheless, designers should be aware that shapes are quicker to "read" than text. When the name is short, like Brillo, there will be little difference between reading the name and recognizing the letters as a shape. Longer names take more time to read and the use of a graphic device as a consistent part of the logo becomes more desirable.

As a packaging designer, you are most likely to be faced with the task of creating a new logo as part of a wider corporate identity programme. Typically, even for a small company, this is likely to include signage, letterheads and stationery, vehicle livery, brochures, clothing and website—as well as packaging. So, in addition to a logo, a corporate identity programme considers typography, layout and colour. Here, however, we shall begin by considering the origination of a new logo.

The examples shown below illustrate four commonly used types of logo. While the brands are all easily recognized, we have to rely on advertising to convey the full scope of the activities that each brand is involved with.

Logo using stylized lettering

Stylized lettering together with a graphic device

Use of symbols and lettering

Symbols alone

Research

There is limited value in considering the logos of other companies as a source of inspiration, as many of the most successful brands have a long heritage, pre-dating modern brand requirements and incorporating the name of the company. Nevertheless, it is fascinating to see how logo design has been influenced by the Bauhaus, Art Deco, Picasso, Miró, Mondrian, Peter Blake and other influential artists, periods and movements. Look around you, starting with some of the references at the back of this book. You will be captivated, and probably influenced, by what you will see but, actually, designing a new logo (and the basis of a corporate identity programme) begins by considering the company itself. What you seek is the fundamental philosophy on which the organization is based. Logos and corporate identities are not add-on extras or slick badges to aid sales; they are in-depth representations of the company ethos, paring the company back to the bone, revealing all. Anything less and it will not work. The key question to ask is "What is this company about?" This sounds simplistic and easy to answer but, in practice, many companies rarely ask this question. They may provide an answer but, frequently, they may fail to recognize what their business actually is. Until recently, many electricity providers thought their business was the generation and provision of electricity. Actually, a wider view might identify that they are in the energy business. This gives them the freedom to include other energy types within their portfolio, such as bio-fuels, solar power, wind power, gas and oil. This might entail a logo change if the original design was centred on electrical power generation alone.

So, in a study of this type for a company or organization, begin by asking the vital question "What business are you in?" to staff at all levels in the organization. If possible, arrange to meet senior executives and discuss the business plans for growth, their customer base, competitors, customer profile, factors that affect the company's ability to perform and the prevailing business climate. If the company is a manufacturer, try to spend time visiting every aspect of their production cycle. You are looking for clues and, with a fresh pair of eyes, you may spot something that they are simply too close to see for themselves. If the company runs a fleet of vehicles or maybe just one small van, include that in the research. Companies are likely to give permission for you to take photographs and this can be the basis of a superb record-keeping system. Make sure, however, that people know you are not spying or checking up on them.

Collate research material, photographs, existing company brochures, competitor material and, if there is an existing logo or corporate identity, visual reference to how and where it is used. As with most design studies, it is useful to create a mood board but, in this instance, it seeks to identify the company and the values it stands for. Honesty is important but be prepared to be tactful, as companies can often become sensitive to proposals that appear to be critical.

Design concepts

When considering design concepts, as with most design studies, a spider diagram or brainstorming session might be used to stimulate thinking. The key often lies in being able to encapsulate the company's real business in a sentence, or better a phrase, in the same way as producing a strapline to an advert. When doing this, it helps to consider how customers themselves might view the company, for example, as one providing positive solutions to their problem.

Brand values can be expressed visually through the logo design so it is always worthwhile researching the designs favoured by competitor brands with similar brand values. This does not mean copying, but identifying design elements that work and those that do not.

Initial conceptual design work should be through sketches and should not move to screen-based software too early.

A simple amount of visual information ensures that a logo may be read quickly. When designs become complex, there is too much visual clutter and it either takes longer for the brain to read it or it is simply ignored. Simple designs are more effective and often more elegant.

›› Tip

Work in black and white, using tints to achieve greys if required, as it helps to eliminate colour as an additional variable in early work. Logos should work without colour anyway to ensure good reproduction in faxed or black and white photocopied formats.

Use photocopies of concepts to examine the effect of scale.

Below It is best to work initially in sketch format, as with these logo sketches. Later, concepts can be cleaned up on screen.

Design development

Right It is not advised that designers modify existing logos unless it is specified in the brief. Here, however, the designer is using an existing logo and experimenting with changing the background to create a sense of movement.

» Tip
When tracing over a bitmap image, set the path to a contrasting colour in the tools palette before you start. This makes the traced path easier to see.

Photoshop is not the programme to use when developing graphics as the output is raster-based, causing pixelation when the image is enlarged. Both Freehand and Illustrator offer the designer vector graphical methods of developing concepts. If a logo includes elements of text or graphic devices, it is useful first to scan in a sketch of the proposed logo and import this into Freehand or Illustrator. The raster or bitmap image can be traced to convert it to a vector graphic.

If existing logos incorporate text, most will have used hand-drawn lettering to achieve distinctive styles. When making tweaks to existing logos or evolutionary changes, use the method above to scan and draw the text as a vector graphic. This allows perfect scaling, filling and, ultimately, printing at any size. It also allows keylines, drop shadows and other effects to be added, while maintaining vector accuracy. There are often many subtle variations to consider, so be prepared to produce a range of design options.

If a new logo is being developed and you wish to include text or lettering, you may want to create distinctive letterforms. There are specialist software programmes for typographic use but, where only a few letters are being created, both Illustrator and Freehand are suitable alternatives. Letters can be created from scratch but it is easier to select a typeface that approximates your requirements and modify it. Converting the appropriate letters to "paths" allows individual letterforms to be manipulated and a new letter design to emerge.

Having developed logo concepts it is advisable to carry out some checks to see how it will perform in every application. A web-based version, signage, letterheads, vehicles and uniform decoration can all be mocked-up using Photoshop to explore its suitability. It is, in any case, useful to have this visual reference to present to the client. Seeing a new logo in the context of its use makes a far more compelling argument than viewing an isolated logo on its own.

Creating brands, sub-brands and brand extensions

It is far more usual for packaging designers in commercial practice to be involved in the creation of sub-brands and brand extensions rather than the creation of a new brand. In most instances, clients bring an established brand to the designers as part of the design project. Some projects, however, and student projects in particular, call for the creation of a new brand. There are many professional branding companies that originate brands, using conventional name-generating sessions and specialist software to produce brand names. It is an expensive and time-consuming business, involving checks to find out if the proposed name has been used before in any of the countries where the new brand will appear. Students will probably have more modest requirements and can check if a name is already in use, in most instances, on-line with their national government trade-mark organizations.

Care needs to be taken in the choice of brand name to avoid offence. Even the experts get it wrong sometimes, adopting a brand name that translates badly in other languages. This also applies to any imagery (and colours, as described in Chapter Three) that accompanies the brand and might be inappropriate for other cultures.

Above left A European audience may associate this product with cat food—but this popular Brazilian product is in fact chocolate shaped as cats' tongues.

Above right There is always great sympathy for translations that do not work well. The choice of brand name has uneasy associations for this Japanese product.

Brand extensions

A brand extension is a distinctly new product marketed by an existing brand that may target a different market segment to the parent brand. This is becoming an increasingly common practice, with major brands moving into quite different markets for a variety of commercial reasons. Some cigarette brands, for example, have moved into branded clothing in an attempt to broaden their commercial base away from reliance on potentially declining cigarette sales. It is an obvious strategy for such companies to adopt. Others find that their customer base, and others outside it, are receptive to products in addition to those associated with the parent brand.

Right This vodka mixer is directed at the existing FCUK audience. Retaining the same market but broadening the offering is one way of gaining sales.

French Connection is a high-street, fashionable clothing company, operating in Europe, Canada, the USA and the Far East. In 1996, the company commissioned an advertising agency to revitalize their image and differentiate the brand from competitors. FCUK was the abbreviation used by the London office of French Connection. By transposing the letters, FCUK, into the vernacular English equivalent, a challenging and controversial campaign was created. It immediately found resonance with the young adult target audience as the company relentlessly pursued a campaign to exploit the word associations, using word combinations such as "Guaranteed FCUK" superimposed on models. Despite an advertising ban in New York and adverse criticism from scandalized members of the public, brand attention and product sales increased. Brand extensions were introduced, including toiletries (Eau de FCUK) and vodka-based drinks.

In this instance, the brand extensions, although removed from the company's core fashion business, were accepted by the public as just another example of FCUK's eccentric marketing stragegy. In order to work successfully, it is important that the purchasing public can understand the brand extension and believe in the rationale that underpins it. It is this believability factor that packaging designers may be required to incorporate into their designs. Care is needed, however, to use restraint, avoiding clichés or parodies of the parent brand, in case consumers become confused about the nature of the product.

It is also becoming common for brands to incorporate famous characters through negotiation with license holders. In effect, two brands are represented on the pack, usually with the character being displayed prominently to provide visual interest, particularly to children. Characters from cartoons, animated films, superheroes and TV/movie portrayals such as Harry Potter or James Bond are all used, together with the main brand, in appealing to niche market sectors.

In the main, brand extension decision makers lie within the marketing staff of the brands themselves. Some companies have formed separate organizations just to consider where the brand could go next. Most of the world's leading brands now have some form of think tank as part of their structure. These operate in

Above This is one of a range of Barbie toothpastes featuring Barbie wearing different outfits, designed to appeal to pre-teen girls. Colgate is using Barbie, a licensed character popular with this market sector, as a vehicle for increasing sales of toothpaste.

Left The extension from soap bar to facial cleanser in a pump dispenser, retaining the distinctive shape and colour of the soap, was misunderstood by purchasers who anticipated a liquid hand soap. Retaining the pack and re-launching the expected hand wash retrieved the situation. The shape is so distinctly based on the soap bar that it is not credible to use it for non-soap products.

Above Evian, with an established reputation for mineral water, have moved into a different market by using their water not for drinking, but as a cooling spray.

Below Skin care has traditionally been the realm of topical products, creams and lotions. Olay have interpreted their own strapline "Love the skin you are in" to mean inner health leading to outer beauty, and this has allowed the brand to extend comfortably into vitamins.

different ways, with some staffed by mixtures of artists, engineers, poets, musicians, designers and others, all seeking creativity through the interaction of different disciplines. Other organizations draw on outside consultancies or set up loose groups of creatives, including their advertising agency, packaging designers and product development staff.

This last team-based approach can be tasked to look at the problem in a number of ways. One, which was used by an advertising agency for a leading dairy company, involved the organization of an event where teams were given a sum of money each and allocated two hours to buy products into which the company could diversify. A different approach was adopted by a multinational company with a portfolio of soft drinks. They posed the question to a design team, "How will we drink in the future?" Both of these approaches to generate ideas rely on the creativity of individuals and their ability to share ideas as part of a team.

These examples show how teams can be encouraged to explore a wide range of ideas, often outside conventional parameters, but there is also a place for considering a more evolutionary approach, where packaging design skills can be highly relevant.

By first analysing the brand and attempting to assess what business the brand is in before posing the question "Where can it go now?", the resulting extensions will be more believable. This is the process that many of the petroleum brands have had to face and has resulted in an extension of the brand into the energy business, including solar, wind and hydrogen power. If this model were to be applied to Persil, a major laundry detergent brand, for example, we might speculate that actually the Persil brand is not just about laundry but has a broader market sector context that we might label "cleaning care for the family". This opens the door to new products such as easy-clean, spill-resistant fabric treatments, impregnated fabric cloths, spray cleaners, baby wipes, disinfectants etc.

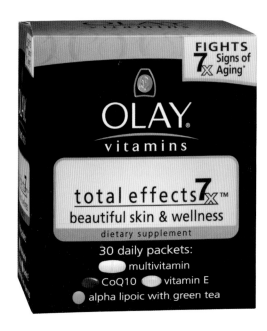

A common theme running through the rationale of the Evian and Olay brands concerns the relationship between inner health (water in the case of Evian; vitamins in the case of Olay) and outer skin care products. It would be unbelievable for Olay to extend the brand into water, as the Olay heritage is still established in oil-based creams; it would be less difficult, however, to imagine Evian extending into vitamins.

In designing packaging for brand extensions, therefore, it becomes important firstly to understand the link between parent brand and extension and secondly to be able to express this visually in a manner that will be believed by the target audience. It helps if an advertising strategy is in place and accessible to the packaging designer. Advertising agencies use both their experience and research to great effect in developing brand extension concepts.

» Tip
Consider adverts featuring the brand. Advertising agencies are adept at visual summaries of brand values.

Above and right Although initially there may be little connection between an off-road vehicle and an infant's stroller/pushchair, the common link is transport and, as the styling of the stroller suggests with its knobbly tyres, off-road transport for the family, both from the General Motors "Jeep" brand.

Above left and right From muscular military-derived vehicles to aftershave seems almost effeminate but, no doubt, the Hummer fragrance is sufficiently aggressive to win over anyone who dares to stand in its path.

Conclusion

Branding is a key activity within packaging design but, as this chapter has shown, a brand is much more than just a badge. Brand values form the character of a company and extend to every activity it undertakes, both internally and externally. This implies that there must be a consistent application of brand values across the spectrum of company activity. Externally, the brand is visibly represented to consumers through packaging and advertising, both key areas for creating brand values. Equally, consumer contact with the brand by phone or in person must also provide the same message. The most successful brands are those that understand the importance of emotional involvement between brand and audience. Branding is now moving into the creation of experiences for its devotees and, as packaging designers, the branding tasks ahead will increasingly be in this arena. Opening a gift pack or using a meal kit must become part of the brand experience, providing convenience, emotional involvement, intrigue and engagement.

Further reading and additional resource list

Robert Goldman and Stephen Papson, *Nike Culture*, Sage Publications 2004
In-depth description of the Nike philosophy and approach to business
John Grant, *The New Marketing Manifesto: The 12 Rules for Building Successful Brands in the 21st Century*, Texere 2000
Naomi Klein, *No Logo*, Flamingo 2000 One of the most influential books about brand culture
Martin Lindstrom and Patricia Seybold, *Brand Child*, Kogan Page 2004
Study of "tween" attitudes and knowledge of brands in 15 countries
John O'Shaughnessy and Nicholas O'Shaughnessy, *Persuasion in Advertising*, Routledge 2004
Jane Pavitt (ed.), *Brand.New*, V&A Publications 2000 Really useful explanation about branding today with good examples. If you don't read anything else, read this
Lisa Silver, *Logo Design that Works: Secrets of Successful Logo Design*, Rockport 2001

Reports on-line
www.interbrand.com
Interbrand, "Global Brands", July 2006
www.warc.com
C.F Hite and R.E Hite, "Reliance on Brand by Young Children", Journal of the Market Research Society, 1994

Websites
www.dragonbrands.com Assessment of brand communication via the Internet and seminars on brand issues
www.magazine.org/Advertising_and_PIB/Case_Studies Advertising case studies
www.superbrands.org/uk Branding case studies from around the world—a must-see reference for anyone interested in brands

Packaging obligations and responsibilities

Responsible design

Packaging designers have to be aware that, frequently, packaging is required to comply with legislation. This can be product specific, category specific, transport method specific and on national and international levels. In addition, packaging should not mislead consumers in any way but, instead, act positively as a means of communicating information, often important information about the product and how to use it safely. Most companies have a legal department that ensures packaging complies with the law.

Corporate social responsibility has now also become an essential activity within business. More than ever before, designers now need to be sensitive to social, moral and ethical issues to ensure that all sectors of the public are treated fairly and not stigmatized, misrepresented or otherwise offended. Without doubt, however, packaging has achieved its highest profile within the environmental debate, where it has attracted a largely negative consumer response.

Packaging designers, therefore, need to understand these issues and, while using design to promote the brand and sell products, use design responsibly. This chapter explains these obligations and responsibilities and provides guidance on how routinely to incorporate them into packaging design projects.

Changes in greenhouse gas emissions 1990–2004 (%)

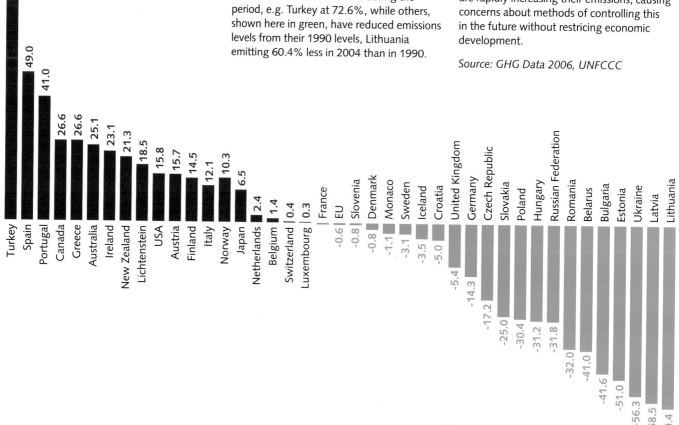

The chart uses data where greenhouse gas (GHG) emissions are presented in CO_2 equivalent terms. It can be seen from the pink lines that many countries have dramatically increased their GHG emissions during the period, e.g. Turkey at 72.6%, while others, shown here in green, have reduced emissions levels from their 1990 levels, Lithuania emitting 60.4% less in 2004 than in 1990.

While the chart indicates emission changes, it does not show actual tonnages produced. The USA leads the table in this respect but the developing economies of China and India are rapidly increasing their emissions, causing concerns about methods of controlling this in the future without restricting economic development.

Source: GHG Data 2006, UNFCCC

Environmental impact—fact and fiction

An increasingly frequent calendar of natural disasters, accompanied by unusual weather patterns around the globe, all serves to alert us to the reality of climate change. Scientific studies present evidence that, on the whole, supports the view that global warming is taking place due to atmospheric changes brought about directly by human actions. The predicted effects of global warming include rising sea levels, ocean current changes and extreme weather patterns, all of which will have catastrophic consequences for entire populations. In order to understand what impact packaging has on the environment it is necessary to familiarize ourselves with the issues. We, as designers, need to know the facts so that we can identify areas of design activity within which we can reduce the burden of packaging on the environment.

There is absolutely no doubt that the levels of carbon dioxide emissions, the major component of a basket of greenhouse gases that retain the solar heat reflected back from the earth, have increased. Despite the United Nations Kyoto Protocol agreement to limit carbon emissions, they continue to increase, unhindered by a carbon trading system that allows wealthier nations to spend their way out of their agreed targets rather than making fundamental measures to reduce emissions. The USA alone emits more greenhouse gases than any other nation yet the Bush administration has, so far, not become a signatory to the Kyoto Protocol.

Carbon dioxide is a naturally occurring gas produced, among other sources, by animal and plant respiration. Much of the additional, human-made emissions of the gas are the result of burning fossil fuels, used to create electricity and power transport. As with the production of most products, packaging requires energy inputs right from the extraction of raw materials, through every production process to final delivery, filling and eventual disposal. Much of this energy currently stems from fossil fuel use, resulting in carbon emissions.

Using energy from such sources as wind farms, tidal schemes and solar power would reduce carbon emissions but, in an increasingly energy-hungry culture across the globe, it is apparent that there are no sustainable ways of meeting projected energy demands. In addition to replacing fossil fuel energy with renewable energy, a massive sacrificial reduction in energy use is also required. This is evident when one considers that a giant wind farm may save 178,000 tonnes of carbon dioxide emissions per year while one return transatlantic flight between London and Miami, flying daily for a year, releases the equivalent of 520,000 tonnes of carbon dioxide: the environmental benefit of three giant wind farms.

The type of personal sacrifice made by changing habits and reducing flights is just one example of the action that individuals can take. There are many ways of saving energy in our homes, how we choose to use transport and in our consumer lifestyles. There is no doubt that a reduction in carbon emissions has become a global priority. Equally, this has highlighted packaging as being a contributor to gaseous emissions. It is a contributor, of course, but, as we shall see in the following section, its environmental impact is far less than the high visibility of packaging might suggest. It does also make some positive contributions by, for example, reducing product spoilage and maintaining product hygiene.

Greenhouse gases— the "basket" of six gases

CO_2	Carbon dioxide
CH_4	Methane
N_2O	Nitrous oxide
PFCs	Perfluorocarbons
HFCs	Hydrofluorocarbons
SF_6	Sulphur hexafluoride

Source: Greenhouse Gas Inventory Data, 2006, UNFCC

Global Warming Potential (GWP)

Designers should be aware that, under the Kyoto Protocol, six gases are measured. Some, such as nitrous oxide, have a GWP of 310. This effectively means that nitrous oxide retains six times more heat than carbon dioxide. As it is also emitted by burning fuel, it underlines the need for reducing movement of goods.

In packaging terms, environmental action might mean less product choice, with less pre-packed exotic food flown in at the expense of aircraft emissions and more locally sourced, fresh, seasonal produce. Although there appears to be public support for this more traditional, as well as greener, change, it is not yet clear what the impact of lack of choice will be. It can seem acceptable in theory but what practical consumer reaction will there be when bananas and other exotics become a rarity? While the environmental focus is currently on the emission of greenhouse gases, environmental performance extends beyond this and must also include considerations of the depletion of finite resources, seeking opportunities for reuse and improved methods of recycling and disposal.

Against such a complex and dramatic background, what is the contribution that packaging makes to environmental damage and how can designers influence its reduction?

Right Packaging waste is highly visible and should be a reminder of the environmental impact of consumer lifestyles. This photo, shot in 1994 in Jakarta, Indonesia, is typical of any landfill site or waste dump across the globe. It provides a compelling reason for packaging designers to reduce levels of packaging and packaging waste.

Domestic packaging waste and the packaging lifecycle

Unlike exhaust gases from cars or aircraft, packaging waste is highly visible as it blows through the streets of cities, collects under hedges in the countryside and pollutes the seas. Buying packaged products and, in consequence, trying to dispose of packaging responsibly is an everyday experience for most people, sometimes resulting in frustration at over-packed products or discarded packaging that refuses to compress into rubbish bins. These factors contribute to packaging being given a high profile in the environmental debate. Although the method of recording waste statistics varies from country to country, making it difficult to make accurate comparisons, packaging represents, on average, under 10% (by weight) of domestic waste, less than one might think, perhaps. The city of Stuttgart in Germany, for example, with a population of around half a million, reports packaging to be 4% of total household waste, while the Danish Environmental Protection Agency reports packaging to represent an average 6% of household waste across that country. (Elsewhere, many countries do not differentiate between commercial and household waste, and include automotive scrap, tyres, institutional waste and waste from street cleaning, park maintenance etc. in their waste statistics.) Non-packaging paper, in the form of newspapers, magazines, leaflets, household paperwork etc., is consistently the most significant contributor to domestic waste in most areas, for example, running at between 10% and 24% of domestic waste by weight across South East Asian countries. (The UN Environmental Programme, "State of Waste Management in South East Asia" considered municipal solid waste in Manila, Kuala Lumpur, Bangkok, Singapore and Jakarta, arriving at these figures for 2001.)

While packaging may present less of a waste problem than might be supposed, it is, nevertheless, significant enough to attract governmental intervention. The EU introduced the Packaging and Packaging Waste Directive 94/62/EC in 1994, amended by subsequent directives, that set specific targets for recovery and recycling that Member States are obliged to write into their national laws. Many other countries have adopted a similar approach to help reduce waste.

The chart on page 172 illustrates the typical lifecycle of packaging, sometimes referred to as a "cradle to grave" scenario. Considering energy-use first, we can see that at each stage, energy is required and that, between stages, transport is involved. The exact quantity of energy used not only depends upon the type of packaging materials involved and transport distances, but also the design of the packaging itself. Lightweight, space efficient packaging is likely to require less material and use transport more efficiently than heavier, bulkier pack designs. It becomes evident, even at this initial glance, that design has an environmental role to play and later in this section (see pp.174–180) we shall expand on what this might mean for designers. Although the energy requirements for specific packs can be calculated, this still does not provide a clear environmental profile or assessment of carbon emissions, as the sources of energy also require definition. Using hydro-electric power to provide energy for production processes rather than fossil fuels, for example, will not alter the quantity of manufacturing energy required to produce specific packaging materials and pack forms, but will provide the same energy with minimum carbon emissions. (Note that renewable energy sources such as hydro-electric power may also have a negative impact on the environment, such as, in this case, flooding previously inhabited areas to create reservoirs.) Substituting more energy-efficient forms of transport, however, such as barges rather than trucks, or ships rather than aircraft, makes real energy savings at each of the many transport operations within the packaging lifecycle.

The packaging lifecycle

As the chart indicates, the production of raw packaging materials to produce paper, plastics, glass and metals begins the process. Packaging manufacturers' processing plants produce finished packs or, in some instances, packaging materials that receive further processing at specialist packaging convertors. For example, corrugated board is often shipped to a corrugated case convertor, which then manufactures packs. It is typically at the product manufacturer that packs and products are combined before shipment to retailers, often via an intermediate warehouse. Consumers have the task of sorting discarded packaging, according to their local waste authority strategy, while discarded transit packaging at the retailers is normally recycled by contractors. Material for recycling may be processed by raw material suppliers or by packaging manufacturers, depending upon the material involved. Note that transport energy is used at each stage.

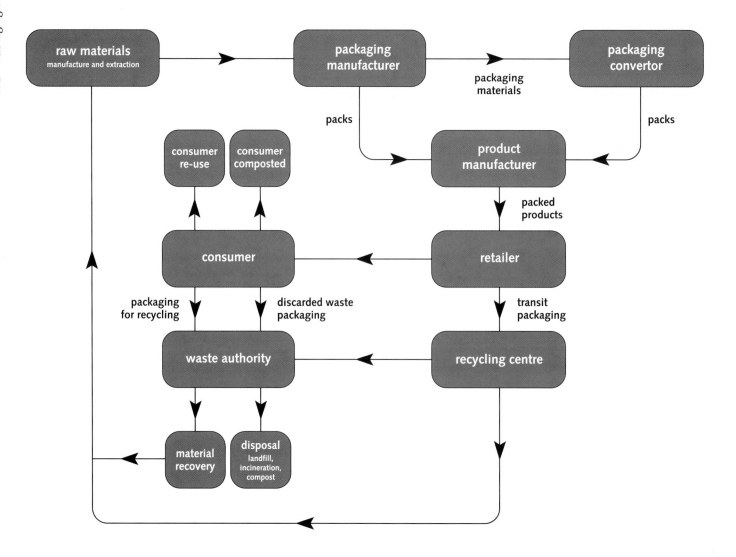

Energy and energy protection

One of the fundamental roles of packaging is to protect products against damage. This, frequently, means protection against physical damage in transit from accidental dropping and vibration. Some products, however, also require protection against extremes of temperature, UV light or infestation by insects and rodents, while others may require packaging that preserves the contents against degradation and prolongs the product's shelf life. By protecting the product, packaging is protecting the energy used to create the product. Put another way, the energy invested in the product is protected by the energy invested in the packaging.

A laptop computer manufactured in Malaysia, for example, represents an investment in the energy used to extract the raw materials, convert these materials into usable forms, produce components from them and assemble the finished product in the Malaysian production plant. As the laptops are sold around the globe, this product energy must be protected at every stage of distribution until the laptop is finally in the purchaser's hands. The packaging to do this task also has energy invested in it through its own production cycle but the packaging energy levels are likely to be much lower than that of the laptop. The small energy investment in packaging protects the large energy investment in the laptop. If the product is damaged during distribution, it is likely that both packaging and product energy inputs have been wasted. To compound matters, a replacement laptop would effectively double the energy investment. The packaging must, therefore, be designed to withstand the normal transit hazards during distribution, not just to provide customer satisfaction but also to preserve the energy used in creating the product.

The same argument applies to perishable goods and food, even where the major component of the product energy input results from agriculture or farming. The challenge for packaging designers is to minimize the energy used in packaging while still maintaining product integrity. In practice, achieving a zero percentage damage rate often indicates over-packing and, depending upon product type, a small percentage of damage is usually tolerated. Clearly, if the products are tins of beans, it may make economic and environmental sense to accept a low damage rate rather than increase packaging levels to eliminate damage. The opposite is the case when the product is expensive or energy hungry in production. A 1% damage rate on the laptop example discussed above may be economically difficult to accept. It is important to note here the apparent correlation between economic values and environmental values. Reducing energy also reduces costs. The pursuit of reduced financial costs may sometimes be the driving force that also results in environmental cost reductions. (For some product categories, however, the "rules" may be different. Packaging for kidney dialysis machines or aircraft navigation systems, for example, must ensure zero damage because of the product's critical nature and is not simply a matter of protecting their energy inputs or reducing packaging costs.)

Energy invested

Energy is invested in the following:
—Raw material extraction
—Conversion and processing
—Component manufacture
—Assembly
—Transport at all stages

Total energy invested

The energy invested in the product is much greater than the energy invested in the pack, yet the pack is protecting their combined energies during storage and distribution. Should the product be delivered to the consumer in a damaged condition, the energy invested is not only lost but involves additional energy in obtaining a replacement. As energy also has environmental implications, unless the packaging fulfils its task, there will be a greater negative effect on the environment.

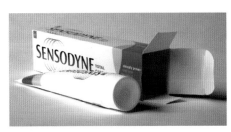

Above top Do we really need the outer carton on a tube of toothpaste? In Germany, environmental legislation forced manufacturers to rethink their packaging strategies, resulting in the elimination of secondary packaging on many products—including toothpaste cartons. As designers, we have to begin to think of ways to remove packaging while still maintaining product integrity.

Above This substantial clamshell-style blister pack is being used here for physical protection and not to extend shelf life. The cauliflower is trimmed, making the florets vulnerable to damage. As there is little consumer convenience, why not rely on nature's protection, instead of using excess packaging? Purchasers will still be able to see if the florets are fresh and unbruised.

Remove, reduce, reuse

Disposal of packaging remains a key focus of environmental attention and the starting point for designers considering environmental packaging performance. There are four strategies to consider, the first being removal of packaging.

Remove

In some instances, it is possible to remove secondary packaging without compromising the integrity of the primary pack. The example shown on the left illustrates the principle where the outer carton around a tube of toothpaste seems to be unnecessary. Toothpaste manufacturers, however, will point out that the exposed tube is prone to damage and that cartoned products become much more efficient to handle in production, storage and transport. The carton can also carry more information than a tube. This example merely demonstrates the problem that might be applied to a whole range of packaged products and could be solved by design thinking. Inevitably, there might be consequences for the way products are manufactured and/or displayed at point of sale but, to achieve environmental benefits, some fresh thinking might be necessary.

Many small products, such as razor-blade refills, drill bits, pens etc., are blister packed to deter theft rather than to protect the contents, so could such inexpensive products be sold unpacked from refillable dispensers, even if this meant a slightly higher risk of product "shrinkage" through theft? More expensive products could use the same method but be tagged with RFID (radio frequency identification tags), particularly as new RFID technology is dramatically lowering costs. Many expensive (and portable) products are already displayed in locked cabinets, requiring staff service to purchase them. These include perfumes, mobile phones and electronic devices, where the consumer invariably discards the packaging immediately after purchase. Could 12 MP3 players be delivered unpacked in a custom moulded returnable tray and then simply placed into a bag by a sales assistant at point of purchase, thereby eliminating the outer pack? Increasingly, designers will need to adopt this "systems" approach, considering not just the design of primary and secondary packaging but also the total involvement of the product with its surroundings. This will involve greater cooperation with other disciplines, from production through to retailing.

Reduce

If the pack cannot be eliminated, its environmental impact can be limited by reducing the number and weight of components. For example, the development of lightweight containers allows more containers to be carried per truck than before, reducing energy requirements during transport.

Reuse

Western society has become used to a throwaway mentality, discarding and replacing rather than keeping, repairing and reusing. In part, at least, this has resulted from the need to constantly update consumables to keep up with fashion, from rapidly changing technology that quickly makes some products obsolete and from economics where repair costs are in excess of replacement costs. Many products are also designed for disposal, such as disposable razors, nappies and pens, where convenience is also a factor. By contrast, in poorer economies or those facing economic restrictions (including, historically, a war-torn Europe during the 1940s) the culture of reuse is widespread. Here, ingenuity fashions discarded packaging into household objects, tools or art out of economic necessity rather than for environmental reasons.

Even in prosperous countries, some packaging is reused. Tins and jars make useful storage containers while plastic bottles can be cut to make scoops and, if the plastic is clear, cloches for young plants. It would be relatively easy to design a plastic bottle, for example, with clearly indicated areas for cutting so that, once its primary role is completed, it could be converted into a scoop. The prime use of such containers designed in this way may be to raise public awareness of recycling issues, as, in reality, the impact of this type of reusable packaging is limited. A scoop converted from a plastic bottle, for example, will probably be inefficient and not long-lasting because of its light construction (the result of the material grade to minimize the costs of packaging); its life as a scoop will merely serve to prolong the time before it is recycled. The only environmental gain is that it saves the materials and energy involved in creating a "proper" scoop. Yet, a "proper" scoop, robustly made for the purpose, might last for many years and never need replacing. Some supermarkets have used this argument to introduce robust shopping bags, a "bag-for-life", to stop the issue of millions of carrier bags to shoppers. (Lightweight, "disposable" bags are often thrown away or perform only one reuse function as rubbish containers.)

A more effective reuse strategy is to create closed loop systems. The classic example is the returnable glass beer bottle. These are bottles designed to be returned by the purchaser to the brewers, via retail outlets, for cleaning and reuse. Each bottle would typically expect to make ten trips before being recycled. (A similar system exists in the UK for milk, although it no longer extends across the nation as it once did.) There are positive environmental benefits with this strategy, despite additional handling, as there is a reduced energy requirement compared to producing one-trip bottles, providing that the system works at a local level. Transport costs for heavier reusable containers on longer journeys may offset any gains from the closed loop system.

Above Some pack forms, such as these three-piece steel cans, are robust and suitable for secondary use around the home. It can be argued, however, that this type of reuse only postpones the time of disposal, making few environmental gains. It would be more accurate to say that packaging has been appropriated for another use.

Closed loop system

The concept is simple but far more complex in practice. The environmental and financial cost of transporting containers to and from a filling plant have to be viable, requiring the total operation to be at a local level. The supermarket would have to find a method of collecting empty containers that does not involve additional burdens on space and labour. Glass bottles could probably survive ten trips before being replaced. Similar systems have long been established in many countries for milk, soft drinks and beer. With increasing penalties on packaging waste, this system is likely to be reintroduced in some form.

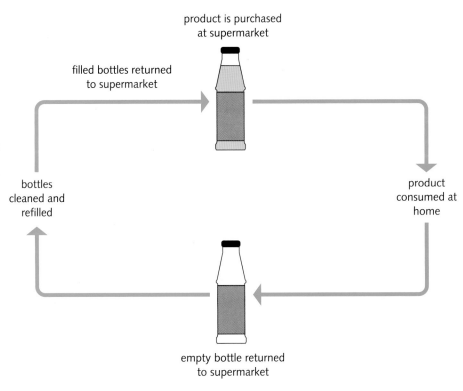

product is purchased
at supermarket

filled bottles returned
to supermarket

product
consumed at
home

bottles
cleaned and
refilled

empty bottle returned
to supermarket

Body Shop, in their chain of franchised stores, experimented with the same technique for plastic containers during the 1980s but found that uptake of the scheme by the public was disappointing and, ultimately, it was discontinued. Similar systems have been trialled with liquid laundry detergents in Germany where empty detergent bottles could be refilled in-store. As the environmental debate becomes more pressing, it is perhaps timely for packaging designers to once again consider closed loop systems.

Recycle

The German Packaging Ordinance was the first legislation that enabled consumers to remove secondary packaging in-store and oblige the retailer to accept it back for recycling or reuse. It was a bold initiative. Now, the "green dot" (Grüne Punkt) symbol of the organization, Duales System Deutschland, is frequently seen on packaging and, in Germany and now in many other European countries, guarantees collection and recovery of the marked packaging by doorstep collection. The symbol indicates that a fee has been paid by the company responsible for marketing the product.

As packaging designers, it is always worth considering if recycled materials can be specified for the production of packaging, which reduces the environmental pressure on material resources. In many instances this is not a problem, but there are three areas, applying to all material types, that designers need to consider.

Below The Grüne Punkt logo originated in Germany but is now widely used on packaging in many countries. It indicates that a fee has been paid for the recovery of packaging for reuse or recycling.

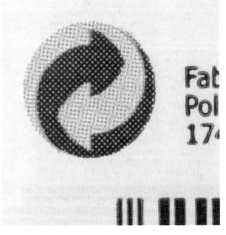

—For some applications using recycled materials is not always possible if there is any risk that products might be contaminated by the impurities contained in the recycled materials. This effectively excludes their use for food and drink, if there is likely to be direct contact between the product and recycled material. This can sometimes be overcome by selecting materials that use a thin lamination or coating of virgin material onto the bulk of the recycled component.

—When specifying recycled materials, anticipate increased costs. Recycled material is generally more expensive than virgin equivalents, because the recycling process is often costly. As with all commodities on the market, the price of recycled materials varies and, eventually, could reduce if stock levels rise or improved sorting methods are introduced.

—The physical and chemical properties of recycled material may not match that of virgin material and so may be unsuitable for some uses. To take paper as an example, it is the length of cellulose fibres in paper that provides strength. The recycling process chops and shortens these fibres, reducing paper quality in terms of physical properties and the ability to accept print. There comes a point at which repeated recycling cannot produce a paper of usable quality. By creating a "sandwich" of virgin and recycled paper, however, some of these problems can be overcome.

It is good environmental practice to use recycled materials where possible, but, when virgin materials are the only alternative, choose materials that are easy to recycle. The characteristics of some of the most widely used packaging materials are briefly outlined below.

Paper and board
Paper and board have become familiar waste products as part of household recycling schemes. Corrugated fibreboard manufacturers, in particular, have used recycled paper for many years to manufacture lower grade paper liners for corrugated board. Apart from the considerations discussed above, recycled paper and board is a well-established design option.

Glass
Glass can be recycled repeatedly without any decline in quality. Any special colours, other than brown or green, may create distinctive packaging but the colour causes contamination with other glass and, therefore, such colours are usually excluded from the recycling process. It can become a design decision, whether to opt for a better environmental solution and use clear glass or use colour for marketing reasons. Here, there may be a third option of using clear glass but with a coloured plastic shrink sleeve. This is typical of the situation that packaging designers often face—finding a compromise between environmental and marketing performance.

Metals
Metals, principally steel and aluminium, are both easy to segregate and recycle from domestic waste, particularly steel, which is magnetic. Both require large amounts of energy for reprocessing but this is offset by gains in avoiding mineral extraction and processing. Recycled metals regain their original properties without any deterioration in strength, quality or food contact problems.

Below The glass recycling logo requests that the container should be placed in a bottle bank. There are no legally imposed international symbols and some variations will be encountered.

Below bottom The steel recycling logo depicts a magnet, indicating the magnetic properties of steel and hinting at the recovery process that uses electromagnets to separate steel from other materials in domestic waste. Symbols such as these assist consumers in sorting waste for recycling.

Plastics

Plastics have received a bad press on environmental grounds but, as they provide such a useful and versatile spectrum of materials, the environmental emphasis tends to be on reuse and recycling rather than replacement. For this reason, rather than using a universal plastic recycling symbol, the major plastics are identified by polymer type. The chart detailing rigid plastics (see p.65), shows the symbols used. Plastics, in domestic waste, present recycling problems, not least because of their diverse range of polymers, copolymers, grades, colorants and additives. Segregating the different types and grades of plastic waste from domestic sources is difficult and expensive, although some automated segregation is achieved through water immersion, with different plastics having different flotation characteristics. Often, it is more economical to recover the energy content of the plastic materials through incineration. This action, however, ignores the fact that nearly all plastics are derived from mineral oil—a finite resource.

Composite materials using plastic

These are a further problem, especially where they are used as a coating on paper-based materials, or as a laminate with metals. A typical single-portion sauce sachet, for example, may use the following laminate structure:
—Layer 1 Polypropylene (reverse printed)
—Layer 2 Low density polyethylene (white opaque)
—Layer 3 Aluminium foil
—Layer 4 Low density polyethylene (extrusion coated)
—Layer 5 Low density polyethylene (film)

Although it is a superb and cost-effective method of maintaining vinegar-based sauces, this pack cannot be conventionally recycled because the layers cannot be separated. Most board-based aseptic (sterilized) drinks cartons contain even more layers, typically seven, again being unacceptable for recycling unless they are segregated and specially processed (although one process merely shreds them and uses the resulting material for thermal insulation). Technology is being developed that claims to solve the problem, but it will require either consumers or local authorities to segregate discarded drinks cartons into dedicated collection systems.

Faced with the task of designing packaging for a fruit juice, it becomes apparent that the aseptic carton option may be less environmentally viable than metal cans or glass jars. On the other hand, the carton may be more cost-effective, space efficient or acceptable to the target market than other options. The choice has implications for the brand and/or client and their stance on environmental performance in relation to marketing performance. Resolving issues like these will require designer/client meetings.

As with paper, processing techniques (often co-extrusion where two or more layers of material are extruded together) allow a thin layer of virgin material to be combined with recycled plastics, overcoming problems of recycled material coming into contact with food or drink. Recycled plastics from domestic waste are often used for non-packaging uses. For example, PET (Chapter Three has more details on PET) is a particularly useful material as it can be used to produce polyester fabrics. Mixed plastics, unsuitable for segregation, can also be heat treated to form waterproof boards and timber substitutes for agricultural and construction use.

Designing for recyclability

Designing packaging that is specifically aimed at being recycled requires some materials knowledge, structural design skills to ensure that components can be separated for recycling, a knowledge of the consumer base that the pack will be directed at and their needs and, finally, a way of clearly indicating how to recycle the pack. From the materials information discussed above, some points to address will already be fairly evident. Any mixed materials will require consumers to separate them, so pack designs should make this both obvious and easy. Try out your concepts yourself and test them on others. No tools should be required to segregate packaging—if they are needed, the pack has failed. If possible, avoid plastic overwraps. A shrink-wrapped CD, for example, may be a cost-effective and secure pack, but it causes injuries as consumers attack the impregnable film with sharp implements, plus the film cannot be recycled efficiently. A better design solution might be a paper band, or to reconsider the whole concept and just download from the Internet. We have to be open in considering ways in which packaging can be removed entirely. It will not prejudice our opportunity to work as packaging designers but simply enhance our standing if we can provide a better environmental solution for presenting products.

Biodegradable and compostable packaging

Some plastics have been designed to be biodegradable—to break down in the soil or under UV light. It seems to be a reasonable solution but these materials are, in effect, a network of plastic and (frequently) starch molecules. The starch or other active component breaks down, leaving plastic particles intact. The concern is that small plastic particles may find their way into soil and water systems causing long-term pollution. Before choosing the biodegradable option, designers need to become aware of the possible drawbacks.

Typically, compostable packaging is made from polylacticacid (PLA), using corn or other vegetable starch as a raw material. In landfill conditions, however, where air is excluded, these materials produce methane gas—a contributor to global warming. Compostable materials, therefore, need to be segregated and composted by consumers or local authorities. Unfortunately, little information is given to the consumer about this and it is difficult to identify the biodegradable material, particularly as it is often used to replace plastic trays, which it resembles. (PLA is often transparent and looks like plastic.) Compostable containers do carry the symbol shown above but there appears to be little public understanding or knowledge of it.

Before specifying biodegradable or compostable packaging, therefore, check the disposal system(s) to which it may be subjected. It is also worthwhile finding out how it is made. One starch-based tray, for example, proclaimed by a UK supermarket as being "eco-friendly", was manufactured from genetically modified (GM) potatoes. Consumers concerned about environmental issues are

» **Tip**
When designing packs that use both plastic and non-plastic components, you should try to make it easy for consumers to separate the materials. For blister packs, avoid sealing the plastic blisters to board. Instead, use sliding blisters or "clamshell" blister designs with card or paper inserts. For plastic-based packaging, try to design containers constructed from simple single polymers, rather than co-extrusions of different materials or mixtures of polymers. Providing these are identified with the appropriate polymer symbol, they are at least capable of then being segregated.

» **Tip**
The packaging of consumer durables also requires an environmental eye. All too often we are faced with the disposal of expanded plastics, corrugated board and plastic films in some abundance. Expanded polystyrene can be effectively recycled but many local authority recycling schemes exclude it. Consider the use of moulded pulp as an alternative or, by clever design, suspending fragile goods using corrugated fibreboard fittings which are easier to recycle.

Above The German DIN (German Institute for Standardization) organization has long provided technical standards for industry that are widely accepted around the world. The DIN compostable standard has been incorporated into EU packaging legislation. The symbol shown here is applied to products and packaging meeting the specified test regime. For packaging applications the symbol should be set within a solid hexagon but, in practice, perhaps because it is often embossed, the hexagon frequently does not appear.

likely to also be concerned about the potential dangers associated with GM crops, their potential for contaminating native species and their unproven effects on humans and animals. Most European countries have banned GM crops but, in the UK, trials have been conducted. These have been met with vigorous public protests leading to retailers refusing to stock any GM products. Despite public protests and media fears about "Frankenstein foods", the UK government continues to dabble in further trials. Clearly there would be an incompatibility between packaging manufactured from GM products and any environmental benefits to be gained through composting.

To summarize, packaging, like all human activity, can have a negative impact on the environment. There are no truly "environmentally friendly" packaging options, only some options that are less environmentally antagonistic than others. Because of our interaction with packaging as consumers, it has assumed a higher profile within the environmental debate than, perhaps, is deserved. It is often overlooked that packaging also contributes positively to our lives by preserving products, improving hygiene and providing choice, whether this is for medical products, food or drinks. As a packaging designer, however, it is important to exercise design judgement in a way that meets client requirements or the brief but is also sensitive to the environment. Always, for example, consider if packaging is really needed and find solutions for removing it. If packaging is required, it is the designer's job to see if the level of packaging can be reduced while still containing and protecting the contents, providing consumer information and promoting product and brand. Consider, also, using both recycled materials and designing the pack to be easy to recycle.

Finally, be aware that claims of environmental superiority are usually ill-founded since, as this chapter has indicated, the issues are so complex that such claims are difficult to substantiate. In addition, there may be legal challenges. The International Standards Organization produced ISO:14021 in 1999 that defines what environmental claims may be made and how they must be substantiated. Designers please note that natural objects such as trees, flowers, butterflies or globes may not be featured in a symbolic way on the pack unless there is a direct (and explained) link between product, object and the environmental benefit being claimed.

Issues of age, gender, sexuality and ethnicity

Attitudes to these issues are constantly changing but at different rates and with different outcomes in different cultures. As designers, we must ensure that we understand the underlying sensitivities of the target audiences we are addressing and avoid visual clichés, offence and consequent brand damage through the use of inappropriate imagery, colours and text. This is not an optional extra but a serious design obligation. Environmental issues tend, on the whole, to unite peoples, while the issues in question here are largely divisive, alienating sectors of our communities.

Age

Many products are specifically directed at older age groups, including many health, mind and body rejuvenating treatments that claim, in one way or another, to turn the clock back. It has not escaped the notice of marketing gurus that older people are also those, generally, with a higher disposable income than their younger counterparts. Age now represents a lucrative and growing market.

By 2020, many countries will experience a population change, where more than half the adults will be over 50 years of age. While this raises serious social issues concerning housing, health care and pension provision, we also have to remember that this group will include a diversity of students, chief executives, judges, marathon runners and lovers. Within the 50+ market, there are some important sectors, with characteristics relating more to ability than to age: fit and active | elderly and infirm | those in care.

Working with a team of design students in the UK, mostly in their late teens and early twenties, on a project that concerned a range of aromatherapy products directed mainly at 50+ women, revealed some initial misconceptions about the nature of the market. They assumed the target market would have the following characteristics: poor eyesight | stiff joints, particularly fingers and knees | wrinkly skin | no grasp of technology | slow and careful drivers | no interest in fashion | social life consisting of coffee mornings, library visits and gardening | loneliness | deafness | poor speech | dribbling | incontinence.

While it is undeniable that the ravages of time eventually affect us all, most students did not associate the "fit and active" sector as being in the target group and, in consequence, missed some of the more interesting features of ageing, as shown on p.182.

Interestingly, none of the students mentioned sex, maybe presuming that it is the perogative of the young, although, when quizzed on the subject, none felt confident about predicting a personal cut-off date.

The student market analysis was expressed in fairly unimaginative graphics. There were happy, smiling elderly folk on rocking chairs and in gardens, waggy-tailed retrievers and other clichéd, age-related images. Alternatively, there were images of 50-year-olds, impossibly elegant and sophisticated, representing those that bore their age well. Nothing had much edge to it. Clearly, the market had failed to excite them, perhaps because they had little personal experience of it.

Below Wine importers and merchants frequently use unusual labels to target specific niche audiences. There are many examples where unusual graphics, heat-sensitive inks or quirky names have been used, as a quick Google search under wine labels will reveal. Here, the label of this French beer targets those enjoying the fun of the carnival. Rather than being an everyday beer, it is intended for a special occasion.

Aged 50+ group

As the chart shows, niche audiences must be targeted with care. Here, the over-50s group is shown to include those enjoying wealth and health. The same broad sector would also include those in poor health and impoverished. We need, as designers, to be very clear about defining market sectors where age is an issue, avoiding the use of inappropriate clichés and also not being afraid to consider introducing humour.

> Highest proportion of Porsche and BMW cars are bought by this group

> Highest proportion of Harley Davidson motorcycle riders are 50+ males

> Affluent members of this group are frequent travellers abroad

> Over-50s attend more live music events than those under 30

> They are the most active group in the stock market and Internet trading

> They own 80% of national wealth

Once, however, the target market was investigated more carefully and the full scope had been understood, the work changed dramatically. Humour was introduced, wrinkles celebrated and sex made a subtle entrance with couples enjoying a bath together. The pack designs depicted the fun, liveliness and sensuality that the products could help induce, celebrating age rather than regretting it.

Unfortunately, age does inevitably bring with it both physical and mental problems and we may be unfortunate enough to progress from fit and active pensioners to those less mobile and less able to use the assets of youth. Packaging has to cater for this group too, not sidelining them but including them in the overall plan. Much has been written about inclusive design, making products accessible to all through considered packaging design. It is an area that packaging designers should become familiar with, partly as a discipline to consider other groups in society, and partly to explore how this growing market sector can be addressed. The "Oxo Good Grips" range of products illustrates the approach by producing products across markets but which address the manipulation problems of elderly people. Packaging should follow this example.

Right Humour has been used to portray that these "Naked chips" are not "dressed" in salt. The image of naked women here is inoffensive to most but designers have to be very sensitive in their selection of imagery when portraying nakedness or attempting to be humorous.

Gender

It is part of the packaging designer's job to design packs that appeal to specific markets, which, frequently, include those defined by gender. There can hardly be a more contentious area of design than this one, involving the interpretation of shapes, pack sizes, textures, colours, typography and graphic devices. Clearly, there are physical differences in strength and size between males and females that may determine pack configuration from the outset. A little research into ergonomic data will soon reveal information regarding differences such as average hand-span measurements or weight-carrying ability, together with any other physical attributes that may be relevant to particular packaging studies. The real problems lie, not with physical differences, but within social codes and conventions. It is easy to fall into the trap of producing stereotypical designs that are offensive to segments of society and so we, as designers, have to be aware of what these conventions may be within the society for which we are designing.

Below The Dove campaign "Real Beauty", devised by ad agency Ogilvy & Mather, featured women aged between twenty-two and ninety-six. Here, the advert breaks with the dominant trend of showing super-slim models, and instead features ordinary women with real figures. Fashion photographer Rankin chose deceptively simple shots to bring out the personality of the women. Following this campaign, Dove sales increased by 700%.

curvy thighs, bigger bums, rounder stomachs.
What better way to test our firming range?

There's not much point in testing a new firming lotion on size-eight supermodel thighs, is there? That's why Dove's Firming range was tested on ordinary women with real lives to live – and real, curvy thighs to firm. After using Dove's nourishing and effective combination of moisturisers and seaweed extracts, we asked if they'd go in front of the camera. What better way to show how they felt about the unretouched, unairbrushed results?

new Dove
Firming Range
Gel Cream · Body Wash · Lotion

There are many gendered objects that are manifestations of a previous generation of cultural values, which, in themselves, have little relevance today but, nevertheless, still remain in place. For example, there seems to be little logical explanation for maintaining male and female versions of hair dryers, umbrellas or the right/left button convention on clothing. Nor can there be much medical evidence to support the suggestion that men and women need different handkerchief sizes, yet we see larger "mansize" packs of tissues. Designers are often in a position to challenge such conventions when they arise during a project, either through addressing questions to the client or by designing packs that tackle the issues. In the instance of tissues, perhaps the larger tissue size could be retained (or a new size proposed) but the pack designed to appeal to both men and women. There is a parallel here with products that are designed to be unisex, such as the eau de toilette CK One, by Calvin Klein.

Products in the laundry detergent sector also conform to stereotypical perceptions of the male/female share of work in the home. Such products employ graphics that show them to be directed at women. Many packs feature young children and mothers, the pack confirming the advertising promise of cleanliness,

Below left and right The Venus razor, produced specifically for women, features packaging with soft graphics and pastel shades. The Venus brand is prominent, playing down any masculine associations with the manufacturer, Gillette. Biotherm is another product for women that uses colours selected from the "feminine" spectrum.

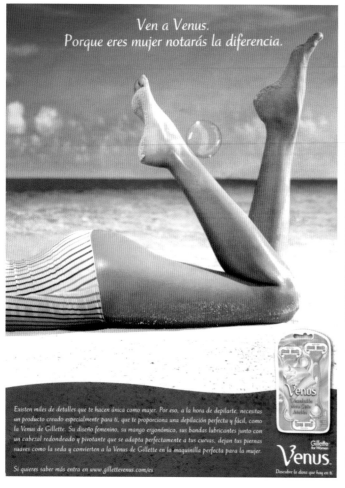

care for the welfare of children and, therefore by implication, confirmation of the mother's love for her children obtained at the price of the product. Fathers who also care for the family and who may also wash clothes are not featured on the packs. This is still perceived by the manufacturers as a female market, not even a dual-parent market. This creates opportunities, in design terms, to design for two male markets: firstly, to consider how fathers can be engaged in the process; and, secondly, how mainly young independent men living on their own can be persuaded to buy a brand directed at them. Both these sectors have little knowledge of washing and remain unengaged with detergents, preferring to ignore colour segregation of fabrics, variable temperatures and other programming features. Despite multi-programming machine capabilities, these cohorts are most likely to simply choose one setting for everything. How can packs be designed to appeal to these audiences in order to encourage male engagement with the laundry task?

A UK-based student project looking at the young, independent male market sector yielded some interesting results. They rapidly identified the need to provide some basic instruction but also to simplify the process. Most concepts also required the detergents to be reformulated into one general type suitable for all colours and fabrics. One concept, that demonstrates the possibilities, used a circular pack where tablets of detergent could be pressed out, making it easy to use and removing the need for measuring. The graphics incorporated a cartoon style instruction panel, designed to give an edgy, urban feel to the product. It was right for the sector. With European sales of laundry detergents now static due to market saturation of washing machines, and low birth rates reducing the need for purchase, laundry brands are desperate for innovation that might increase brand share. The opportunity exists for a gendered pack.

Sexuality

Sexual imagery has been used for many years in advertising to demand attention and persuade us to purchase products. Some imagery has been explicit or, at least, as explicit as the cultural taboos of the time would allow. Such imagery is almost exclusively of women and has been used to promote a diverse range of products and brands from cosmetics and toiletries, alcoholic drinks, cars, chocolate and pretty much everything in between, to both male and female markets. The adverts invariably offer the spectator a dream of some future pleasure.

Other techniques have been more subliminal, suggesting sexual associations through hidden codes incorporated into the advert.

Packaging imagery, however, has not generally followed this route and usually if sex is a product attribute, as it might be on women's underwear and hosiery packs, it simply illustrates the product as it is meant to be, an accessory that will make a woman feel confident of her sexuality.

Sexual references using shape have often been deliberately used in packaging to create containers, particularly for both men's and women's toiletry products. Occasionally some design work may accidentally include features that could be open to sexual interpretation. While this can be highly amusing to examiners and tutors, it is possibly less so to clients. It is worthwhile reviewing structural design work prior to presenting it to avoid any subsequent embarrassment.

Above Yorkie is a well-established brand and began to develop its male target market by featuring truck drivers in its TV ads. The ad campaigns and joke symbol, prohibiting women, have largely been accepted as humorous. The product format shown here is new, moving away from the chocolate bar configuration—aimed, perhaps, at boys' lunchboxes rather than working men. Interestingly, the "not for girls" message encourages female consumers who want to defy the strapline.

» Tip
What might seem to be humorous or cheeky to the designer might be offensive to others. If there is any element of sexual imagery in a design, seek the opinion of colleagues and those within the target audience.

Ethnicity

In designing packaging that contains images or illustrations of people, decisions have to be made regarding the depiction of skin colour, race, ethnicity and their role in the image. You may wish to make a positive statement about ethnicity, or to make no particular reference at all, but a definite decision must be made and reviewed. Not to do so can lead to problems. For example, a pack for Fairtrade coffee showed black African workers with their baskets of beans being checked by

Above This type of racial imagery should be avoided, even if the company has a historical precedent for using it. Happily, it is now rare for such blatant images to be used but care still needs to be taken to avoid stigmatizing any particular sectors of society.

a white man with a clip board. Unhappily, this is probably an accurate reflection of reality but it undermined the value of Fairtrade.

It is often difficult, in a multicultural society, to use images that adequately represent the population. In the UK, nearly all detergent products show middle-class white mothers with white children. It would be unrealistic to suggest that one image should contain representatives from every ethnic group but it would be refreshing to see a wider range of people on packaging.

Products that are specific to ethnic characteristics, for example, shampoos and cosmetics for the Afro-Caribbean market sector, would be expected to reflect their market. The difficulty, here, when designing packaging, may be getting an image that is not a racial stereotype. Scottish products do not always need to be represented by a kilted warrior nor do Australian products require hats with corks. It is fine to make historical references in designs but take care to avoid clichés.

Working with all of the cultural issues described in this section requires sensitivity and it is always useful to discuss any design proposals with colleagues, particularly if their background or knowledge-base corresponds with that of the target audience. Many clients may be unaware of the changes in viewpoint taking place in society that make previously-accepted practice offensive. This is particularly important when packs cross borders into other states with differing cultures or where companies expand their activities. For example, a packaging company in the Czech Republic featured provocatively posed female models in its literature and on its website but were persuaded by the designer that this would be inappropriate for a company with serious ambitions for pan-European expansion. The designer's role, in instances like this, is to work alongside the client in finding out what design solutions are appropriate for the market, using client knowledge and also finding sources of local knowledge about the cultural issues involved.

Corporate responsibility

Successful brands have become the most valuable asset of many companies, representing, in terms of revenue and goodwill, a monetary value way in excess of the company's financial assets. The problem with high-profile brands is that they are vulnerable, indeed the higher the brand profile the more vulnerable they become. Designers work hard to ensure that the brand is seen and subsequently bought. This also means, however, that when the brand becomes the subject of

Home grown food.
For cattle.

George believes in quality.

That's why he not only rears cattle,
he raises the food they eat too.

On his Wiltshire farm he grows wheat, maize, barley
and grass, stirs in minerals and serves it to his herd
all year round. Putting home grown goodness into his
cattle helps George deliver quality British beef.

Overall, we use 16,000 beef farmers and make
our hamburgers from 100% beef. M

2 medium
Extra Value Meals
for £3.99.
Present voucher before placing order.

2 cheeseburgers
for 99p.
Say cheese again!
Present voucher before placing order.

Left Following criticism, McDonald's demonstrated their purchasing policy of buying fresh produce from approved farms. This campaign was accompanied by TV advertising reinforcing the company commitment to fresh produce and menu changes that included salads and healthy-eating options. Although the fresh and healthy approach has increased choice, particularly for families, McDonald's is still associated with its core offering of fries and burgers.

any negative press, it is easily identifiable. Non-governmental organizations, consumer organizations, pressure groups, web blogs and the power of electronic communications make it possible for the media to inform brand purchasers around the world of any company wrongdoings, resulting in action such as a consumer boycott of the brand. The effects can be instant and devastating. Morgan Spurlock, in his film *Supersize Me*, chronicled his decline in health when eating McDonald's meals for 30 days. This had immediate financial implications for McDonald's, which responded by a programme of menu simplification, eliminating super-size meals and introducing healthier options.

Many companies have suffered in similar ways, some through revelations of worker exploitation, others through environmental damage, poor animal husbandry, inadequate hygiene, social injustice, disregard for local communities and so on. The list is a long one where profit has come before ethical behaviour. In response, the big brands have introduced "corporate social responsibility" (CSR) departments, charged with guiding ethical behaviour and sustainability issues throughout their organizations. The cynical view is that some brands are merely cranking up the PR machine, with corporate responsibility and accountability being a veneer to appeal to shareholders and consumers, while underneath the company is concerned with risk management, damage limitation and in using CSR to generate additional profit.

As discussed earlier in this book, the brand and its values should penetrate every aspect of company behaviour if it is to succeed and, to embrace corporate responsibility, the brand must also embrace the ethics and values for which it stands. Only then can it express those views to its major stakeholders and be believed. The world's fastest growing brands do this well partly through flat management structures, where the older multi-layered management pyramid no longer exists, and through building cult-like followings. Apple and Harley Davidson, for example, have cultivated a brand-loyal consumer base, while Google, Amazon and eBay have created vast communities around their brands. These newer companies encourage an ethical dimension flowing through their operations that many older brands, with complex management structures, are struggling to emulate.

Packaging design is not generally represented in the company boardroom so does not have a strong voice within company strategies but, nevertheless, its role as a communication channel between brand and consumer makes it an important part of the debate. There are specific CSR issues where packaging is involved:
—Deception *size, contents, product claims, imagery*
—Environmental performance and superiority
—Confusing messages *too much copy or too small type sizes*
—Cultural representation *Fairtrade, ethnic origins*

Deception

Packaging has always been the subject of weights and measures legislation, among other legal obligations. While CSR policies are largely perceived as being in addition to legal requirements, company reputation and customer satisfaction are clearly linked. Consumers finding fault with products are not particularly interested in distinguishing between CSR and legal non-compliance; the perception is simply that it is the brand that is at fault. From time to time, successful legal action has taken place against brands and companies marketing products that are deceptive, appearing to offer more than they actually do. Jars that contain inserts reducing the measurable amount of their contents, bottles that are tall but very flat and excessive outer packaging masking inner contents are all examples of deceptive containers. Whereas a small regional claim would pass unnoticed, now negative media interest can influence corporate profitability.

These are areas where designers can take direct action to avoid deception by exercising a responsible design approach, guided by common sense. More difficult for the designer, however, are apparently spurious claims made by clients. Product claims such as "Destroys the molecules that cause smells" may have no grounding in science or truth. Similarly, cosmetic products making claims of anti-wrinkle, anti-ageing properties may also be stretching credibility. If the client insists that copy featuring such information appears on the pack, what does the designer do? There is no clear answer, but remember that designers also have social responsibility, with accompanying legal implications.

Below Only when the lid on this jar is opened does it become evident that the contents occupy only a fraction of the apparent volume.

Environmental performance and superiority

Environmental issues and sustainability are keystone policies within any corporate social responsibility strategy. Packaging itself, as discussed earlier in this chapter, is the subject of environmental criticism and, to any CSR policy group, an area of concern. Responsible companies should, from the top down, be reviewing their strategy on packaging, aiming to reduce negative environmental impact. This would include a review of energy consumption, renewable resources, waste reduction and other environmental and sustainability issues. It is only recently, compelled by the marketing value of appearing to be green, that company executives have begun to react and implement real environmental reviews. What should be resisted, however, are claims of environmental superiority by CSR groups used for PR purposes. Inevitably with such a complex issue, they will be proved to be wrong. (See p.169 on the environment.)

Instructions:

Apply preparation at temples, behind ears, nape of neck, underarms, inner elbow creases, behind knees, base of backbone and top of pubic bone, while confidently repeating until self entranced, "I feel sexy, I am sexy. I feel so sexy. I feel so damn sexy. I am *so* damn sexy!"

Scent for
Secret Places
[damn
sexy mix]

Warning and Disclaimer:

This preparation comprises a sensually activated potion which when applied correctly may induce unpredictable behavioural responses from anyone in your intimate vicinity including yourself. Neither Barefoot Doctor, nor anyone involved in the production, distribution or sale of this preparation will be held responsible for any radical alterations to your personal sphere of action which may result. Always apply care.

www.barefootdoctorglobal.com

Confusing messages

Packs are required by law, in many product areas, to carry information about contents, hazard warnings, allergies and safety procedures so that it sometimes becomes difficult also to accommodate instructional and promotional text at readable levels. In addition to the legal responsibilities, corporate responsibilities extend to ensuring that consumers are adequately informed. Those designers who are guilty of using small type sizes for aesthetic reasons need to be aware that people reading them may not have perfect sight. Type size, font, colour, kerning and leading require careful selection to ease the access to information by consumers. Designers should not become too carried away by the desire for aesthetic perfection.

Where practical considerations seem to demand small type, for example, where the container size is too small to accommodate the text requirements, it is worth considering a fix-a-form label, which adheres to the container but opens out in a series of "pages".

The necessity of avoiding small type also poses problems in some countries that have dual (or more) languages and, therefore, it is often a legal obligation, as well as a social necessity, to incorporate more than one language on the pack. The problem also occurs when multilingual packaging is adopted to reduce packaging costs, allowing economies of scale by using the same pack for different countries. In principle, this is acceptable, but consumers have the right to read packaging in a language they can understand and should not have to search the pack in order to find their language from a selection of eight or more. There are techniques to assist in these circumstances:

—What are the implications for using, say, eight different packs (it may just be a black printing plate change)?

—Can a generic pack be overprinted/overlabelled?

—Can language groups be compiled, say of three or four languages, accommodating adjacent distribution areas?

—What are the stock control and purchasing implications of the above?

This is frequently a difficult area, sometimes complicated by company protocol in selecting language combinations for multilingual packs. Even the language order can be a problem, alphabetical order being different for different languages, for example Germany translates as Deutschland and Almania, among others. Once market groupings are agreed for countries, perhaps a solution to the language order might be to order them according to sales revenue per country.

Opposite The instructions on this pack use fashionably small type in line with the playful nature of the product and a design conscious target audience. Reversing out small sized type, however, can cause letters to fill, as can be seen on the red panel, reducing legibility.

Below Multilingual packaging is usually used for economies of scale but it can be overdone. Here, the languages have been well identified and ordered but probably represent the limit for this size of pack.

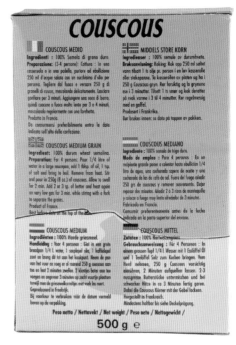

Above It is becoming increasingly common to find both organic and fairtrade symbols on packs, as illustrated by the quinoa pack shown here.

Above right All three tinned products highlight their organic nature in large type. In the case of Heinz, however, the text for "organic" remains relatively small, while the distinctive Heinz "tombstone" uses a green fill to differentiate the organic product from its non-organic version.

Ethical trading

A cornerstone of many corporate responsibility strategies is to demonstrate their commitment to ensuring fair conditions for their suppliers in countries where the economy is depressed. This means paying workers a reasonable wage, caring for employee welfare, maintaining good working conditions and respecting the environment. Shamefully, many Western corporations and brands have exploited their suppliers to achieve greater profit, leaving communities impoverished but dependent on the work. The effect was to keep prices low in the West but at huge social, economic and political costs in other areas of the world. Fairtrade, an international non-profit organization, aimed to change that, and has moved from being a fringe operation in the 1980s to a mainstream organization operating in some 20 countries.

Previous sections have referred to the depiction of ethnicity and it is an issue with Fairtrade products and other products that wish to express their ethnic origins. Suffice it to say, when working on pack designs where visual reference is being made to other cultures, care must be exercised to ensure that their dignity as co-workers in a Fairtrade project is respected.

Organic food

There has been a steady increase in the purchase of organic food, moving it from being a specialist niche market to becoming part of the mainstream shopping experience. Nevertheless, the graphic presentation of organic food is still being developed, reflecting its greater popularity and marking a move away from speciality food. Many designs still incorporate the word "organic" in a flowing style, reflecting natural origins. Now, however, this is beginning to be challenged as complete ranges of supermarket own-label food become united under organic sub-brands.

The subject of incompatibility between pack form and organic contents has been mentioned before but it is of considerable importance both to the sale of organic produce and to the benefit of the environment. There are still packaging materials being used that are not entirely satisfactory, such as the examples shown here. Packaging manufacturers, however, are aware of these problems and are striving to solve them.

It is tempting for companies to demonstrate environmental performance by incorporating logos underpinning their environmental claims. There is a danger, however, that if too many such logos appear, the public may become cynical about their value. National schemes may have to be replaced by internationally agreed alternatives to replace diverse logos with a more unified and authoritative approach. As organic products find widespread consumer acceptance, these symbols will migrate to the rear panels of the pack.

Above The Soil Association is just one organization that licences companies to use its symbol, shown here. The food producer has to comply with strict standards but then gains widespread market acceptance by consumers looking for organic produce.

Left Individual countries have developed their own organic labelling standards. Within Europe, all organic certification is to agreed EU standards although symbols vary between member states. This French organic soup majors on the "bio" symbol to communicate its organic origins, with a more formal certification appearing below.

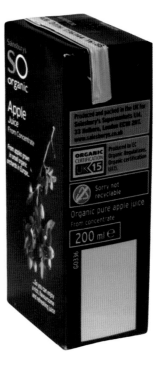

Above It seems incongruous to combine organic food with packaging that cannot be recycled. In this example of a juice carton, the UK-based multiple grocery company, Sainsbury's, are honest enough to apologize for this while still persisting with the pack.

Conclusion

Packaging designers have a responsibility and, sometimes, a legal obligation, to design packaging that is safe, effective, not misleading, accurately informative, environmentally sound and inoffensive to consumers. That may seem like a formidable list but each of these areas requires consideration to ensure that packaging responsibilities are properly discharged. Fortunately, some companies have their own legal team to advise on these matters but usually only at the artwork sign-off stage, which is too late in most design studies. Designers can, perhaps, become so involved with the task of meeting a brief that important issues, such as those discussed here, may be overlooked. It is important to ensure that for each project all the obligations and responsibilities of packaging design are considered.

Further reading and additional resource list

Joshua Berger, *XXX: The Power of Sex in Contemporary Design*, Rockport 2003
Pat Kirkham, *The Gendered Object*, Manchester University Press 1996
> Some interesting examples and case studies

Reports on-line

www.mintel.com
> Mintel (March 2005), "British Lifestyles"

www.dti.gov.uk
> Department of Trade and Industry (2003)
> "Sustainability and Business Competitiveness", on-line resource

www.environment-agency.gov.uk
> Environment Agency (2005), "Greenhouse Gas Emissions—Background and Data"

Websites

www.monbiot.com UK environmental activist

www.euractiv.com EU news and policy

www.europa.eu.int EU documents and information.
> Check out the packaging legislation

www.foe.co.uk Friends of the Earth, environmental group

www.unep.org United Nations Environmental Programme

www.sasems.port.se Scandinavian airlines emission calculator. Lets you calculate all emissions for different aircraft and condition for any specified international flight

www.ucsaua.org Concerned scientific community in USA has collated this database of global warming statistics

www.gruener-punkt.de German Duales System—environmental leader in Europe

www.ttura.com Recycled glass used as flooring

Finding your role VIII

First steps

Having now equipped yourself with the tools to begin a packaging design career, it is time to consider some of the alternative career paths that you may take. Of course, decisions made at this stage are not likely to be so binding that you can't change direction later. In practice, this is exactly what most people do. The important thing is to get started and, as experience is gained, you will begin to get a clearer picture about the career path that you particularly want to pursue. Many students may already have had some experience with work placements, which helps to generate career preferences. Importantly, however, no matter how brilliant you may think you are, inevitably you will begin as a junior. Yes, this does mean doing some of the more mundane jobs. Don't be insulted by having to make coffee, run off photocopies and all the other small tasks that come your way; your turn will come to strut your stuff and prove just how much potential you have. Always stick it out for six months before making any decisions, even if, at the beginning, you are not enjoying it. This length of time is crucial so that you are in a position where you can make rational informed decisions.

Packaging is a fast moving, ever-changing business so, as your chosen career, it is a good idea first to look ahead into the future of packaging design and see how this may affect you.

The future of packaging design

Although we tend simply to accept our current experiences as being entirely normal, for design practitioners and students alike, it is important to attempt to understand both the magnitude and the pace of change that impinge on the business of packaging design. Earlier, in Chapter One, it was suggested that packaging design has been driven by the influences of socio-economic change on lifestyles, new technology and changes in retailing methods. The timeline chart (on p.10) considered all three of these factors and showed how they continue to be major factors, projecting their influence into the future. Interwoven through these factors are also deepening concerns for the environment and an increasingly global platform for conducting business. How all of these elements may affect designers at the start of their career is considered below.

Understanding markets

Throughout this book, emphasis has been placed on understanding consumer behaviour and how changing social patterns and economics influence it. So, it will be no surprise to find reference to these important areas here—this time in the context of the role of a packaging designer at the start of their career.

Many design students will have experienced working on projects that focus on the lifestyle that they are most familiar with, that is, their own peer group. There are some understandable reasons for this. One reason can be found when looking at competition briefs, many of which target this dynamic, exciting and radical market sector that will inspire student work. In addition, competition sponsors seek to use student understanding of their own market to provide results that, ultimately, may have commercial value. When this happens, there is no question that it benefits both student and sponsor. Other reasons for students to choose to work in this market sector are because it is often considered to be a fun area, where little market research is needed because of its familiarity. It is all perfectly understandable and potential employers also appreciate seeing portfolios that contain imaginative work and fresh thinking in this important market as people tend to take their preferred brands from youth through to later years.

Design, both for products and packaging, is not, however, always concerned with vodka, surfing, skateboarding, clubbing and all the other activities we assume students are particularly familiar with. Realizing this, students with an eye to the future will balance their portfolios with work that also reflects other markets where research has been required to generate market understanding. In commercial practice, designers will work across many different markets, some in which they may have had no previous experience.

Technology changes

Changes here will affect packaging designers at several levels:

Individual level

New and improved software will allow much simpler text and image manipulation, allowing widespread amateur access to "design" skills for the creation of graphics, web design, animation and video production. In theory, even small companies will have the technical ability to create and manage their own advertising, print, packaging and web-based material. In practice, technical skills also require aesthetic merit to be successful. Companies employing designers will expect them to bring creativity across a wide spectrum of design activities, not just packaging.

Monitoring change

The development of new packaging materials and processes will increase the range of technical options open to designers. The first challenge will be to find a way of being informed of these developments. Secondly, much of the technology may be outside individual designers' knowledge, requiring access to specialist assistance. In both instances, help may be provided through new forms of custom web-based information services, tailored to meet the individual designer's requirements by conducting an electronic "trawl" of global packaging activity and delivering both relevant information and sources for detailed follow-up. We may also see greater reliance being placed on packaging suppliers to carry out technical development of packaging design concepts.

At the corporate level

Companies will face difficult decisions about the nature of their business as new technologies render older ones obsolete. There is nothing new in this process but, in the past, companies have often had time to adjust to change. Now the pace of technological change requires close monitoring and a swift response.

The transition from film to digital photography was rapid and left major photographic film manufacturers such as Kodak and Fuji with factories producing wet process films and papers surplus to market demand. Digital imaging, however, not only took photography away from traditional film and camera manufacturers but delivered it into the hands of mobile phone companies where no previous track record of photography existed. Converging technology now means that mobile phones, personal organizers, computers and MP3 players can also incorporate digital photography, increasing competition and making it more difficult for companies like Kodak and Fuji to define their business activity. Their responses have included, in the case of Fuji, production of high-specification SLR digital cameras for serious photographers, while Kodak have concentrated on providing convenience through camera docking systems and photo printers.

Dilemmas such as these will continue to challenge conventional corporate thinking and this provides an opportunity for designers because challenging convention is an integral part of design activity, and also because designers must be in tune with lifestyle issues. For example, a pack that actively monitors pollen levels and then dispenses the appropriate dosage of medication to hay fever sufferers, begins to reposition the company from a manufacturer of drugs to a more proactive health caring role. This is a subtle distinction, perhaps, but critical in the way a company views itself and how it is viewed by others. As a packaging designer, you have the key to making these changes in company strategies happen through presenting design concepts that demonstrate this level of thinking. The future of corporate viability will depend on flexibility and employers will actively seek those capable of providing it.

Environmental concerns

In looking to the future, it is clear that environmental matters are going to achieve a high priority and impact on all our lifestyles. It is of such significance for the immediate future that we must return to it here in some detail.

As discussed in Chapter Seven, changing weather patterns attributed to global warming and the apparent increase in the frequency of natural disasters have helped to focus public attention on environmental issues. As ordinary citizens, we can see the folly of over-packaging, appreciate that unnecessary flights cause environmental damage, know that air conditioning consumes power and that driving a four-by-four V8 engined "gas-guzzler" is a burden on the environment. Most people are aware of such issues and are prepared to make some compromises within the constraints of their own lifestyles but, often, we find ways of justifying some of our recognizably poor environmental choices while salving our consciences by taking some, often limited, environmental action. We may, for example, decide to use public transport occasionally rather than drive, or recycle our domestic waste while still opting to fly on our annual vacation. It is a matter of personal compromise and priorities, balancing lifestyle choices with environmental impact.

Despite the lack of governmental progress internationally so far and a disappointing response to the United Nations Kyoto Protocol, the environmental debate does now seem to be gathering momentum. It appears that governments are likely to respond, with the notable exception of the Bush administration in the USA which continues to defy scientific evidence and, in consequence, has not ratified the protocol. Worryingly, it is far from clear what actions countries will take or how the key margins between the developed world and developing world will coordinate their actions.

In seeking to limit carbon emissions, it will come as no surprise, however, if taxation and carbon trading are the options favoured by governments, probably applied to air travel and fuel in the first instance but, at a later stage, possibly extending to some form of consumer packaging tax. We might speculate that this could be based on the carbon footprint of non-essential packaging or perhaps as a levy on materials that are difficult or expensive to sort and recycle. Any move of this sort might stimulate further negative consumer opinions regarding packaging and increase the pressure to reduce the levels of packaging used. Whether such a tax will come about or not is simply speculation but, in any case, it is clear that the design community will have to start seriously considering reduction in the levels of packaging. Taxes are simply monetary devices and, in themselves, fail to address the fundamental issues of surviving, as a planet, on less energy. The carbon funds and possible packaging taxes are likely to look rather pathetic when submerged by waters from melting ice. Perhaps the design community can introduce some sanity to the debate by exercising its unique position to inform public debate and create a meaningful dialogue with those currently in power.

Rethinking packaging design alone, however, will not be enough, as it will also require a change in thinking throughout the entire distribution chain, from product sourcing, packaging, logistics and retailing industries through to waste management. This is because, for example, any proposed packaging reductions or the introduction of closed loop systems will have implications throughout the production and distribution cycle. Among many effects, these could include higher levels of product damage, reduced product shelf life, redesigned store fixtures and fittings, less product choice, more pack standardization and modified transport systems. An integrated approach on this scale has not taken place before, particularly when many of the participants are now global players. This would represent a major change of direction for all the parties involved in the distribution chain, but would also involve trade associations, which represent the voice of the packaging industry.

Currently, there tends to be a largely unhelpful regime of environmental claim and counter-claim among trade associations, championing the environmental performance of their particular material sectors. Regrettably, these arguments tend to negate one another and obscure the real value of what is being said. Overall, the packaging industry appears defensive and has made little progress to persuade consumers about the positive benefits of packaging. It has also resulted in confusion among designers in trying to measure design outcomes in environmental terms, balanced against other design criteria. If, as suspected, packaging becomes enmeshed in the environmental debate, we shall expect a greater degree of transparency and cooperation from the industrial spokespeople.

As young designers beginning their careers, it is now essential that the environmental implications of design decisions are fully understood. Clients who commission packaging design will expect to be informed about the environmental performance of the pack. Where packaging unexpectedly encounters consumer resistance, attracts higher green taxes or otherwise incurs a reduction in profit margin, clients will soon wish to seek redress from their appointed design team.

Clearly, environmental action is going to have a significant effect on the future of packaging design, changing both the balance and the interface between design, marketing, manufacturing, retailing and distribution. Products and brands will still have to compete in our new greener world, and the design challenge will be to achieve this for our clients while meeting our environmental responsibilities.

Global marketing and production

The characteristics associated with the successful companies of the future will be their ability to adapt to new business climates, embrace new technologies and be prepared to locate into new territories. Kenichi Ohmae, in his book *The Next Global Stage* (2005), refers to a post-globalized, borderless world where the traditional hierarchical company model has no place and where the concept of "multinationals" with a national home base is superseded by more dynamic and adaptive companies. Throughout the book, Ohmae illustrates how companies are evolving in this direction, citing examples such as the rise of Chinese companies producing sophisticated electronics and how they are competing successfully in the global market place. We have all become familiar with seeing "Made in China" on leading brands of electronic products. Ohmae, however, tends to overlook the environmental burden of shipping products across the planet and it may be that this detrimental aspect will eventually become a powerful enough argument to cause a rethink of global production strategies.

For example, an AppleMac mouse is printed with the legend "Designed by Apple in California, assembled in Malaysia". If a green tax is levied on the transport between Malaysia and the computer's destination, is it still going to be cost-effective to manufacture it there? We shall see and, along the way, find out if politicians will be able to resist manipulating the figures to suit their domestic policies.

Armed with the most up-to-date background knowledge required to convince a potential employer of their depth of understanding, the student can then prepare to launch themselves into the job market.

Design consultancies

For many design students, consultancies represent their career of choice. It is here that creativity seems most highly prized and that award winning, cutting edge, media highlighted design takes place. Our design heroes tend to be from this background rather than from any other. It is portrayed as the sexy end of packaging design, populated by design enthusiasts working in exciting environments. It is seen as weird, wired and wonderful—but is that true?

The answer is "Yes", immediately qualified by "Coming at a price", but more of that later. Design consultancies range from small one-person businesses up to complex conglomerates. They organize themselves in different ways and are variable in quality and offering so it is very difficult to generalize. Wise students who want to join a consultancy will already be monitoring websites, reading the design press and pestering studios for placements. It is essential to know what each consultancy specializes in and to decide which ones seem to offer the right mixture of service to suit your ambitions. Like all design activities, research the market first.

Design consultancies are becoming ideas factories rather than just places that solve design problems. Along the way they have to do that too, but the big players in design are really selling big ideas. They appreciate that brands now have to offer an experience to differentiate themselves in a crowded market, and consultancies are keen to demonstrate that they can provide the vision to create brand experiences. This is very much the arena that Imagination operates in. Here

Opposite Working in this environment is the dream job for many and you may be sure that having a company like Imagination on your resumé is an accolade and marks you as a serious contender in design. There is greater specialization in large companies, however, with larger clients, longer and more complex projects and so perhaps not the diversity and fast project turnaround experienced in smaller studios.

Below Bloom, the London-based design studio, have rapidly established a reputation for packaging design with an impressive client list. Small enough to be friendly and personal, they successfully compete with design companies of all sizes and are receptive to providing student placements. For many students this represents the ideal environment to be involved in all aspects of design.

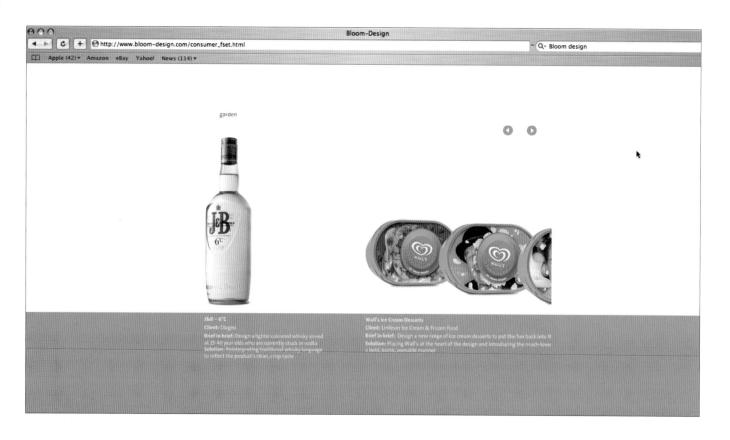

packaging is a small part of a much larger whole that includes graphic designers, architects, multimedia, theatre, lighting and acoustic designers, all housed in one of the most exciting buildings in London. Behind the glamour, Imagination has huge technical and logistical resources sufficient to enable them to turn ideas into reality on a dramatically large scale. Perhaps this may be the way design will develop, where the principal creative role will be idea generation and a secondary role will see the drawing in of different disciplines to make ideas come to life. This multi-disciplined approach requires a large number of staff and, with so many mouths to feed, a steady source of income. Imagination does this by dealing at a high level with some of the world's largest organizations. Ford, for example, is a long-term client and Imagination has worked on most of the automotive brands in the Ford stable. Imagination has offices in Tokyo, Hong Kong, New York, Los Angeles, Detroit, Cologne, Toronto, Sydney, Stockholm and London.

A similar ideas-based approach to creativity is taken by Pentagram. The accent, tone and way of working, however, are very different between these companies. Pentagram is responsible for creating some of the most enduring design work ever produced. Many examples of their typographic and graphic design work are widely regarded as design classics, for example, the V&A logo for London's Victoria & Albert Museum created by Alan Fletcher, one of the company's co-founding partners. Pentagram, unusually, is an amalgam of partners. All earn the same salary and share the same bonuses. The company works across a wide range of project types, including packaging but extending to interior design, product design branding and corporate identity. In addition to the London office, it now has offices in San Francisco, New York and Austin, Texas.

To work as a designer at either of these organizations would, without doubt, be a superb opportunity. It will not be surprising to learn that finding a job at either company is difficult, with competition being intense. Packaging designers with knowledge of three-dimensional structural design, however, may have an edge, as structural design is important to both companies. While few consultancies can match the scale of Imagination's work or the plaudits received by Pentagram, there are plenty of companies with the skills to compete.

Many consultancies now include packaging design as just one option, with web design, brand consultancy and original concept generation as commonly quoted other options. It is easy to understand why studios are moving away from concentrating just on packaging design as a specialization when many clients are now looking for a more comprehensive one-shop solution to all their design and branding requirements. Packaging has become recognized as just one part of an integrated marketing strategy rather than a stand-alone activity. This is probably prudent, in that to be successful in tackling increasingly competitive markets demands a more deeply embedded strategic plan affecting all company activities. The days of adding a sales flash to packaging graphics being seen as a way to boost sales have gone. Consumers are now better informed, brand-aware and prepared to cast their brand vote in an intensely competitive market place.

For packaging designers, the implications of this are that, while specializing in designing packaging, successful designers will also need to develop their communication skills to work alongside other specialists in areas such as web

187

design, advertising and even animation and film. Inevitably this means developing an interest and basic understanding of other design disciplines and the technology that underpins them. Packaging design must integrate with the marketing strategy used across a broad spectrum of media types to form a concerted message that explores consumer benefits and addresses consumer desires.

Although we have become accustomed to seeing celebrity designers or, at least, leading figures in the design world, appearing on television and in the press, the reality is that design studios work as a team. Claims of "I designed that", more often than not really mean "We, the studio, designed that". Sharing ideas and showing work to colleagues can sometimes seem difficult at first, especially after a student experience where it is your own work that is assessed rather than a team's work. Hopefully, however, your student experience will have been structured to provide you with the opportunity of working in groups, giving a flavour of consultancy practice. The comparison can be made with playing in a band. Each member of the band contributes to the total sound, even though someone might be playing lead guitar. In design terms, when working on a project, your idea might be good enough to be the equivalent of lead guitar but it almost certainly will require the input of others to get the right sound.

Above If you work at Pentagram you are probably at the pinnacle of design. It does not really become more prestigious than this. Here is an example of their packaging design work—creating the Tesco "Finest" range. By using photography worthy of haute cuisine cooking, together with a consistent use of black and silver, they have established a successful formula for Tesco and created a template that other retailers would follow.

A design studio is usually an interesting and lively environment to be in. Alongside the usual array of Macs, there are likely to be design magazines, project work at various stages of completion, images, colour swatches and printouts. Working alongside like-minded individuals can generate a real buzz, where ideas are exchanged, modified, worked up, thrown out or developed. Inevitably, there are time pressures on every project, with deadlines that must be met. There are no opt-out clauses or excuses for failing to meet deadlines. That might mean working long hours, perhaps through the night on occasion, and a last minute sprint to prepare work for a client meeting seems par for the course in most studios. Having made the deadline and presented models where the paint is barely dry and graphics are still warm from the printer, there is a great sense of relief, particularly if the client likes the work. When the client has gone, amid the studio debris of coffee cups and pizza boxes, celebration can commence, if tiredness does not strike first.

Another issue that is raised by the AppleMac mouse, designed in California and manufactured in Malaysia, is that design, enabled by technology, is increasingly becoming an activity that can be carried out at locations remote from production sites. On a strictly design origination level, designs can be created in Tokyo, Los Angeles or Delhi and electronically sent to clients in any part of the world. You know, however, from reading this book, that design is concerned with people and its success is very much connected to knowing the wants, needs and desires of the target audience. This cannot effectively be done remotely. There is a need for local knowledge of the market in terms of consumer lifestyles, competitor activity, retail methods and any local taboos or opportunities. Many of the large design companies, as we have illustrated, already replicate their studios across the globe. Smaller design consultancies sometimes establish satellite offices in other countries or form associations with local design companies. Here, the design work might originate from a remote location but to a brief researched locally.

So, if you want to work at the cutting edge of design, possibly in glamorous parts of the world, then working for a consultancy might be for you. But it is not all plaudits and media attention. Changing packaging is often a cost-effective way for brands to refresh themselves and so there is a fast turnaround of design work. This can mean working for the same client on a range of products almost on a constant basis, sometimes making very small changes. This might not sound so, but is often very difficult to do. Also, consultancies often become known for activities that they are particularly successful at doing. It might be designing alcoholic drinks, for example, where their portfolio of design success attracts yet more drinks companies, addressing a similar target audience. There might be a limit to the number of new concepts that you can generate for vodka mixers and so you may decide to move on to other areas inside a company or attempt to interest others elsewhere in your vodka-mixer biased portfolio. For this reason, studios do attempt to bring in a range of different projects but it is very easy for design studios to become stereotyped. It might be advisable, as a young designer seeking employment, to look for variety in the portfolios of design companies.

Packaging manufacturing

Many young designers find careers within companies that manufacture or convert packaging. It is a vast and diverse industry, making a significant contribution to most national economies around the world. Estimates suggest that it is worth $500 billion world wide, including the manufacture of packaging machinery. Rather than being one industry, as the title to this section might suggest, the packaging industry is actually fragmented into many industrial sectors, each being defined largely by the packaging material produced. Major manufacturing categories include glass, steel, aluminium, corrugated fibre-board and cartons. The plastic material category, alone, is so diverse that it tends to split according to production techniques and includes injection moulded packs and components, blow moulded containers, thermoforming and expanded foams. Some companies may be classed as converters rather than manufacturers. Here packaging material is purchased from manufacturers and converted into packaging. Examples of this are widespread but typically might involve a company buying sheets of corrugated board and then printing the board, before cutting and creasing it to manufacture point-of-sale material.

It is a highly competitive industry, where the purchasing power of global organizations can squeeze profits. With an increasingly high proportion of packaged products (both food and non-food items) being sold through supermarkets, the multiple grocery companies play a significant part in controlling costs and, therefore, the profit levels of their suppliers. Converters, in particular, either supplying directly to supermarkets or to brand manufacturers, can become vulnerable to such financial pressure, sometimes seeing their output becoming a commodity competing with rival companies only on price. In order to prosper and, on many occasions, just to survive, packaging manufacturers are increasingly using design to add value to packaging and to seek out new markets. An example here would

Above Lantero are just a part of the SCA company empire, originating in Scandinavia but now manufacturing paper-based packaging world wide. Designers in packaging manufacturing companies become expert in their knowledge of a small range of materials and help develop new materials, pack forms and markets.

be a converter of corrugated board, normally supplying shipping cases but beginning to design a range of play furniture for children under their own brand. This might, for example, take the form of easy-to-assemble castles, trains, cars etc., that young children can climb into. The same packaging materials, machines and processes are being used but the output is a product with higher profit margins. Another approach may take the form of having a small design team to work directly with clients in producing design concepts or to create new pack forms and finishes that represent a commercial advantage and demonstrate innovation in the packaging market place. Some glass manufacturers have adopted this approach, exploring the use of thermochromic inks and new technologies to add value, gain publicity and, ultimately, attract new business. Occasionally packaging manufacturers introduce outside teams of consultants to work alongside them and help generate ideas to drive the company into new areas.

Much of this book has been directed at consumer goods because the elements of graphic and structural design are best demonstrated by these categories. However, packaging manufacturers design and supply packaging for many different businesses where clients are looking for technical as well as graphical solutions. These range from supplying large runs of packaging, perhaps printed cartons designed to run on particular packaging machinery, through to designing packaging for specialized products where packaging may be critical. The packaging for titanium replacement hip joints, for example, requires a pack that protects the highly polished surface from scratches yet allows gamma radiation sterilization in the pack, and can present the components to the medical team in theatre without danger of dropping, yet be easy to remove. Getting this right really matters and it is easy to understand the fascination with the design task here, quite unlike that of designing retail packaging. This example is not just structural; graphics are also a requirement, primarily for identification but also instruction—and they should, if possible, not be language dependent. These packs are exported to surgical teams worldwide. The challenge is evident. Producing packaging for the armed services is another equally challenging specialist area where defence standards may require product protection and storage for three months in both tropical and arctic conditions.

Working as a designer for a packaging manufacturer means developing knowledge of a smaller range of materials but in much greater depth than would be possible in a consultancy. Often, this entails being flexible and adaptable, moving between structural and graphic design, and having the confidence to represent the company to clients. You might be the only designer in a small company, an exciting prospect where the rewards may be high and the challenges demanding. Alternatively, many large packaging organizations have manufacturing plants spread across the globe and are working for major client accounts. They too are looking for design innovation. In addition to design skills, this environment demands close cooperation with others. Production departments may have to make whatever you design and almost certainly will have expertise to provide a positive contribution to any project. It will be a similar story with other specialist departments, together with the client, and so the designer is working as part of a team closely involved in developing the company.

Brand owners

The term "brand owners" once more embraces a broad collection of business models. At one end of the spectrum there are multinational manufacturers such as Unilever and Procter & Gamble, each with a portfolio of brands most of which we would all recognize and some that might surprise us. At the opposite end of the spectrum are companies with one brand that is used across a wide product range. Examples include supermarket own-label brands, product manufacturing companies such as 3M and non-manufacturing companies that exist only as a brand (Tommy Hilfiger being an example where the brand is effectively a design house rather than a manufacturer). Of course, between these extremes lies just about everything else.

Above 3M is a global organization manufacturing a wide and diverse range of products for industrial, retail, commercial and specialist markets. Innovation in product and packaging is fundamental to the company. Designers in this type of organization are likely to have divisional design and management responsibilities that may take them to other locations, domestic or abroad.

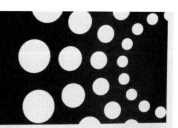

Above The ad here is looking for a packaging
designer to create own-label products under
the W.H. Smith brand. These will be produced
by outside suppliers where imaginative design
will need to be tempered by commercial
awareness and consumer understanding.

Unlike working for a packaging manufacturer, where the material is likely to be specific, here it is the brand or brands that remain a constant and the packaging design challenge is to promote the brand through new products or new packs. It is important that brands are presented consistently so that consumer recognition is triggered, which usually means that there will be a corporate identity manual or guidelines in place to achieve such consistency. All design decisions must reflect the brand values; either the current values, or new values if the brand is trying to reposition itself. You may also find pressure within the organization to reduce costs or increase the efficiencies of the packaging process while, at the same time, attempting to produce innovative designs. Some students have suggested that working in this environment, with its restrictions on design and cost, might repress the creative flair they are keen to demonstrate. In many ways, however, the imposition of restrictions really does demand creative solutions. It adds several new dimensions to the design process. For example, a design for a new shower gel may look elegant, stand out well against competition and accurately represent brand values, but do the graphics work when they are translated into German or Chinese? How elegant will the container look when a 1-litre version is required, in addition to the 250ml version you have been working on? How will you ensure that the pearlescent pigment you have specified is consistent when the container is produced by five separate companies in two different continents? Obtaining answers to questions like these are part of working for a brand. Effectively, in this situation, you are likely to be much closer to the details and in a position of considerable responsibility.

A graduate's experience

A recent graduate, Verity, got a job working for a major food producer. Although the company is a multinational and has a diverse portfolio of products and brands, her first appointment as a designer was in a small team that concerned a pet food brand. Her task was to develop new packaging concepts for the brand. This involved close cooperation with the production and manufacturing teams where technical requirements for packaging were critical. Any radical departure from the current design of primary pack had cost implications in terms of new plant and equipment. There was, however, more opportunity for innovation in the design of multipacks, both structurally and graphically. Marketing liaison was with the company's French headquarters, responsible for European distribution. Even within Europe, she learned that pet owners have different attitudes to their animals, requiring variations in food variety, pack size and multipack format. Design decisions in this environment are critical, where results are swiftly assessed in terms of financial performance of the brand. It is a career path, often, where creativity is required within tight parameters, in many ways, making this the most challenging of creative roles.

Down the line...

As with every human activity, a carefully planned career path is seldom followed. Events intervene, new interests arise, skills are developed opening fresh prospects, others inspire you to change direction, but, above all, fate has a hand to play in whatever destiny you may seek. Whether or not there is any cosmic strategic plan for this is open to speculation. What appears to be consistent is that the road travelled by those in the creative disciplines seems to have more forks in it than most other career paths. Perhaps this is because what we think of as the design world is both highly fragmented and fast changing, creating an environment where chance encounters, or simply luck, may point the direction for future development.

Not everyone who trains in a discipline goes on to practise it. There are many examples of design students pursuing successful careers outside design. The nature of this book, however, compels us to look at just a few of those who deliberately pursued careers in the world of design.

James

James studied packaging design at Sheffield Hallam University in the UK at both undergraduate and Masters levels, where, as a spin-off from his packaging work, he began to demonstrate a talent for branding and advertising. Clearly these were the areas he wished to develop and he felt that New York would be the place to do it. With little money, James took a job at the Hampton Coffee Company in East Hampton and, on his days off, came into the city with his portfolio, obtaining interviews with many companies including Interbrand and JWT.

Meanwhile, back at the coffee shop, James served a couple who, intrigued by his English accent, wondered what he was doing serving coffee in New York. James explained and, as chance would have it, the customer headed up an advertising company and invited James to an interview where James's portfolio would be reviewed. The company was Robert A. Becker, a specialist healthcare advertising agency, and James jumped at the chance of a one-year contract. In fact one year became two before James decided to move on, joining the healthcare advertising sector of JWT as an account supervisor. Now, a year later and in another move, James is working for Interbrand in their strategy division.

In this instance, James moved away from packaging design and developed new skills in account handling, branding and advertising. The ability to think creatively and strategically, however, remains paramount. It is this and the flexibility to adapt to change that allows designers to explore new avenues and discover fresh talents. No doubt luck played a part in this story, but determination, personality and talent stacked the odds in favour of success.

José

Having graduated with a first from a UK-based packaging design course, José returned to his home country of Spain to find employment. His work, as might be expected from a first class degree, had always been exemplary both in creative output and in the standard of presentation. Some of his student work can be seen in Chapter Five, displaying his design flair and attention to detail. It was no

Above James, Interbrand, New York

surprise that he quickly found employment in Valencia as a designer with ITENE. This is an interesting organization that might be equated, in some ways, to a packaging institute, having a considerable voice within the packaging industry in Spain. Its role is diverse, including research, package testing, material testing and pack design. Much of this work stems from developing the competitive advantages of Spanish produce for export. In terms of packaging design, the emphasis was on technical performance and structural design. Having gained experience in this arena, José is now working in the design team of the international corrugated fibre-board company, SCA (Grupo Lantero), in Valencia.

Bernhard

Bernhard had already had commercial design experience in his homeland of Germany when he joined a packaging design postgraduate course. In addition he had worked professionally as a photographer, a skill used to good advantage in his project work. His particular interest was to explore the use of modern discarded materials in a way that could be compared to the use of natural materials in simpler times. The work was also concerned with the contrast between expensive, luxury products and inexpensive packaging. To explain the theoretical direction of his work can be made easier by illustrating what he did. For example, he considered traditional materials that would have been cheap and readily available. This included bulrushes, leaves and fibres, which produced a packaging material when woven. He learned how to do this by sitting alongside craft workers skilled in these tasks. He then replicated their efforts using discarded synthetic packaging materials, weaving industrial strapping, shredded plastic carrier bags from Tesco and making packs from glue-impregnated string. These "new" materials then formed the basis for packing expensive products such as watches and perfumes. It sounds odd, perhaps, but the packs were beautifully crafted and the contrast between what had been waste and the expensive product that now lay packed within it was visually intriguing. Experiments followed using discarded fire hose and industrial hoses, to create a range of packs, some for designer perfume. To ensure that these packs, with their origins in waste, would never return to the waste-stream, he crafted solid silver closures. Nobody would throw the pack away!

This is not mainstream packaging design and we don't expect to see solid silver caps on our detergent bottles. The work, however, was reflective, showing a depth of thinking and a different approach to packaging. It is the ability to demonstrate new ways of thinking that will shape the future direction of design and make designers like Bernhard attractive to the world's top design organizations. Bernhard is now completing a placement as a designer in the studios of the international design organization, Metadesign, in Berlin, developing his own range of products manufactured from recycled material and completing his postgraduate Masters programme.

Above Here, Bernhard has used industrial hosepipe material as a basis for creating an experimental range of cosmetic products. The hosepipe is rubber based, providing a tactile element to the pack. In contrast to the discarded hosepipe material, highly finished metal, possibly silver, closures are being trialled.

Below Also using hose, but this time discarded fire service hose, at this stage the packaging is conceptual, exploring the aesthetic qualities of the materials with no clearly defined product yet established.

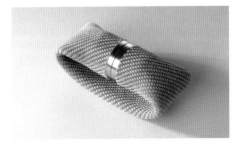

Conclusion

Packaging design is a subject so broad that it is almost impossible for any one book to do it justice. Here, we have managed to raise some of the main issues that designers at the start of their career must understand and some of the basic skills that they will need in order to progress. As changes take place regarding technology, lifestyles, socio-economic conditions and environmental concerns, we shall all have to continue learning. We hope it will leave time for the sort of reflection that Bernhard demonstrated, to provide fresh sources of inspiration. Above all, we want our passion for design to let us enjoy learning and working in this endlessly fascinating world of design.

Further reading

Josh Berger, *100 Habits of Successful Graphic Designers: Insider Secrets from Top Designers on Working Smart and Staying Creative*, Beverly, USA: Rockport 2005 How successful designers work

John Grant, *The Brand Innovation Manifesto: How to Build Brands, Redefine Markets and Defy Conventions*, Chichester, UK: John Wiley & Sons 2006 Cutting-edge insight into branding strategies with useful case studies throughout. The role of brands in today's and tomorrow's markets is critical for designers

Donald Norman, *The Design of Everyday Things,* Cambridge, USA: The MIT Press 1998 Vital reading for anyone embarking on a career involving design for real people

Kenichi Ohmae, *The Next Global Stage, Challenges and Opportunities in our Borderless World*, New Jersey, USA: Pearson Education Inc 2005 A readable account of globalization and what the outcome may be for societies around the world—important information for designers beginning their career

Hideyuki Oka, *How to Wrap Five Eggs: Japanese Design in Traditional Packaging*, New York, USA: Harper & Row 1967

Hideyuki Oka, *How to Wrap Five More Eggs: Traditional Japanese Packaging,* New York, USA: Weatherhill 1975 Thought provoking reading providing design inspiration that is relevant to today

Shan Preddy (ed), *How to Market Design Consultancy Services: Finding, Winning and Keeping Clients,* Aldershot, UK: Gower Publishing Ltd. 2004 Insight into the philosophy of different design agencies and how they operate

Glossary

Acetate (CA) cellulose acetate. Transparent film manufactured from wood cellulose, often used as window in cartons

Ambient temperature uncontrolled temperature of environment a product is in

Artwork drawing, illustration, image, text or graphic device prepared for reproduction

Aseptic process where product and pack are sterilized separately before combining and sealing under aseptic (sterile) conditions

Barrier properties ability of a material to prevent the passage of gases, flavours and aromas through it

Biodegradable ability of material to break down through biological activity to naturally occurring end products

Bitmap images defined by pixels. Resolution is often described as dots per inch (dpi)

Blank cut-out portion of material for subsequent conversion into a container

Blanket roll rubber roller that receives wet image from a printing plate and then transfers it onto surface to be printed

Bleed printed area beyond the cut edges. Bleeds allow graphics to extend to the complete surface

Blister pack thermoformed blister is secured to a backing sheet

Cardboard not an accepted technical term; commonly used to describe paperboard

Chipboard 100% recycled fibres, often containing ink, foil and other contaminants, used for rigid box construction

Closed loop system where original object or pack is circulated on a continuous cycle, avoiding the waste-stream

Closure generic term used for any device used for closing a container

Co-extrusion extrusion of two or more materials simultaneously from a single die to form one continuous material, combining the properties of each component

Colour separation separation of artwork into process printing colours by photographic or electronic means

Composite container container made from more than one material, e.g. paper tube with plastic ends

Compostable the ability to degrade naturally in the soil under composting conditions

Continuous tone image where the graduation from black to white is continuous, e.g. black and white photograph

CAP (controlled atmosphere packaging) storage or warehousing of bulk products in a modified atmosphere to extend shelf life

Convertor company that takes in pre-manufactured materials and converts them into packaging

Copolymer polymer produced from two or more monomers

Corrugated fibreboard facings or liner material separated by a fluted or corrugated medium

Crashlock base pre-glued carton base flaps that form automatically when carton is erected

Cullet crushed recycled glass

Dead-fold the ability of a material to retain the geometry of a fold, e.g. aluminium foil has good dead-fold properties

Debossing creation of hollow patterns on a substrate

Decoration inclusive term for graphic treatment on pack, includes printing, foil-blocking, embossing, shrink-sleeving and labelling etc.

Demographics numerical measurement of a specific category

Die-cut operation where sharp cutting edges cut out a specific shape from a substrate

Embossing creation of raised pattern on a surface

EPS expanded form used for thermal insulation and shock protection

Extrusion process of forming a thermoplastic through a shaped orifice or die

Extrusion blow moulding a parison (see entry opposite) is extruded and clamped between two moulds prior to inflation forming the container

Flexible packaging all packaging that is made of flexible materials such as pouches, sachets and bags

Foil a thin metal membrane of less than 150 microns. Also used to describe any thin material

Folding cartons die-cut blank glued and stored flat for subsequent erection

Font complete set of letters, numbers and punctuation of a particular design

Form-fill-seal technique using flexible film fed to a machine that forms the pack, fills it with product and seals it

Gable top carton generic name for Tetra Pak style carton

Glassine "greaseproof" paper, made from chemical pulp with highly beaten fibres

Gob measured amount of molten glass to make one container

Gravure print areas made up of engraved, laser or chemically etched cells of different depths varying ink density when printing. Used for long runs on flexible non-absorbent films

Halftone image created by dots of varying size

HDPE high density polyethylene, milky white, used for blow-moulded bottles

Hot stamping decorating method that uses heat to transfer material from a carrier web onto an object. Referred to as hot foil when metallic foils are used

Impact extrusion container, usually a tube, produced from metal slug in a mould impacted by a punch

Induction sealing electrically generated magnetic energy used to raise material temperatures sufficient for bonding to take place

Injection blow moulding a pre-form is produced by injection moulding prior to following the blow moulding process

In-mould labelling process that places heat-sealable labels into a mould before the container is blow moulded, bonding the label onto the container

Just-in-time elimination of storage by arranging delivery to correspond to manufacturing schedule

Kerning adjusting the space between letters; typographical term

Keyline drawing indicating main pack features and boundaries. Allows graphic design to be accurately positioned

Kraft paper light brown paper, strong because of long fibre length. Bleached Kraft is white but loses a little strength

Land the flat sealing surface on a container, e.g. top of the neck on a bottle

LCA (lifecycle analysis) technique to quantify environmental performance at all stages of manufacture and disposal. Cradle-to-grave analysis

LDPE low density polyethylene, clear, used for bags

Leading the space between lines of type

Liner paperboard, usually Kraft, component of corrugated fibreboard

Line-work solid colour used in text, illustration and diagrams

Litho, lithography uses flat plates that contain water-attracting and oil-attracting areas, ink sticking to the oil-receptive areas only. Usually plates transfer image onto blanket cylinder to prevent plate wear, hence offset lithography

Makeready all activities involved in setting up a machine prior to a production run

Manufacturers joint the flap of a shipping case used to glue or staple the blank

MAP (modified atmosphere packaging) introduction of a gas into a pack to modify rate of product degradation. Usually involves mixtures of nitrogen, carbon dioxide and oxygen

MD (machine direction) direction of material flow through a machine. Often imparts properties to materials due to direction, e.g. directional paper fibre alignment during manufacture

Metallizing (vacuum metallizing) deposition of vapourized metal (aluminium) onto film giving opacity, metallic appearance and improved barrier properties

Nylon polyamide—makes strong film with good oxygen barrier. Heat resistance allows boil-in-bag applications

OTC (over-the-counter) pharmaceutical products that are sold without prescription

Pantone trade name of company operating the Pantone Matching System (PMS) used to specify colours for printing

Parison partially formed semi-molten plastic or glass shape prior to conversion into a container

PE polyethylene

PET polyester (polyethylene tetraphthalate)—used for carbonated drinks bottles. In crystalline form (CPET), temperature properties are further improved for use in dual ovenable, pre-prepared food trays

Pinch off line left on the base of a blow moulded container base where mould closes, removing excess plastic

Plasticizer chemical lubricant added to plastics to assist processing

Polycarbonate (PC) high-impact resistance polymer with high temperature resistance. Used for sterilizable baby feeding bottles

Polylactic acid (PLA) biodegradable/compostable chemical resembling plastic, used for compostable packaging trays

POS (point-of-sale) retail display stand constructed to promote or merchandise products. Some secondary packaging can have this feature built in

Polymer scientific term for plastic consisting of large numbers of monomers forming a large molecular structure

Polypropylene (PP) high-strength properties used as component of laminates for flowwraps, e.g. biscuits, chocolate, etc. Injection-moulded containers use "live-hinge" properties that resist cracking with repeated use

Polystyrene (PS) clear, glossy, hard material, used for injection moulded packs, e.g. CD cases. Film forms used for vacuum forming as blisters or trays

Polyvinyl chloride (PVC) clarity makes it suitable for clear bottles. Easy to thermoform into clear blisters. Plasticized forms used as stretch/shrink wrap. Chlorine content raises environmental issues

Preform injection moulded preliminary shape for subsequent transfer to blow moulding machine

Preprint printing of material before conversion into a pack, e.g. preprinted paper liner laminated onto corrugated fibreboard prior to case manufacture

Process printing colour reproduction using the three process colours: cyan, magenta and yellow (black is usually added as a fourth key colour)

Psychographics study of behaviour and motivation of groups of people. Often referred to as lifestyle

Raster digital image created by scanning, forming a bitmapped file

Relief printing uses a raised surface. Flexography and letterpress

Reverse printing printing on the inside of transparent film

Rigid box non-folding box, ready to fill

Rotational moulding used to produce large drums. Plastic is placed into a heated metal mould that is rotated to distribute the liquid plastic around the mould

RSC (regular slotted container) corrugated cases cut from rectangular blank, having all slots, scores and creases in either machine or cross directions

Score an impression on material for ease of bending

Screen printing metal or plastic mesh, normally photo-generated seal in non-print areas, using squeegee to spread ink

Spirally wound tube/can constructed from overlapping layers (usually three) of Kraft paper

Spot colour specific colour used instead of using process colours. Often corporate colour may be used this way for consistent appearance

Sprue the passage that brings plastic material to an injection moulding cavity

Tampo print ink transferred onto a silicon pad from an etched image plate before transfer to pack. Used for complex curved surfaces or raised features, e.g. wristwatch numerals

Test paper recycled paper used for corrugated fibreboard liners

Thermoplastic polymer or plastic that will become flexible under heat, e.g. PVC

Thermoset polymer or plastic that will not melt but degrades with temperature, e.g. nylon

Three-piece can constructed from welded body and two ends

Tinplate sheet steel coated on both sides with a thin layer of tin

Triplewall corrugated board with four liners and three fluting media used for heavy-duty transit

UHT (ultra high temperature) process to sterilize milk and fruit juice. Temperatures of 135–150°C (275–300°F) are applied for a few seconds

UV coating coatings that are polymerized by ultraviolet light. Often applied as varnish to cartons as last stage of printing

Vacuum forming heat-softened plastic sheet is drawn into the mould by a vacuum

Vignette image that changes tonal value or colour from solid to halftone

WVTR (water vapour transmission rate) the rate that water vapour migrates through a barrier

Web any material that is unwound from a roll and passed through a machine

Bibliography

B

Phil **Baines** and Andrew Haslam, *Type and Typography*, London: Laurence King, and New York: Watson-Guptill, 2005

John **Berger**, *Ways of Seeing*, London: Penguin Books, 1972

Joshua **Berger**, *XXX: The Power of Sex in Contemporary Design*, Gloucester, Massachusetts: Rockport, 2003

—, *100 Habits of Successful Graphic Designers: Insider Secrets from Top Designers on Working Smart and Staying Creative*, Gloucester, Massachusetts: Rockport, 2003

Rachel **Bowlby**, *Shopping with Freud*, London and New York: Routledge, 1993

Albert **Bregman**, "Asking the 'What For' Question in Auditory Perception in Hillsdale, NJ", *Perceptual Organization*, Mahwah, New Jersey: Laurence Erlbaum Associates, 1981, pp.99–118

British Medical Association, "Preventing Childhood Obesity", June 2005, www.bma.org.uk/ap.nsf/content/childhoodobesity

C

Giles **Calver**, *What is Packaging Design?* Hove, East Sussex and Mies, Switzerland: RotoVision, 2004

Contact 21, *Illustration*, Reigate, Surrey: Elfande, 2005

James **Craig**, *Production for the Graphic Designer*, New York: Watson-Guptill, 1990

D

David **Dabner** (ed.), *Graphic Design School*, London: Thames & Hudson, 2004

Terence **Dalley** (ed.), *The Complete Guide to Illustration and Design Techniques and Materials*, London: QED, 1984

Edward **de Bono**, *Lateral Thinking: A Textbook of Creativity*, London: Penguin Books, 1990

John **Desmond**, *Consuming Behaviour*, London and New York: Palgrave, 2003

Department of the Environment, Transport and the Regions, "Green Claims Code, revised June 2000", www.defra.gov.uk

Department of Trade and Industry, "Sustainability and Business Competitiveness", on-line resource, 2003, www.dti.gov.uk

Xavier **Drèze** and Françoise-Xavier Hussher, "Internet Advertising: Is Anyone Watching?", *Journal of Interactive Marketing*, 2003, 17(4)

J. **Driver** and G.C. Baylis, "Edge-assignment and Figure Ground Segmentation in Short-term Visual Matching", *Cognitive Psychology*, 1996, 31(3), pp.248–306

E

Environment Agency, "Greenhouse Gas Emissions—Background and Data", 2005, www.environment-agency.gov.uk

F

Catharine **Fishel**, *Packaging: 50 Real-life Projects Uncovered*, Gloucester, Massachusetts: Rockport, and Hove, East Sussex: RotoVision, 2004

Alan **Fletcher**, *The Art of Looking Sideways*, London: Phaidon, 2001

G

Mark **Gatter**, *Software Essentials for Graphic Designers*, London: Laurence King, 2006

I. **Gauthier** and M. Tarr, "Becoming a Greeble Expert: Exploring Mechanisms for Face Recognition", *Vision Research*, 1998, 37, pp.1673–1682

Global Market Information Database, "Carrefour SA", 5 October 2005, www.gmid.euromonitor.com

—, "Consumer Lifestyles in China", 25 April 2005, www.gmid.euromonitor.com

—, "Consumer Lifestyles in Denmark", 14 July 2005, www.gmid.euromonitor.com

—, "Consumer Lifestyles in Germany", 1 October 2004, www.gmid.euromonitor.com

—, "Consumer Lifestyles in Japan", 15 February 2005, www.gmid.euromonitor.com

—, "Consumer Lifestyles in Mexico", 1 November 2004, www.gmid.euromonitor.com

—, "Consumer Lifestyles in South Korea", 1 February 2005, www.gmid.euromonitor.com

—, "Consumer Lifestyles in Spain", 1 November 2004, www.gmid.euromonitor.com

—, "Consumer Lifestyles in the United Kingdom", 1 October 2004, www.gmid.euromonitor.com

—, "Retailing in the Czech Republic", 1 May 2004, www.gmid.euromonitor.com

—, "Retailing in France", February 2004, www.gmid.euromonitor.com

—, "Retailing in Japan", August 2004, www.gmid.euromonitor.com

—, "Retailing in Mexico", May 2004, www.gmid.euromonitor.com

—, "Retailing in Spain", May 2004, www.gmid.euromonitor.com

—, "Tesco Plc", 5 October 2005, www.gmid.euromonitor.com

Robert **Goldman** and Stephen Papson, *Nike Culture: The Sign of the Swoosh*, London and Thousand Oaks, California: Sage, 2004

John **Grant**, *The New Marketing Manifesto*, London: Texere, 1999

—, *The Brand Innovation Manifesto: How to Build Brands, Redefine Markets and Defy Conventions*, Chichester, England and Hoboken, New Jersey: John Wiley, 2006

Jane **Graves**, "The Washing Machine: Mother's not Herself Today", in Pat Kirkham, *The Gendered Object*, Manchester: Manchester University Press, 1996

Kalanit **Grill-Spector** and Nancy Kanwisher, "Visual Recognition: As Soon As You Know It Is There, You Know What It Is", *Psychological Science*, 2005, 16(2), pp.152–160

Christoph **Grunenberg** and Max Hollein (eds), *Shopping: A Century of Art and Consumer Culture*, Ostfildern-Ruit: Hatje Cantz, 2002

Barrie **Gunter** and Adrian Furnham, *Children as Consumers: A Psychological Analysis of the Young People's Market*, London and New York: Routledge, 1998

H

Cynthia **Hite** and Robert Hite, "Reliance on Brand by Young Children", *Journal of the Market Research Society*, 1994, 37(2) www.warc.com

Jenny **Hogan**, "Climatologists Pursue Greenhouse Gas Danger Levels", *New Scientist*, 1 February 2005, www.newscientist.com

I

John **Ingledew**, *Photography*, London: Laurence King, 2005; as *The Creative Photographer*, New York Harry N. Abrams, 2005

Institute of Alcohol Studies, "Binge Drinking", July 2005, www.ias.org.uk/resources/fact sheets/binge_drinking.pdf

Interbrand, "Best Global Brands", July 2006, www.interbrand.com

K

E. **Ketibuah**, "Comparative Analysis of Household Waste in the Cities of Stuttgart and Kumasi – Options for Waste Recycling and Treatment in Kumasi", 2003

Pat **Kirkham** (ed.), *The Gendered Object*, Manchester: Manchester University Press, 1996

Naomi **Klein**, *No Logo: Taking Aim at the Brand Bullies*, London: Flamingo, and New York: Picador, 2000

L

La Caixa, "History of La Caixa", www.portal1.lacaixa.es

Martin **Lindstrom** and Patricia Seybold, *Brand Child*, London: Kogan Page, 2004

Jeffrey **Liter** and Heinrich Bülthoff, *An Introduction to Object Recognition*, 43, Tübingen, Germany: Max Planck Institute for Biological Cybernetics, 1996, www.mpik-tueb.mpg.de/bu

Mark **Lovell** and Jack Potter, *Assessing the Effectiveness of Advertising*, London: Business Books, 1975

M

Beryl **McAlhone** and David Stuart, *A Smile in the Mind: Witty Thinking in Graphic Design*, with a foreword by Edward de Bono, London: Phaidon, 1998

Catherine **McDermott**, *Design Museum: 20th Century Design*, London: Carlton Books, 1999

Robert **Mason**, *A Digital Dolly?: A Subjective Survey of British Illustration in the 1990s*, Norwich: Norwich Gallery, Norwich School of Art & Design, 2000

Paul **Messaris**, *Visual Persuasion: The Role of Images in Advertising*, Thousand Oaks, California and London: Sage, 1997

The **Mind** Gym, *The Mind Gym: Wake Your Mind Up*, New York: Time Warner, 2005

Mintel, "Snacking on the Go", April 2004, www.reports.mintel.com

—, "Organics—UK", November 2005, www.reports.mintel.com

—, "Childhood Obesity—UK", June 2000, www.mintel.com

—, "Frozen Ready Meals—UK", March 2006, www.mintel.com

—, "Impact of Celebrity Chefs on Cooking Habits", July 2002, www.mintel.com

—, "British Lifestyles", March 2005, www.mintel.com

N

K. **Nakayama**, Z.J. He and S. Shimojo, "Visual Surface Representation: A Critical Link between Lower Level and Higher-level Vision", in S.M. Kosslyn and D.N. Osherson (eds), *An Invitation to Cognitive Science: Visual Cognition*, Cambridge, Massachusetts: MIT Press, 1995

Quentin **Newark**, *What is Graphic Design?*, Hove, East Sussex: RotoVision, 2002

Dorte **Nielson** and Kiki Hartmann, *Inspired: How Creative People Think, Work and Find Inspiration*, Amsterdam: BIS, 2005

Donald A. **Norman**, *The Design of Everyday Things*, New York: Basic Books, 2002

O

Kenichi **Ohmae**, *The Next Global Stage: Challenges and Opportunities in our Borderless World*, Upper Saddle River, New Jersey: Wharton School Pubications, 2005

Hideyuki **Oka**, *How to Wrap Five Eggs: Japanese Design in Traditional Packaging*, New York: Harper & Row, 1967

—, *How to Wrap Five More Eggs: Traditional Japanese Packaging*, New York: Weatherhill, 1975

Robert **Opie**, *Sweet Memories*, London: Michael Joseph, 1987

— (ed.), *The 1950s Scrapbook*, London: New Cavendish, 1998

John and Nicholas **O'Shaughnessy**, *Persuasion in Advertising*, Oxford and New York: Routledge, 2004

P

Haresh **Pathak**, *Structural Packaging Designs*, Amsterdam: Pepin Press, 2003

Jane **Pavitt** (ed.), *Brand. New*, London: V&A Publications, and Princeton, New Jersey: Princeton University Press, 2000

Pentagram, *Pentagram Book Five*, New York: Monacelli Press, 1999

Mary **Peterson** and Bradley Gibson, "Must Shape Recognition Follow Figure-Ground Organisation? An Assumption in Peril", *Psychological Science*, 1994, 5, pp.253–259

Mary **Peterson** and Jee Hyun Kim, "On What is Bound in Figures and Grounds", *Visual Cognition*, 2001, 8, pp.329–348

Shan **Preddy**, *How to Market Design Consultancy Services*, Aldershot, Hampshire: Gower Publishing, 1999

R

Gillian **Rose**, *Visual Methodologies: An Introduction to the Interpretation of Visual Materials*, London and Thousand Oaks, California: Sage, 2003

Edgar **Rubin**, "Figure and Ground", in David Beardslee and Michael Wertheimer (eds), *Readings in Perception*, Princeton, New Jersey: Van Nostrand, 1958

S

Andrew **Seth** and Geoffrey Randall, *The Grocers: The Rise and Rise of the Supermarket Chains*, London: Kogan Page, 1999

Adrian **Shaughnessy**, *How to be a Graphic Designer Without Losing Your Soul*, London: Laurence King, 2005

Lisa **Silver**, *Logo Design that Works: Secrets for Successful Logo Design*, Gloucester, Massachusetts: Rockport, 2001

Walter **Soroka**, *Fundamentals of Packaging Technology*, revised by Anne and Henry Emblem, Grantham: Institute of Packaging, 1996; 3rd edition, Naperville, Illinois, 2002

SRI Consulting Business Intelligence (SRIC_BI), www.sric-bi.com/VALS

Bill **Stewart**, *Packaging Design Strategies*, Leatherhead, England and Portland, Maine: PIRA International, 2004

U

UNEP/UNFCC, 'Climate Change Information Kit', www.unfccc.int

V

Roger **Von Oech**, *A Whack on the Side of the Head: How You Can Be More Creative*, New York: Warner Books, 1990; London: Atlantic Books, 1992

W

John A. **Walker** and Sarah Chaplin, *Visual Culture: An Introduction*, Manchester: Manchester University Press, 1997

Guy M. **Wallis** and Heinrich H. Bülthoff, "Learning to Recognize Objects", 84, Tübingen, Germany: Max Planck Institute for Biological Cybernetics, 2000

Warhol Foundation, "Andy Warhol: Biography", www.warholfoundation.org

Wucius **Wong**, *Principles of Three-Dimensional Design*, New York: Van Nostrand Reinhold, 1997

Sources of inspiration

In addition to the resources shown at the end of each chapter and the Bibliography on pp.218–219, there are some sources of information listed here that may help to trigger inspiration. Do, however, go on-line and use a search engine to find other similar sources, regionally, nationally and globally.

Books

Dorte Nielson and Kiki Hartmann, *Inspired: How Creative People Think, Work and Find Inspiration*, Amsterdam: BIS, 2005
Some of the best designers describe where they find inspiration.

Adrian Shaughnessy, *How to be a Graphic Designer: Without Losing your Soul*, London: Laurence King, 2005
Specifically graphic design but contains some good information on how to become a designer and how designers work.

Magazines

Campaign, www.brandrepublic.com/magazines/campaign
Design Week, www.designweek.co.uk/Home/Home.aspx

Europe
Emballages, www.emballagesmagazine.com

US
www.packagingdigest.com
www.packagedesignmag.com/index.shtml

Art and Design Galleries

Australia
Perth
Art Gallery of Western Australia, www.artgallery.wa.gov.au

Austria
Graz
Kunsthaus Graz, www.kunsthausgraz.at
Vienna
MAK, www.mak.at
Technisches Museum Wien, www.tmw.at

Belgium
Gent
Design Museum, design.museum.gent.be

Hornu
Grand-Hornu, www.grand-hornu.be

Denmark
Copenhagen
Dansk Design Center, www.ddc.dk

Humlebaek
Louisiana Museum of Modern Art, www.louisiana.dk

Germany
Berlin
Guggenheim, www.guggenheim.org
Düsseldorf
NRW-Forum, www.nrw-forum.de

Italy
Milan
La Triennale di Milano, www.triennale.it
Rovereto
MART, www.mart.tn.it
Venice
Guggenheim, www.guggenheim.org

Ireland
Dublin
Irish Museum of Modern Art (IMMA), www.modernart.ie

Netherlands
Amsterdam
Beurs van Berlage, www.beursvanberlage.nl

Portugal
Porto
Museu Serralves, www.serralves.pt

Spain
Bilbao
Guggenheim, www.guggenheim.org

Valencia
IVAM, www.ivam.es

Sweden
Malmö
Form Design Center, www.formdesigncenter.com
Stockholm
Arkitekturmuseet, www.arkitekturmuseet.se

UK
London
Design Museum, www.designmuseum.org
Museum of Brands, Packaging and Advertising, www.robertopiecollection.com
National Portrait Gallery, www.npg.org.uk
V&A, www.vam.ac.uk

London, Liverpool, St Ives
Tate Galleries, www.tate.org.uk

Manchester
CUBE, www.cube.org.uk

USA
Boston
The Institute of Contemporary Art, www.icaboston.org
Los Angeles
Guggenheim, www.guggenheim.org

New York
Cooper-Hewitt, National Design Museum, www.ndm.si.edu
Guggenheim, www.guggenheim.org
The Metropolitan Museum of Art, www.metmuseum.org
MoMA, www.moma.org
Oklahoma
Oklahoma City Museum of Art, www.okcmoa.com
Phoenix
Phoenix Art Museum, www.phxart.org

Trade associations

Institute of Packaging (UK), www.iop.co.uk
Institute of Packaging Professionals (USA), www.iopp.org
The Design Council (UK), www.design-council.org.uk
IAPRI (International Association of Packaging Research Institutes), www.iapriweb.org

Index

Page numbers in **bold** refer to picture captions

A

Adidas **49**, 148
advertising
    and brands 144, 145, 151, 155, 165
    in conceptual design 103
    and target audiences 53
    use of images 88
Albers Super Mkts, Cincinnati 28
Amazon 22, 188
A&P 27, 144
Apple 10, 149, 150, **153**, 188
Apple Mac 35, 149, 201, 206
Armani 49
ASDA 10, 30, 33
Auchan **28**
Audi 101
Autodesk Alias **133**

B

Barbie **163**
Berger, John 48
Biotherm **184**
Blackburns 105
Blake, Peter 107, 109, 158
Bloom 35, **202**
BMW 153
Body Shop 176
Bonne Maman **103**
Bovril 81
brands and branding
    advertising relationship 144, 145, 151,
        155, 165
    brand extensions 152, 161, 162–5
    brand names 161, 163
    brand owners 11, 209–11
    brand terminology 152
    brand values 101, 142, 148, 151, 152,
        153, 159, 166
    and celebrity 143, 147, 163
    colour 79, 80–1, 161
    in conceptual design **100**, 101, **102**, 114
    consumer involvement 144, 146, 147, 150–1,
        166, 187–8
    creating 161–5
    design relationship 11, 142, 143
    emotional involvement 145–8, 151, 161, 164,
        165, 166
    as an experience 147–8, 166
    history 10, 11, 143–4
    personality brands 11, 152
    shape **142**, 154–5, **163**
    sound 155
    sub-brands **11**, 152, 161, 192
    and tribal behaviour 20–2, 146, 149
    winners and losers 148–50
    see also logos
Branson, Richard 11, 152, **153**
British Gas 11

C

Cadbury's **11**
Capa, Robert 109
Carbonell **71**
careers in packaging design
    brand owners 209–11
    design consultancies 202–6
    environmental issues 200
    examples 211, 212–13
    getting experience 196
    packaging manufacturers 207–8
    technological advances 197–8
    understanding markets 197
Carrefour 10, 30, **31**
Cartier-Bresson, Henri 109
cartons 63, 75, 115, **126**, 127, 128, 129
    see also Tetra Pak containers
Chanel 101
China 10, 14, 18, 30, 200
Coca-Cola 19, 80, **142**, 143, 150
Colgate 143, **163**
colour
    and branding 79, 80–1, 161
    category conventions 79, 81–2
    in conceptual design **116**, 118, 159
    corporate requirements 79, 80–1
    cultural meanings 21, 79, 82–3
    emotional associations 79, 83
    gender associations 84, **184**
    selection 79, 82
    vignettes 84
commercial television 8, 11, 28
The Complete Guide to Illustration and Design
    (Dalley) **34**
computers
    computer-aided design 84, 118, 125
    for design presentation 135, 136, 138–9
    design software 10, 35, 91, 125, 131–2,
        133–4, 160, 197–8
    history 10
    for mock-ups and models 128, 129, 130,
        131–4, 137
    see also Internet; websites
conceptual design
    and brands **100**, 101, **102**, 114
    the brief 95–6, 110, 111
    concept generation 110
        colour **116**, 118, 159
        mock-ups 115 see also under
            developing designs
        shape 110, 111
        sketches 110, 111, **112**, **116**, 117–18, 159
        stand outs 110, 114
        visibility of graphics 114
    logos 159
    planning projects 94, 96, 110
    presentation 110, **116**, 117–18, 122
    research 97, 110, 111, 118
        advertising strategy 103
        branding strategies **100**, 101, **102**
        competitor activity 100–1

point of sale 82, **98**, 99, 118
    the product 97
    product usage 100
    sources of inspiration 104, 109
        art and design influences 107, 109, 158
        brainstorming 104–5
        notebooks 106
        product history 105
        product origins 105–6
convenience food 17, 33, 44–5, 149, 150
    see also packaged food; ready meals
Cora supermarkets 10
"Crystal Palace" store, San Francisco 28

D

Dairy Milk chocolate **11**
Dasani 150
Delhaize, Louis 10
design consultancies and studios 10, 34–5,
    202–6
Design Futures (Sheffield Hallam University)
    104, 105
design practice changes 8, 10, 11, 34–6, 202,
    204–5
Design Week magazine **46**
developing designs 120, 123, 140
    assessing concepts 121–2
    the brief **120**
    computer-aided designing 125, 128, 129, **130**,
        131–4, **137**, 160
    graphics 121, 125–7
    logos 160
    mock-ups 115, 121, 125, **126**, 127, 128–9
    models 121, 128, 130–1, 135, 136, **137**, **138**,
        139
    outline specifications 95, 123–4
    presentation 121, 122, 135–6
        computer projection 135, 136, 138–9
        models 135, 136, **137**, **138**, 139
        presentation boards 135, 136, **137**, 138
        when things go wrong 139–40
        see also under conceptual design
    structure 121, **126–7**
DKNY **145**
Dove **183**

E

Eastern Europe 14, 29
eBay 149, 188
Elemental **56**
environmental issues
    consumer awareness 168, 170, 179–80
    corporate social responsibility 188, 190, 193
    energy use and protection 171–2, 173
        the future 199–200, 201
    greenhouse gas emissions 10, **168**, 169, 170,
        199
    packaging waste 33, **170**, 171–2
    remove, reduce, reuse 174–6, 180, 199–200,
        213
    of technological advances 26
    see also recycling

Euromonitor 14, 17, 39, 52
Europe 10, 20, 28–9, 30, 32, **193**
   see also Eastern Europe
Evian **109**, **164**, 165

F
Fairtrade products **88**, 146, 186, 192
FCUK **162**, 163
Fletcher, Alan 204
food photography 89, 90
food safety issues 19, 26
Ford 149, 204
Ford, Henry 38
France 10, 18, 28, 30, 33, 143
Freehand (Macromedia) 91, 125, 131, 132, 160
French Connection 163
frozen food 10, 16, 24–5, 44–5, **114**
Fuji 198
the future of packaging design 197–201

G
Gap 149
Gates, Bill 150, 152
Gaultier Classique fragrance 49
General Motors **165**
Germany
   brands and branding 143, 144
   environmental issues 171, **174**, 176, **180**
   socio-economic changes 12, 16, 17, 18
Gillette 143, **184**
GlaxoSmithKline (GSK) **102**
Glenrothes **105**
Google 188
Great Atlantic and Pacific Tea Company *see* A&P
Gucci **48**, 49
Guerlain **146**

H
Harley Davidson 188
Harriott, Ainsley **50**
health issues 18
   alcohol consumption 20
   of brands and branding 165
   "functional food" 19, **103**
   GM food 180
   "healthy" food 19, **101**, **103**
   obesity 18
   organic food 18–19
Heinz 149, 150, **192**
Hello! magazine 20
history of packaging 8, 10–11
HP Sauce **105**
Hummer **165**
hypermarkets 10, 28, 30, 33

I
IKEA 46
illustration 88, 90, 91, 107, **108**, 109
Illustrator (Adobe) 91, 125, 131, 132, 160
images
   in advertising 88
   art and design influences 107–9

and branding 161
   gender issues **184**
   as surface decoration 88–91
Imagination 202, 204
Innocent **101**
Interbrand 212
Internet 10, 31 *see also* websites
iPod 21, 149
ITENE 213

J
Japan 10, 16, 17, 18, 30, 143
J&B Whisky **77**
Jean Paul Gaultier 49
"Jeep" (General Motors) **165**
Jobs, Steve 152, **153**
Johnson's **144**, 154
JWT 212

K
Kallo 81
Kellogg's **144**
Kid Acne **108**
King Kullen "Food Market," New York 28
Kleenex 84
Knorr 81, 82
Kodak 143, 149, 198

L
La Caixa Bank 107
Lab 21 38
Landor Associates 107
Lantero **207**, 213
Letraset **34**, 35
Lichtenstein, Roy 109
Linux 150
Lipton, Thomas 27, 144
logos 156
   art influences 158
   audio logos 155
   as corporate identities 81, 158, 159
   defined 144, 156
   design concepts 159
   developing designs 160
   emotional involvement 146, 156
   history 143
   research 158
   types of 156–7
London Pride **146**
L'Oréal 77, 107

M
McDonald's 10, **187**, 188
McKinsey 52, 54
Malboro 80, 81
manufacture of packaging 62, 66–70, 71–2, 123, 124, 207–8
marketing 8, 11, 144, 200–1
Marks & Spencer **104**
Marvelo 144
materials
   glass 61, 71, 77, **115**, 175, 177

metals 61, 72–3, 75, 77, **97**, **115**, 177
   aluminium 72, 73
   steel 72, 73, **177**
   tinplate **73**, **77**
paper and board 61, 63–4, 77, 177
   carton board 63, 77, 115, 128–9
   corrugated fibreboard 63, 64, 207–8
plastics 61, 65–70, 75, 77, **109**, 178–9
   biodegradable 179
   extrusion blow moulding 66, 67
   flexible plastics 68–9
   foamed plastic **115**, 129
   form/fill/seal machines 69
   injection blow moulding 66, 67
   polystyrene 179
   rigid plastics 65, 178 *see also* PET
   thermoformed packaging 70, 179
recycling issues 63, 123, 176–9, 213
selection 60–2, 78, **115**, 124, 176–9
speciality packs 73
wood 61, 129, **130**
Mercedes-Benz 156
Metadesign 213
Mexico 14, 16, 17, 30
Microsoft 10, 150, 152, **153**
Mini (BMW) 153
Mintel 18, 39, 41, 52
Miró, Joan 107, 158
Mobius Awards 35
Mondrian, Piet 107, 158
Morrison's 30

N
Nestlé **11**, **156**
Netherlands 18, 144
Nike **21**, 147–8

O
Ogilvy & Mather **183**
OK! magazine 20
Olay **164**, 165
organic food 18–19, **87**, 149, 192–3
Oxo 81, 82

P
Package Design magazine 35
packaged food 15, 16, 18, 19 *see also* convenience food; ready meals
Pampers **145**
Penney (J.C.) 144
Pentagram 204, **205**
Peroni **146**
Perrier 143, 154
PET (polyethylene terephthalate) 10, **23**, 24, 65, 66, 67, **109**, 178–9
photography 89–90, 91, 109
Photoshop (Adobe) 90, 125, 131, **137**, 160
Picasso, Pablo 158
"Piggly-Wiggly" stores 28
Poweraid 150
PowerPoint 135, 136, 138–9
Procter & Gamble 209

R

ready meals 16, 19, **23**, 33
"Real Beauty" campaign (Dove) **183**
recycling
  biodegradable and compostable packaging 179–80
  consumer awareness 175, **193**
  design issues 33, 179–80
  in material selection 63, 123, 176–9, 213
Red Bull **19**
Red or Dead **63**
responsible design
  age issues 181–2
  and alcohol consumption 20
  closed loop system 175–6
  corporate social responsibility 168, 187–8
    confusing messages 191
    deception issues 189
    environmental performance issues 188, 190, 193
    ethical trading issues 188, 192
    organic food 192–3
  environmental issues 168, 199–200
    consumer awareness 168, 170, 179–80
    energy use and protection 171–2, 173
    the future 199–200, 201
    greenhouse gas emissions 10, **168**, 169, 170, 199
    packaging waste 33, **170**, 171–2
    remove, reduce, reuse 174–6, 180, 199–200, 213
    see also recycling
  ethnicity 186
  gender issues **182**, 183–5
  legal issues 168, 194
  packaging lifecycle 172
  sexuality issues **182**, 185, 186
retailing changes and packaging design 27
  bar codes 10, 25, **26**, 30, **114**
  brands and branding 143–4
  diversification 10, 11, 29, 32–3, 81
  future of retailing 33
  global retailing 30, 200–1
  history 10
  home shopping 10, 31–2
  self-service shopping **8**, 10, 28–30
  see also hypermarkets; supermarkets
RFID tagged packaging 10, 25–6, 33, 174
Rhinoceros **133**
Ribena **77**, **130**
rigid boxes 63
ring pulls 10, 155
Robert A. Becker 212
Rockware Glass **133**
Royal Ahold 144

S

Sainsbury's 27, 28, 30, 144, **193**
Saunders, Clarence 28
SCA (Grupo Lantero) **207**, 213
Schweppes 143

Sheffield Hallam University, UK **104**, 105, 156, 212
Shell 143
SiebertHead 10, 34
Skoda 103
Smith's (W.H.Smith) 144, **210**
socio-economic issues and packaging design 8, 10, 11
  cult of celebrity 20–2
  eating habits 15
    convenience food 17, 149, 150
    packaged and processed food 15, 16
  health issues 18
    alcohol consumption 20
    obesity 18
    organic food 18–19
  social trends 14–15, 22, 28
    freedom of choice **12**, 14
  social values 12–14
Soil Association **193**
South Korea 16, 17
Spain 16, 17, 18, 30
Spencer, Percy 23
Sprite 3G **19**
SRI Consulting Business Intelligence 40
Stamp, Terence **107**
Starbucks **147**, 148
Starck, Philippe **19**
sugar rationing **8**, 10, 28
supermarkets 10, 28, 30, 33, 53–4, 150
surface decoration 60, 74
  embossing/debossing **63**, **71**, 73, 77
  foil blocking 77
  printing 74
    flexography 74
    gravure (rotogravure) 76
    lithography 73, 75
    offset letterpress (dry offset) 73, 75
    offset lithography 75
    planographic printing 75
    relief printing 74–5
  screen printing 77
  selection 78, **115**
  stretch/shrink sleeving 77
Swoosh (Nike) **147**, 148

T

target audiences
  identifying aspirations 48, **181**
    aspirational packaging 49, 50
    celebrities and role models 20, 22, 48–9, 50
    emotional involvement 49, 146, 147–8
    motivation **15**, **24**, 31
  identifying market sectors 197
    demographics and psychographics 39–41
    lifestyle profiling **15**, 40, 42–5, 46
    multiple influences 53–4
    virtual customers **24**, 41, 48
    visual referencing 46–7
market research 51
  active research 52

the brief 52, 95–6
collating research **46**, 51, 55
desk research 39, 46, 51, 52
ethnographic research 53
mood boards 46, 47, 55, **56**
multiple influences 53–4, 84
observational research 47, 51, 52, 53–4
see also research under conceptual design
types of audience
  children 18, 41, **163**
  over-50s 181–2
  working mothers 19, 41, 44–5
  young people 14, 20, 21, 148, 149, 150, 163
Tea Direct **192**
technological advances and packaging design 8, 10, 23, 35, 197–8
  bar codes 10, 25, **26**, 30, **114**
  film technology 25
  frozen food 10, 16, 24–5 *see also* frozen food
  microwave cookery 23, 25
  modified atmosphere packaging 25
  nanotechnology 10, 26
  paper batteries 26
  polyethylene terephthalate *see* PET
  RFID tagged packaging 10, 25–6, 33, 174
Ted Baker clothing 137
Tengelmann 144
Tesco 27, 30, 33, 144, **205**
Tetra Pak containers 10, 97, **114**, **130**, **154**, 155
3M 209
Toblerone **154**
Toilet Duck 154, **155**
Tommy Hilfiger 209
trademarks *see* logos
Tretorn **145**
Tŷ Nant 109
typography 85–7, 160, 191
Tyrrells "Naked Chips" **182**

U

Unilever 209

V

Venus razor **184**
Virgin 11, 81, 152, **153**

W

Wal-Mart 10, 26, 30 *see also* ASDA
Warhol, Andy 107
websites 10, **31**
W.H.Smith 144, **210**
Woolworth's 144

Y

Yardley 143
Yorkie **185**
young people 14, 20, 21, 148, 149

Picture credits

Frontispiece Caffarel, Italy

Chapter 1
9 Robert Opie Collection; 11/L ©Cadbury Schweppes PLC; 11/R ©Nestlé UK Ltd; 12 Corbis/Gideon Mendel; 15/T, 19/T ©OAO, Belgium; 15 B ©Wm Morrison Supermarkets PLC; 17, 29 Photo: the author. Courtesy and ©Sainsbury's Supermarkets Ltd; 19/B Courtesy and © of Coca-Cola Company; 21 Advertising Archives/©Nike Inc.; 23/L Corbis/ Bettmann; 23/R ©LINPAC Plastics Limited; 24 ©FRoSTA AG; 25/T, 28/B ©Groupe Auchan; 25/B Queen's Setan, Japan; 26/T Courtesy and ©Kellogg Company of Great Britain Ltd; 26/B Staples UK; 27/L, 28/T Museum in Docklands/The Sainsbury Archive; 27/R ©A&P Historical Society; 31 ©Carrefour Group; 34 ©Letraset Ltd

Chapter 2
46/L Design Week Magazine, UK; 46/R ©IKEA France S.N.C.; 47 Natalie Turner, Sheffield Hallam University; 48/TL ©Armani Group, Italy; 48/TC ©Gucci Group N.V.; 48/TR, 49/T ©Jean Paul Gaultier Parfums; 49/B ©Adidas AG; 50 Brand Partnership, UK; 56 Sheffield Hallam University

Chapter 3
62 Peoples Republic of China; 63/BR ©Red or Dead Limited; 64/B ©Campingaz, France; 65/B ©Procter & Gamble, Germany; 71/T Carbonell De Cordoba, S.A.; 73/T GDH-Lebkuchen; 73/B ©Merisant, Chicago, Illinois; 74 ©OAO, Belgium; 75/L Angelo Parodi, Italy; 77/L ©L'Oreal, UK; 77/CL ©GlaxoSmithKline, UK; 77/CR Czechexpo; 77/R ©Justerini & Brooks; 80 Courtesy and ©Coca-Cola Company; 81/L-R ©Unilever UK, ©Kallo Foods UK, ©Oxo UK; 83/T ©Beiersdorf A G, Germany; 83/B ©Masterfoods, UK; 84/T ©Société BIC, France; 84/B ©Kimberly-Clark, UK; 87 ©Quaker Oats, UK; 88 Escale Equitable, France; 89/L William Saurin, France; 89/R ©Glico Group, Japan; 91/B Jeenhuat Foodstuffs Industries Sdn Bhd., Malaysia

Chapter 4
97 Santa Rosa, Italy; 98 Corbis/Reg Charity; 99 Photo: the author. Courtesy and ©Sainsbury's Supermarkets Ltd; 100/T Iliada, Greece; 100/B with permission from Lindsey Stewart; 101/T ©Chanel, UK; 101/B ©Innocent Ltd; 102/L ©Siemens & Co, Germany; 102/TR ©Flexicare Medical Ltd.; 102/BR ©GlaxoSmithKline, UK; 103/L ©Unilever UK; 103/R Bonne Maman, France; 104 ©Marks and Spencer PLC; 105/T Berry Bros. & Rudd Ltd; 105/BL ©Cardini, USA; 105/BR ©H.J. Heinz; 106/L Polarbageriet Bredbyn; 106/R Medrano Estate, Argentina; 107/T Tesori D'oriente, Italy; 107/BR ©Stamp Collection Foods Limited; 108/T Wall by Kid Acne, outside Yorkshire Artspace, Sheffield; 108/B ©Cadbury Schweppes PLC; 109/T ©Groupe Danone; 109/B Tŷ Nant, Wales; 110 the author; 112, 113 Sheffield Hallam University; 114/TL Courtesy and ©Sainsbury's Supermarkets Ltd; 114/TR ©Young's Seafood Limited; 114/BL ©Masterfoods, UK; 114/BC ©Valfrutta, Italy; 113/BR ©Kronenbourg, France; 115/TL Sheffield Hallam University; 115/TR & B, 116, 117 the author

Chapter 5
125 Ciumachella, Italy; 126, 127, 128 the author; 130/T Jose Navarro, Sheffield Hallam University; 130/BL Sheffield Hallam University; 130/BR Tom French, Sheffield Hallam University; 132 the author; 133/L Sheffield Hallam University; 133/R Rockware Glass Ltd/©Stella Artois, UK; 137, 138/L Sheffield Hallam University; 138/R the author

Chapter 6
142 Advertising Archives/Courtesy and ©Coca-Cola Company; 144/T ©Johnson & Johnson Ltd; 144/B ©Kellogg Company; 145/T & C ©Procter & Gamble, UK; 145/BL Tretorn Sweden AB; 145/BR ©DKNY, New York; 146/T ©Guerlain SA, Paris; 146/BL Fuller, Smith & Turner PLC; 146/BR SABMiller International Brands Limited; 147/L Alamy/Alex Segre; 147/R Peter Kent; 149/L Alamy/Neil Setchfield; 149/R Advertising Archives/Apple Inc.; 151 ©DaimlerChrysler; 153/TL ©Virgin Group; 153/TC ©Microsoft Corporation; 153/TR ©Apple Inc.; 153/B ©BMW, Germany; 154/T ©Kraft Foods Schweitz AG; 154/B Saint Louis, France; 155 ©SC Johnson Ltd; 156 ©Nestlé UK Ltd; 157/T Courtesy and ©Coca-Cola Company; 157/CTL ©H.J. Heinz; 157/CTC ©McDonald's Corporation; 157/CTR ©Procter & Gamble, UK; 157/CBL ©BMW, Germany; 157/CBR ©BP PLC; 157/BL ©Shell International B.V.; 157/BR ©DaimlerChrysler; 159 the author; 160 Sheffield Hallam University; 161/L Kopenhagen, Brazil; 161/R ©Glico Group, Japan; 162 ©French Connection, UK; 163/T ©Colgate-Palmolive Company/Mattel Inc.; 163/B ©Cert Brands,UK; 164/T ©Groupe Danone; 164/B ©Procter & Gamble, USA; 165/TL ©Daimler-Chrysler; 165/TR Kolcraft Enterprises Inc.;165/BL ©General Motors, USA; 165/BR Burston Marketing, Inc.

Chapter 7
170 Greenpeace International/Mark Warford; 174/T ©GlaxoSmithKline, UK; 174/B Courtesy and ©Sainsbury's Supermarkets Ltd; 175 the author; 176 M.A.G.S.A. Jerez, Spain; 177/T SABMiller International Brands Limited; 180 ©DIN Certco, Germany; 181 Biere Artisanal, Arras, France; 182 Tyrrells Potato Chips; 183 Advertising Archives/Unilever, UK; 184/L ©Procter & Gamble, Spain; 184/R ©Biotherm, France; 185 ©Nestlé UK Ltd; 186 Fazer, Finland; 186 ©McDonald's Corporation; 190 ©Barefoot Doctor, UK; 191 Saida, France; 192/TL Tea Direct, UK; 192/BL-R Infinity Foods, UK, S&B Herba Foods, UK, ©H.J. Heinz, Biona, UK; 193/L ©Groupe Auchan; 193/R Courtesy and ©Sainsbury's Supermarkets Ltd

Chapter 8
202 Bloom Design, London, UK; 203 Courtesy Imagination, London; 205 Pentagram, London, UK; 207 Lantero, Spain; 209 3M, USA; 210 ©WH Smith PLC; 212 James Toomey, Interbrand; 213 Bernhard Dutsch

Acknowledgements

I would like to thank the staff and students at Sheffield Hallam University, past and present, who, sometimes unknowingly, have contributed to this book. In particular, my thanks to Chris Rust for his patience and support while this book was being written, and the provision of research time by the Art & Design Research Centre at Sheffield Hallam University to allow me to complete the task. Thanks are also extended to all the following who, in one way or another, influenced the direction of this book. I have singled out only a few, missed out many, but thanks to Don and Charles at Sheffield Hallam for their assistance with photography, Bernhard Dusch, James Toomey, José Navarro, Glyn Hawley, Claire Lockwood, Toby Lyons, Natalie Turner, Jim Roddis, Janet Shipton and the Design Futures team.

My thanks to all those at Laurence King who were involved with this book, particularly Jo Lightfoot who commissioned it, Peter Kent who sourced many of the packs and images featured, Anne Townley and Emily Asquith who, between them, had the onerous task of editing my, sometimes, convoluted text. Support from the team at Laurence King was much appreciated when events mid project caused delays to the schedule. I am also extremely fortunate in having Catherine Dixon design the book. Her patience must have been sorely tried at times.

Thanks to all the companies that also provided contributions to the book, notably Rockware Glass, Linpac and Imagination, all of whom provided images, and to J. Sainsbury who also gave us permission to photograph its Sheffield, Archer Road store. Interbrand deserve a special mention, not only for their superb "Global Brands" information, but also for agreeing to let us include James's story in Chapter Eight.

Finally, I would like to thank my wife and family for their tolerance when my life was dominated by producing this book (expletives deleted). I promise never to mention it again.

Dedication

To Yvonne